VISIBLE WORDS

VISIBLE WORDS

The Interpretation and Practice
of Christian Sacraments

ROBERT W. JENSON

Fortress Press

Minneapolis

VISIBLE WORDS
The Interpretation and Practice of Christian Sacraments

Fortress Press ex libris publication 2010

ISBN 978-0-8006-9713-6 (paperback)

The Library of Congress has catalogued the original publication as follows:
Jenson, Robert W.
Visible words; the interpretation and practice of Christian sacraments / Robert Jenson.
p.   cm.
Includes bibliographical references
ISBN 978-0-8006-0507-0
1. Sacraments. I. Title
BV800.J45

Manufactured in the U.S.A.

For
Valborg Charlotte
on the occasion of
her 75th birthday

Contents

Contents

Preface

The attempt of this essay is simply to *explain* Christianity's sacraments, to myself and to other believers who may find my reflections helpful. The goal is simple; and I hope that the explanations offered are also relatively uncluttered. But precisely the simple comprehensiveness of my purpose compels me to an incautiously comprehensive reflective undertaking: we need to see and understand sacraments merely as religious phenomena; we need to specify individual sacraments' institution and history within the institution and history of the gospel; and we need to grasp such phenomena within a unified interpretation of reality according to the gospel.

So far as I know, modern theology has produced few such attempts. There has been much remarkable research into the sacraments' history, but not often so as to ask what might come of this historical knowledge for present practice and interpretation—the exception being a romanticism that simply wishes to revive the liturgy and piety of the fourth or whatever century. Modern exegesis, of course, illuminates the biblical witness to sacraments, but modern exegetical results have seldom, with respect to the sacraments, been put to much systematic or practical use. And nothing would be so liberating as finally to heed the exhortations of phenomenologists simply to face what is *there,* to say straightforwardly, e.g., "Baptism is a typical initiation rite, a rite of passage from one communally created reality to another," and to ask how we might understand these phenomena theologically.

Such a project takes me variously beyond my specific competence, most alarmingly at two points. For the history of sacramental practice, beyond knowledge of the main liturgical texts, I am almost entirely dependent on others' work. I have necessarily done my own New

Testament exegesis, but my exegesis can sustain responsibility only by fervent consultation of the experts. My dependence in both matters is reflected by plentiful footnoting of certain chapters and parts of chapters. Moreover, this documentation is *ad hoc* to my particular purposes and the further information of readers; it is not a scholarly apparatus.

On the other hand, there are few footnotes to more strictly systematic reflections. This is partly because I here speak in my own competence, and have less need to plead authorities. But I might nevertheless have been expected regularly to refer to assertions and arguments of my fellow systematic theologians. I have not much done so because recent sacramentology has not in fact contributed much of importance to what I find I must say, or even provided much to argue against. Christian theology has been in crisis at the level of fundamental theology throughout the modern period; and most of our truly powerful systematicians have devoted themselves to this, never quite getting to such substantial matters of the faith as sacraments. On the other hand, sacramentologists in the style of Odo Casel have ignored the crises of Christian thought, and so have had nothing fundamentally creative to say. The two great exceptions have been Karl Barth and Paul Tillich. Both went on from foundation-laying to build whole theological structures; unfortunately, the plans of the structures compelled what seem to me simply false doctrines of sacrament.

Therefore, instead of footnotes, I will only make acknowledgements here. My learning from Peter Brunner is, in this matter, especially extensive and deep: in the freedom to think theologically about what actually *happens* in the church's gatherings, and in the doctrine of the Spirit, that it is *Jesus'* spirit. Were more of his fundamental work published, Peter Brunner would be a complete exception to the strictures of the previous paragraph. From my work with Karl Barth I learned to play the trinitarian dialectics which I have here applied to the solution of very un-Barthian questions. Finally, all my sacramentology, at its systematic heart, is the fruit of over twenty years' preoccupation with Martin Luther's tracts, *That These Words of Christ, "This is My Body," etc., Still Stand . . .* (1527) and *Confession Concerning Christ's Supper* (1528), and with the speculative developments of Luther's dicta by Johannes Brenz and Martin Chemnitz.

In venturing so widely, I have, moreover, multiplied opportunities for failure, past the number with which even a systematician can feel comfortable. Each reconsideration of the drafts has revealed new lapses, some beyond my ability to make good. I expect to be informed of more. But in one respect I think I may ask for indulgence. At various points the argument and exposition of this book depend upon theological judgments not argued within it, which readers not familiar with the rest of my work may well find too summary. I find no way to avoid this, when a systematician works with the essay form. If he may not leave some connections dangling and make summary references to existing and future other work, each of his books must expand to incorporate all the rest of them, and become a summa. It is for this very reason that the old theologians indeed each wrote one summa as his life's major work. Such a procedure would now find few readers; and the restriction is more blessing than curse, if only its major disadvantage be allowed for.

I am indebted to Blanche Jenson, for long discussion; to the students of many seminars; for the experience of regularly ministering the sacraments in relatively free situations at Mansfield College, Oxford, and at Gettysburg Seminary; to Leigh Jordahl for much discussion in the course of the latter; to Eugene Brand for putting me to work on various assignments for the Inter-Lutheran Commission on Worship; to Gordon Lathrop for first making the importance of Jewish table-thanksgiving fully clear to me; and to Oliver Olsen for so determinedly espousing positions with which I have utterly to disagree, as to compel me to think through why.

Preliminary versions of some chapters of this work, and segments of material, have been published in *Interpretation, dialog,* and the *Lutheran Quarterly.* Parts of chapters three and four appeared as a contribution to the Festschrift for T. F. Torrance, *Creation, Christ and Culture,* edited by Richard McKinney.

Preface to the 2010 Publication

It is now more than thirty years since I wrote *Visible Words*. During that time, people have sometimes mentioned it to me—to my pleasure usually favorably. And when thus reminded, I have of course had a momentary recollection of what I wrote, but one made increasingly indistinct by the passage of time and by differently situated engagements with the same matter.

But then Fortress Press proposed reprinting the book, with a new preface. To write that, I thought I ought to revisit the text. I rediscovered three things about it.

The first: Checking dates, I remembered how much *Visible Words* was the result of seminary teaching and associated activities. Before coming to Gettysburg Seminary in 1968, I had written and spoken mostly as a philosopher, as a theological culture-critic, and at Oxford as a very free-wheeling speculative theologian. At Gettysburg, I had to consider what a future pastor might need to know. High among such matters was of course the theology and practice of the sacraments. Indeed, I even taught liturgics and was for a time dean of services in the chapel. I took up these responsibilities very much from scratch.

Visible Words is the deposit both of what I actually laid before students in those years and of the sometimes difficult reflections by which I worked out for myself what that should be. Readers may, I fear, sometimes be alarmed by resulting combinations of, for example, practical liturgical advice and complicated reflections on time or perception. The various styles do, I think, eventually fit together, and I can only plead for readers' patience.

The second: Thus suddenly faced with explaining the sacraments, I grasped classical Lutheran theology's version of Augustine as my starting place. Then I went to work on that tradition with the tools at my hand: phenomenology, linguistic analysis, historical-critical exegetical method, and some I think I devised on the spot. Rereading the early chapters of *Visible Words*, I was astonished by how relentlessly I explicated such fundamental sacramental notions as body or divine presence by exploiting one principle: that sacraments are actions to which the word of God comes and that the word is law that anchors us in the past and gospel that promises the future.

I have done nothing like that since. The discussions of sacraments in later articles and in my systematic theology are located in very different contexts and argue in very different ways. *Visible Words* is thus a sort of freestanding unit of my work. If the book is valuable at all, it is irreplaceable within the whole body of what I have written; and I am the more grateful to Fortress Press for making it again available.

The third: I had entirely forgotten how much I relied on historical-critical exegesis of the relevant biblical texts and how assertively I presented it. I do not exactly repent of what I then did, but those pages if written now would be fewer and would be sprinkled with "perhaps" and "It can be argued" and other such escape-words.

The fourth: I would not now make some of the liturgical recommendations I did then. Readers may have some fun deciding which those are.

PART ONE

VISIBLE WORDS

1

Initial Maxims

"The Word comes to the element; and so there is a sacrament, that is, a sort of visible word."   Augustine[1]

"By 'the Word' is to be understood: first a mandate . . . . by which an element . . . is separated from ordinary use and destined for sacramental use; and second a promise, and indeed the gospel itself as it is to be applied and sealed by the sacrament."   John Gerhard[2]

I

Augustine's dictum became the sacramental slogan of the Western church. It has been differently understood by every school or movement that has adopted it, but one fundamental testimony has persisted: when the Bible's God speaks to us, when his word comes to us, it comes to and then with some "element," some piece of the external world. His self-communication in one way or another attaches to itself that "visible" reality that stands out there over against our subjectivity; and then that self-communication comes to us with that reality to be itself an external, "visible" word. Just so God truly *addresses* us; just so he speaks to us from outside us. God's word is a word with a bath or a meal or a gesture.

Augustine is not engaged here in defining "sacrament." The word—taken from standard Roman religious terminology—simply serves as a convenient label for certain occurrences which do in fact take place in the life of the church, and which observably share such characteristics as make it useful sometimes to talk about them all at once. All religions have repeated performances that are done in gatherings and form the

3

concrete and binding actuality of the religious life, and which merely because they are public somehow implicate the external world. Augustine calls these "sacraments," and notes that Christianity has such performances also, Baptism and the Supper most notably.[3]

In the quoted maxim, Augustine is rather engaged in a theological interpretation of these Christian "sacraments:" in this particular group, with its own particular public rites, what is their divine function and reality? He answers, Christian rites have their authority and power from the word, from God's merciful self-communication to his creatures; they are just the ways in which that word establishes itself in the visible world out there, to be sensibly accessible to us. With this interpretation, it is also shown that the church not only has sacraments in fact, but *rightly* has at least some of them; and one criterion is provided by which rites that may claim place in the church can be judged for appropriateness.

II

In speaking of "visible" words, Augustine primarily contrasted the *invisible* word: God's own knowledge and intention of himself and his works, the inner reality of all that truth which God knows and is. This invisible word "comes" to the elements by incarnation as Jesus Christ, and by the sacramentally instituting words the incarnate one speaks—as "Go therefore . . . baptizing. . . ." The divine word is in itself inaccessible to our sense-bound apprehension; but in that the Incarnation of the Word establishes rites using the elements of our sensible world, God's inner truth comes to be spoken "visibly," in ways accessible to our senses.

The Reformation's use of Augustine's saying shifted the context. In Reformation discourse, *visible* is opposed not so much to "invisible" as to "audible." Within God's self-communication to us in the sensible world, we may distinguish between what we hear and what we apprehend in other sensory modes: Augustinian and Reformation use made *visible* cover all the other modes. Reformation theology shifted Augustine's interpretation to emphasize: when God addresses us, he does not speak only in the sentences of language, but also by the kind of signs that are seen and touched—and tasted and smelled and apprehended by whatever other senses there may be. We might say in modern jargon:

the gospel is a complete communication, embracing "verbal" and "nonverbal" communication—though to be faithful to Christian insight into the divine reality of the word, we should say "more-than-verbal" instead of "nonverbal." This more-than-verbal reality of God's self-communication makes the sacramental aspect of the gospel event.

The distinction between God's "visible" and "audible" words carries more metaphysical freight than may at first appear. For beings constituted as are we, the difference between "hearing" and "seeing" is fundamental to experience. Indeed, I think it is the key to Augustine's assertion of the presence in our communication of the "invisible" God—but that is the matter of later chapters. For now, it is enough to note that both contrasts, with "invisible" and with "audible," will be reckoned with in my use of Augustine's testimony.

That testimony initiates my book. That the church in fact has "sacraments" in Augustine's sense is evident to the slightest observation. To someone who denied it, I would have little argument to present: I could only say, "Go and *watch* the church for a while." Church groups that themselves claim not to have sacraments are only indulging a semantic prejudice—though it may prove a disastrous indulgence, tempting them to discard necessary sacraments and create vacuums that will be filled somehow, perhaps most inappropriately to the gospel.

Also the basic Augustinian-Reformation interpretations of the Christian sacraments, as "visible words" of the gospel, seem to me so profoundly and primitively and obviously biblical that I have no special way to argue for them. To someone who attacked their theological rightness, I could only say, "Go and read the whole Bible yet again!"

The specifically systematic agenda of this book is the attempt to carry through the understanding of sacraments as visible words more ruthlessly than has been done in the past. In the first two sections especially, I will try to deal with such classic themes of sacramentology as the presence in them of God-in-Christ and the "bodily" and "spiritual" characters of that presence, by analysis of the particular visibility of Christianity's word, the gospel. It is the fundamental conviction in which this analysis will be conducted, that it is a disastrous mistake to distinguish analysis of Christian sacraments as communication from analysis of them as events of God's real presence and action. Overcoming that distinction is the theological program of this book.

III

John Gerhard defined one term of Augustine's maxim and thereby displayed the entire basic sacramentology of the Reformation. The word that "comes" to the sacrament, like the word of God in all its modes, is both "law" and "gospel," which here as elsewhere are neither to be separated or confused.

In his self-communication, God commands us to do such and such and to be such and such; he speaks "law." God's mandates are not ordinarily delivered by direct inspiration. The whole web of actual ordinary discourse between humans endlessly imposes legitimate obligation on us; Christian theology claims that God himself stands behind this obligation, so that in the totality of the addresses by which we are obligated, we are addressed by him. If my fellows so address me that, e.g., *liberty* becomes my genuine obligation to them, then "Stand fast in liberty" is a word of God to me.

"The law" is a Christian description of humanity's whole web of mutual address, in one aspect. "The gospel" is a label for the particular Christian address itself: the particular message, carried by a succession of witnesses through history and space, that Jesus, the crucified Messiah of Israel, lives. If such an assertion that death has yielded to life is true, it too must be a word of God, indeed the defining word of God.

As theology calls the total web of words "law," so it calls this special word "promise." "Law" is address that imposes obligation; "promise" is address by which the one behind the word assumes obligation, and so opens new future possibility for the one addressed. If "Be free" is law, the corresponding promise is, "I will guard your freedom."

Our promises are normally conditional; though I may promise to work hard for my institution, I will stop if they stop paying me. Behind the conditionality of our promises is the certainty of death: by every promise I commit some part of my future, which I do not surely have. The gospel promise is unconditional, for behind it stands the victor over death. Just so, it is the word of God, who has all the future. If "Be free'" is law, the corresponding gospel is, "I, Christ, with death behind me, will guard your freedom."

Law and gospel, said the Reformation, are not to be mixed up. God's commands are to be obeyed just because they are God's and speak for our fellows' need. We are free to obey in this disinterested fashion because God's unconditional promise wholly and independently guarantees our interests. And no further synthesizing is to be done: we are in no way, however subtle, to make obedience to God's commands a condition for the truth of his promises.

We apprehend law in all our communal discourse. If we belong to the community of believers, we apprehend law also in *its* discourse: the command in turn to speak the gospel, verbally and more than verbally. This mandate too is simply to be obeyed. Then the gospel-promise acquires our action as its referent: it "comes," following the mandate, to the human action. The gospel is then a promise about this action: that we may speak not our own word merely but God's message of unconditional hope. And just so the communication made to those who hear us is this very message.

IV

Thus Gerhard's definition of "the word" elicits from Augustine's maxim a method for understanding sacraments: examine both the word that mandates an action and the specific word of promise made about and by the action, and examine also the relation between the two. It is this method which will be followed through the parts of this book devoted to particular sacraments. Again, it is my ambition to do this more consistently than has been usual.

To be sure, I cannot direct any who doubt Gerhard's saying back to Scripture so peremptorily as I did doubters of Augustine. Gerhard's interpretation of Augustine's dictum is evidently not past all dispute backed by Scripture, since so many devoted readers of Scripture dispute it. As a demand that "law" and "gospel" be distinguished also in respect of sacraments, it involves the whole insistence of the Reformation that God's commands and promises, our obedient works and God's works for us, are not to be synthesized: that the church's word, audible or visible, opens that specific justification for life that faith apprehends in the gospel, without reference to the believer's works. But argument here would mean rearguing the whole Reformation yet again. For this book, I can only make my confession to the Reformation, and go on.

A sacramental mandate is a command to draw some "element," some item of the object-world, into our gospel-address to each other: to use the object in a communal action that speaks promise in Jesus' name. "Give thanks to God," we hear, "with sharing of bread and cup and for Jesus' remembrance." When we do what is mandated in this way, our action is the referent of a promise: that our act will be God's own "visible" self-communication, the visible *gospel*. We hear: "This will be my body."

We should note that this way of understanding the matter eliminates altogether the question of "validity." The question of validity is: "What is the least we can do to get the promised blessing?" This is a blatantly works-righteous question; there is *nothing* we must or can do to get any of God's blessings. The distinction of sacramental mandate from sacramental promise makes the sacramental blessing solely the fruit in us of auditory and more-than-auditory apprehension of the promise. And over against a sacramental mandate unconfused with the promise, we have a quite different question: "What may we do to be fully obeying the mandate?" Reformation theology called this the question of a sacrament's "integrity."

The question of "validity" has a reductionist effect on the practice of sacraments. The answer to it is necessarily the listing of a minimum set of acts; and given the sort of interest in the sacraments that the question encourages, that minimum will inevitably become standard practice. Precisely this process constitutes the sacramental history of the Western church since the early middle ages; our question has always been: "Couldn't we leave this out too, and still make it work?" The question of "integrity," on the other hand, can encourage a creative response to the mandate's challenge.

V

Such mandates and promises come to us from the whole tradition of the gospel, from the whole chorus of witnesses from which we ourselves hear the gospel and by which we are bidden to speak it in turn. For an association of mandate and promise, traditional theology and liturgy have used the word *institution*. An institution is an historical event which creates a distinguishable repeated form of the gospel's life in the church: proclamatory gospel-telling, baptism, anointing of the sick, exorcism, membership instruction, or whatever. Since the gospel's tradition is continuously creative, new institutions are regularly added to the deposit.

There is of course no guarantee that every performance instituted somewhere in the tradition is in fact legitimate. For horrid examples, the tradition also commands: "Sell indulgences" and "Meditate transcendentally." There is and should be continuous argument in the church about which communal performances, somehow instituted sometime, can in fact now belong to the life of the gospel. In this connection as elsewhere, the argument proceeds by using one part of the tradition, the canon of apostolic Scripture, as the norm of the tradition as a whole. Thus the Reformers argued that if the gospel is indeed as St. Paul describes it, indulgence selling could never be its visible form, just as "God loves you only if you love him in return" could never be its audible form.

The institutions of some forms of the gospel are themselves in the scriptural strata of the tradition. Since the Scriptures provide the norm for all other strata of tradition, we have no way to judge the gospel-forms thus mandated. They simply are givens of all Christian reflection. The canonical witness to the gospel commands us to speak it in turn; there is no way to disobey this command except by unbelief. Insofar as this canonical witness mandates specific forms of the gospel and in such a way as to make these mandates integral to the mission-command itself, also these forms of the gospel are simply given with the gospel's historically contingent beginning, and are not subject to believers' judgment. Thus, given the way the Scriptures say "Baptize," we either baptize or resign the faith. Of course, whether or not a particular performance *is* so mandated—whether or not, for example, what I just said about "Baptize" in Scripture is true—is an exegetical decision. Thus it too is a matter of our judgment, but of a different sort.

It can be argued a priori that the speaking of the gospel must *somehow* be visible and not only audible, that the church must have some sacraments—I have already begun and will continue such an argument. But that the tradition institutes the particular visible forms of the gospel that it does, and that the canonical strata of tradition with final authority institute the particular visible forms of the gospel that they do, is historically contingent. If the church had begun in a northern climate, doubtless its sacramental drink, if it had one, would be beer. But just this contingency is what binds us. The gospel is a message about alleged historical events. The contingency of the historical is therefore affirmed by faith, which in this differs greatly from most other religion. God might not have chosen Israel from the nations, or Jesus from among the Israelites, or washing instead of incensing, or bread instead of potato chips. But for Christian faith, "might not have been" does not at all decrease the authority of what in fact is.

I should now also say that the centrality and unconditionality of the gospel-promises made about and by a sacrament are in no way diminished by inquiring into the command that establishes the sacrament and into the acts by which we may obey the command. It in no way diminishes the sole efficacy of a gospel-promise in our lives to ask what this promise is *about,* and how we may so act that the referent is in fact there. A sacramental promise is about some act commanded to be performed by us. If the command is not obeyed, e.g., if no washing is performed to initiate, there is no sacrament at all and the gospel in this particular form just is not communicated—just as, if the preacher disobeys the command to preach and does not open his mouth or discourses about the Buddha, there is no sermon at all, and this form of the gospel does not happen.[4]

VI

The word *sacrament* as used by the theological tradition, picks out only some of the church's repertoire of legitimately instituted gospel-forms. At the simplest level all forms of the gospel might be called "sacraments:" all involve ways of communication that are more than verbal, even if this is only the physical presence of the preacher and the sheer sound of his voice, or the appearance of marks on paper. And all are "visible" presences of the "invisible" God. But theology has used *sacrament* more narrowly. Two sorts of distinctions have been made.

First, the event of communicating the gospel, like any event of communication, can be analyzed into the two aspects for which the Reformation used "audible" and "visible." A full analysis of these distinctions is the task of the next chapter; here I anticipate by mere assertion. In every successful communication, something is shared which is or could be stated by sentences, e.g., "The cat is on the mat," or "God loves you." It is this that is, in Reformation use, "heard." But every communication occurs as a use of *objects*: we make or find sounds, statues, marks, gestures, or whatever, and set them between us, thereby to share a world. These may be objects used to make sentences; but they also function in our communicating in more-than-verbal ways, ways that are inseparable from their sheer givenness and quality as things in our shared world. That, e.g., we do our preaching in a particular building with its particular architecture, manifestly shapes the communication that takes place in ways that could not be duplicated by adding sentences to the sermon. It is in this capacity that communication-objects are, in Reformation use, "seen."

We should therefore start with the adjective: every occurrence of the gospel has a "sacramental" *aspect,* a "visible" aspect. Moving to the noun, we should mean by a "sacrament" a repeatable instituted form of the gospel which is identified as a repeatable type by its sacramental characteristics rather than by what propositions are heard. No two celebrations of the Supper necessarily involve the very same sentences, but there is always the specific use of bread and cup, and it is by this latter that we identify two occasions of gospel-communication as two celebrations of *the* Supper.

Second, if no further restrictions are made, obviously there is still a large and changing number of "sacraments." At various times further restrictions have been made. Thus the final medieval list of seven was made by stipulating that only those performances should be called "sacraments" which are essential to someone's salvation. The Reformation lists of two or three or four were made by stipulating that only those of the seven should be called "sacraments" whose institution has canonical authority.

Such stipulations are made for polemical purposes: to commend certain instituted forms of the gospel and denigrate others. Polemics of this sort are sometimes necessary, but in this book my polemics will be of a different sort and I will make no such stipulations. I will simply take the four "sacraments" mentioned in the Reformation confessions as a minimal list on which there is likely to be ecumenical agreement.

As for the question: "How many sacraments are there *really?*"—it is totally meaningless. There are as many sacraments as we polemically define the word to cover. By Augustine's unpolemical use and mine, there are indefinitely many.

NOTES

1. Augustine, *In Johannem,* 80, 3.
2. Gerhard was the standard theologian of established Lutheran Protestantism. His *Loci communes theologici* (1610–22) is cited, XVIII, 11.
3. Augustine, *Contra Faustum,* 19, 11.
4. Even classic Lutheranism analyzed the matter exactly so. Gerhard, op. cit., XVIII, 11. 24. 142; Martin Chemnitz, *Examen Concilii Tridentini,* II, I. 21.

2

Audible and Visible

All communication occurs by and through "elements," objects that we make or find in the world and arrange out there as signs to each other. With elements made especially for the purpose, the arrangements can be more complex. Most vital human mutuality therefore occurs by products of human art, by objects crafted by us to make a shared world: sentences, buildings, gardens, utterances, postures, and all the rest of culture.

Objects in the world are objects of sense—indeed, what we mean by "a sense" is a mode of apprehending the object-world, however many such modes there may turn out to be. As it physiologically happens, humans are so constituted that two senses carry the burden of our community, apart from technology and special arrangements for the bereft. Sight and hearing have more range and are more predictable in their operation than are our other senses; therefore sounds and sights are the chief constituents of our common world, and it is natural for us to divide all means of communication into the audible and the visible.

As it further happens, hearing and seeing work very differently; and the differences correlate with decisive structures of our life with each other in the world. We emit sound at will and can at will vary our sounds indefinitely; whereas—unlike some fish!—we do not emit light but only reflect it. As direct makers of signs, we are therefore in control of the sounds we make and not of the sights we make; we are audible or inaudible more or less as we choose, while to be the invisible man is an ancient fantasy of the race.

As receivers of signs, we are in the reversed situation. We have efficient flaps on our eyes but not on our ears, and can aim our eyes but not our ears: we are in control of what we see but hear what we must. We use our eyes instantly to locate what we apprehend; only inefficiently and with effort can we locate by hearing. Sight is thus the chief medium of *objectifying* consciousness: consciousness that intends realities as located in that world out there which I am not, and seeks to control my relation to them, to handle them as indeed the "objects" of my subjectivity. The God of Israel willed to be spoken for, but refused to be visually depicted.

Had we a different evolutionary history—so as, perhaps, to glow variously at will—all this would of course sort itself out very differently. But as it contingently is, sounds and sights are the natural materials of two very different sorts of "words." The one sort of words are those of language. A language is a sign-system with grammar; that is, it works by rules. There are syntactic rules by which complex signs are put together from simpler signs—in all ordinary languages, quite literally without end. As we speak in language, we endlessly create new signs as needed, and of whatever degree of complexity we need and can keep track of. The present written paragraph is a sign that has never before existed, which I now create from simpler signs for the particular communication-venture of this moment. There are also semantic rules, that relate simple signs, vocabulary, to the world about and in which we speak, as narrowly or broadly as needed: e.g., "Use 'cow' if there is an udder, otherwise use 'steer' or 'bull'." These rules enable us to invent new simple signs whenever new reality seeks voice, to specify old signs more narrowly or broadly as becomes convenient, and endlessly to create new signs for old meanings and new meanings for old signs.

Because language has grammar, its sentences can be fitted to the sequences and changes of our life in time as closely as any act of world sharing may demand. With the sentences of language, we can share our very histories, our temporal selves. No novelty, no intrusion of new reality, or sudden vision of the future can evade the immediate creation of new signs by which to grasp and share it. Language is thus the very home of *spirit*, of life that transcends itself toward the future and toward other lives. It is our ability to speak sentences with one another that makes our capacity for spiritual being.

Sounds are for us the natural material of language. The artifacts we use for language must be wholly subject to our will; we must be able to produce and withold and shape them as we choose. Their possibilities of articulation, of variation and combination, must be very great. Apart from technology, it is sounds that we can make in such freedom. When the theological tradition talks of "audible" words, it means the sentences of language.

The other sort of words are those that do not belong to languages with grammar and do not make sentences. Some of these are the signs of sign systems with no syntax, as the hand gestures of social conversation. Others are the individually unique signs that we call "works of art." We cannot say in sentences what a handshake or the Seagram Building or Massacio's *Mary and Anna* says. Yet most manifestly they are speech—indeed, at once the most intimate and most inclusive speech, the speech by which we perhaps first come together to create a common world.

Here we are concerned with one sort of more-than-linguistic signs, the "sacraments" of a religious community. These depend for their power to speak on "institution," on an interplay between utterances in language, or what at least could be so uttered, and various characteristics of some actions with objects. It is when a religious founder says, e.g., of a sort of washing, "Do this and be clean," that it becomes a visible word of religious purity. On the side of the water, the possibility of a washing saying "purity before God" lies in washing's intrinsic character as a function in life. In other cases, the institution depends on creating a dramatic correspondence between features of an action with objects, and the divine reality to be invoked: as, e.g., the correspondence between the movements of a rain dance and the union of Father Sky and Mother Earth. Very often, both the functional reality of an action and its dramatic possibilities are together the element of an instituted sign: as, e.g., coitus as a function can be made to mean universal impregnation with Life, and as a performance can be made analogous to the impregnating descent of Father Sky's waters into Mother Earth.

II

A communicating being limited to words without syntax and semantics could not keep his or her world-sharing in pace with time, could not be spirit. But the very lack of grammar gives such words enormous and specific power of their own. Once a language with its rules is established, any of its signs can be replaced by others, merely by providing a definition. If we all agree to it, "cow" can be made superfluous by stipulating "x is a cow" is equivalent to "x is gli." The signs of a language are essentially replaceable.

The ontologically powerful characteristic of signs of the other sort is their *irreplaceability*. Donatello's *David* once created, there is no way to make another statue that will "say the same thing;" for there is no way to say in sentences what the *David* says and so no way to give instructions for its replacement or to test the equivalency. The bread and cup of the Supper once instituted, we cannot decide that from some time on we will say the same thing by forming a daisy chain and passing around a hug. For the way in which the bread and cup speak does not involve grammatical rules and there is therefore no way to give meaning to a definition that would say "Bread-plus-cup is equivalent to daisy-chain-with-sequential-hug." A handshake of peace has in a sense replaced the kiss of peace in many churches; but it most definitely does not say the same thing—as liturgical reformers who try to reverse the process quickly discover.

The ontological power of irreplaceable signs is that they place our discourse at home in the external world of objects. Let me introduce the pair-word for "spirit" and from now on speak also of "bodies." Every word is of course a body of some kind; a sentence made from sounds or marks is as much an object in the world as is a building or a pose. But if we abstract to what a sentence of language says only *qua* sentence, a few definitions will let us say the same thing next time by another object that does not at all resemble it. "X is a cow" can be replaced by "x is gli" or with more definition by "/ gli" or with other definitions by an arrangement of pebbles on the ground. The definitional replaceability of the signs of language means that their mass, non-linguistic function, and appearance, their sheer givenness as bodies in the world, is irrelevant to their purpose. Not so with signs lacking grammar. What the bread and cup say is not separable from their ordinary use, mass, and appearance, from their particularity as bodies in the external world. By the bread and cup, the gospel spoken in the mode of the Supper is an inalienably *embodied* word.

As our chief mode of objectifying consciousness, sight is the typical sensory mode of embodied words. We can of course make languages whose signs are in fact objects of sight—as the one I am now using. And we can make irreplaceable works of art that are in fact sounds. And all the other senses sometimes "see" and sometimes "hear." But the primal difference between communicating by sound and communicating by sight makes "visible word" a natural way to evoke a profound ontological fact: there are words that say what they say only as the bodies that they are. It is this ontological fact which the Reformation indicated by speaking of "visible words."

Our communication with each other is in part by fluid, historically replaceable signs which live in the magic of sentences. Such signs free us to live in time toward the future, to open the novelty each of us is to all the rest of us. And our communication with each other is in part by assertively present, historically irreplaceable signs, which once they are given, simply remain what they are and say until, perhaps, they and their meaning pass away altogether. Such signs embody us in the world for each other. The gospel, like other human discourse, is both. Insofar as the gospel takes established forms defined by embodied and embodying aspects, these are the sacraments.

III

I have asserted that embodied words are necessary to full community between us. Mankind has heretofore indeed supposed that a clan's totem or lovers' coitus or believers' sign of the cross exemplify the most necessary sort of discourse, without which we do not find one another at all. But this supposition is now no longer universal.

Much of modern life assumes that there is not, in fact, anything we must say to each other that could not in principle be said by sentences. The question must therefore be asked: Are there necessary matters of our community for the sharing of which the embodiment of our words is essential? It is hard, of course, to get hold of the question; for all our discourse is in fact embodied, so that we cannot imagine utterly disembodied community. But the development of technology has provided a model, and we may put the question so: Have we humans anything we must say to one another, that one computer simply *could* not say to another? A previous generation would have asked: Have we anything to say that disembodied spirits could not?

It may indeed be the dominance of technology that suggests the essential disembodiment of our communication. The "media," after all, progressively approximate our talk with each other to that among computers. And industrialization of human creation—at least under capitalist or orthodox Marxist auspices—means that few of us ever see an artifact that in fact says anything worth noting.

Whatever the causes, the suggestion is far advanced among us. The history of America since the Civil War could be told as one continuous de-ceremonializing of our communal life. Consider, for trivial example, the abolition of the 4th-of-July firecracker. Merely that it was slightly dangerous could not have sufficed to ban it; equally useless and far more dangerous items proliferate in our commerce: snowmobiles, martinis, hunting weapons, much marriage counseling, etc. We gave up the firecracker because it was "only" the ceremonial embodiment of our patriotic sentiments, and social technologists persuaded us we could be just as patriotic without it. But the whole 4th of July died with it. Read the nineteenth-century newspapers of your town or city: its rich ceremonial life was that almost of another culture.

Have we anything to say that a computer or pure spirit could not? It is almost impossible to argue the matter. For we cannot say in sentences what a firecracker says, and so cannot include its burden in an argument. And basic metaphysical issues are in general inarguable. But we can at least analyze what is at stake; the following chapters are in part such an analysis.

Recently, a priest in England tried to celebrate the Supper by television. Each little group was to have its bread and wine, to be blessed by the man on the tube. The metaphysical divide of our epoch is between those who will regard such an event as an interesting experiment or even a "breakthrough," and those who, like myself, will regard it as a joke in pitiably bad taste.

3

Spirit and Body

I

Along the way of the last chapter, I slipped in two words that have been pivots in the history of sacramentology: "spirit" and "body." They are the correlates of "audible" and "visible," insofar as all words are the communion of persons, the presence of persons in the lives of one another. And with the concept of *presence,* we arrive at a great traditional theme of sacramentology.

Christianity's sacraments are but the visibility of Christianity's constituting message, "the gospel," the promise of final human fulfillment made by what happens with Jesus. This news, when appropriately delivered, speaks to the personal concerns and hopes of its hearers: it is an *address* to them, a second-person intrusion into their self-containment. And every address is someone's personal presence. When I am addressed, I acquire a partner, I acquire a community of those for and against whom I live. There are two steps to show this.

First, if I am so addressed as to evoke hope or fear or decision, this means that human possibility that was not before *my* possibility now becomes mine. But human possibility is always someone's possibility; if not mine, then someone else's. If possibility that is not mine becomes mine, what occurs is the sharing of other humanity with me. There is absolutely no act of choice or anticipation that is purely inward and private: all specifically human experience is communal, the intrusion of other persons into my life and the emergence of my life from self-absorbtion.

In established community, this communication of human future may not, however, always be someone's personal presence. The *common* of any community is some established tradition of obligation and value;

and for any individual member of the community, these always remain partly future, partly new and even surprising. America is communally committed to "liberty," but my personal opening even to such liberty as America at any time offers is a life-long renovation. Thus hope and fear and decision are often, indeed usually, collectively communicated: it is often America, not any American, who calls me to decision and hope for "liberty."

But, and this is the second step, no community is self-sustaining. Over against the very hopes and commitments that bind it as community, every community regularly loses its hold on itself, loses its authority and plausibility for the persons who make it. When Americans now despair of America for the intransigent lack of liberty in the lives of most of us, it is precisely America that taught us we ought not be the state's mere subjects, and thus itself created the possibility of disappointment with America.

When a community—whether a nation, congregation, or family—is thus threatened with dissolution by its own collective hopes, new hope is needed. When Americans despair in the face of America's challenge to be free, it is not merely our performance that is questioned. The very liberty to which we are committed is questioned: is "free" in "free enterprise" really the same as in "free and equal"? Does a ballot between the offerings of two cooperating parties constitute democracy, if a ballot for the offerings of one party does not? Such questions demand moral creation; that is, they demand the opening of human possibility new also to the community and not only to its members. They demand a word that *creates* community, that calls it into being.

Such an address from beyond a community cannot itself be the collective voice. If I apprehend a word that creates community, I am in some *person*'s presence. The occurrence is not rare. For insofar as we do not merely depend upon the moral discourse of our communities, but also contribute to it, we are each of us present as persons to others.

If we did not live together by *word*, our mutual impingements would not be those of personal presence; what behavioral science says about our mutual behavior would be all there was to say. Or if we did not essentially live *together* at all, if at the depth of my free existence I were always alone, there would be no personal mutuality at all. But as it is, we have not yet fully conformed our lives to the nightmares either of Mr. Skinner or Mr. Sartre: other people are neither only the modifiers of our behavior nor yet hell. If we may be at once free and together, it is by our *addresses* to each other. Our presence to one another occurs in that each of us emerges from what might have been the isolation of his life to bring from it what is indeed particular and strange and set it before his fellows, just thereby calling them also from their private selves.

II

Spirit is one aspect of this personal presence. I am spirit in that you are present in my life to set me *free* for yourself and in that I am present in your life to set you free for myself. From the New Testament and especially from Paul, both theology and western philosophy have learned that personal beings are—for good and ill—free in time, liberated from what is by the beckoning and impact of what is not yet. From the New Testament and especially from Paul, theology and philosophy have also learned that the impact upon me of the future is always the impact of some other person, who just as other brings what is new to me. And from New Testament and especially Pauline usage we have learned to call this historical freedom "spirit."

Perhaps you are courageous in some way I would not have thought plausible, or perhaps you entertain an idea that would overthrow a whole set of my ideas, or perhaps you see colors in a way I miss. In some way, you are future to me, and however trivial the differences may be, any joint reality that you and I create with sentences and other signs posits new human possibility for me. Just thereby my future opens; just thereby I am self-transcendent in time. And just thereby *you* appear in my life—not only as my perception and conception of you, not only as the construct I make and manipulate and call "So-and-so"—but as yourself, as the subject of that possibility that is not in this moment mine and that beckons me out of myself and this moment. You appear in my life as genuinely other, as free from me and just so liberating for me. It is this appearance that is personal presence, as spirit. Spirit is the liberating presence of other subjects of my life.

When the theological tradition analyzes our communication as "law" and "promise," the analysis is in respect of the different ways in which words open the future, that is, of the different ways in which they mediate spiritual presence. If you speak law to me, the possibility of some new humanity is indeed opened to me, but I am left alone to achieve it.

If you make a promise to me, you yourself take responsibility for the new achievement in my life; just so, you enter my life to stay.

If you impose a law on me, such as that I must study hard if I am to understand the sacraments, your entry into my life is real enough, but there is also a withdrawal. If you make the law stick, the very structure of my life is altered, and you are the author of this alteration: if indeed understanding of the sacraments becomes a value of my life, and if I am left to my own exertions to achieve it, a causal connection is put into the sequences of my life and you are its guardian and manipulator. But you yourself remain remote; none of your exertions or fears or abilities are in play.

One who was present to me only by law would be present as nobody in particular, as sheer invading foreign subjectivity, as empty naked sovereignty. Such a presence—and it is our salvation that it never quite occurs—would be "pure" spirit, the nightmare dream of philosophers and the religious. Such a presence would be *disembodied* spirit—which brings us to the other matter of this chapter.

III

I introduced "body" as a synonym for "object"; in this sense, the inkwell and pen on my desk and the organism moving them are all bodies. But it is of course that pen-pushing organism, a *person's* body, that is the first matter of my usage and that of the theological tradition. It is as an aspect of personal presence polar to spirit that I will speak of *body*. I will be concerned with such bodies as the inkwell and pen, or the body of water in which we baptize, precisely and only insofar as they too are drawn into personal communication, and so come to belong to personal embodiment.

The spirit must be invoked, the body described. My discussion of the phenomenon of the personal body, and of the language which brings this phenomenon to word, must therefore be somewhat more analytical than was my discussion of spirit. What is a personal body? I perceive five determinents.

First, the body is the *object*-presence of a person. Personal presence occurs always as address, as the word-event by which one person enters the reality of another. This entrance may be destructive: it may initiate a mutual reality of lordship-and-slavery, and of struggle over who will be which. If it does not, it is because the address is such as to enable and solicit reply; i.e., because the one who enters grants himself as object also of the other's intention. Contrary to much of what has been said on the matter, authentic personal mutuality depends precisely on mutual self-objectification. If I address you, I make you my object. If I do not seek to enslave you, I so address you as also to grant myself as your object. Of course, there is indeed that treating of the other "as a thing" which has been so often decried; but what this consists in, is that I seek *so* to make you my object as to withhold my own self-objectification.

The total of possibilities, that I may grant myself as object for those I address, is "my body". The body is the self, as the describable and so intendable object of an other self. The body is the available self.

Second, the body is the object-presence of the person *also to himself.* My body is myself insofar as I am available to myself, insofar as I am not merely identical with myself, but *possess* myself. In that I am body, I have myself as object of my knowledge and will, as something in the world I can work on and make plans for. Just so also, I have myself as an object with whose given and causally involved characteristics I must reckon.

Whether or not there is immediate self-consciousness, there surely is mediate self-consciousness as consciousness of my own body. This consciousness is interpersonally mediated. In that you have me as your object and in that you and I share a world in our communication, I also have myself as a worldly object. And in that I have myself as an object I may address also myself: thus the word becomes my interior reality. Once again contrary to much of what has been said, the inner linguisticality of personal existence, its essential character as choice and hope and knowledge, depends upon the person's objectification in a society.

Third, therefore, the body is the to-be-transcended presence of the person. In that you can address me, and so exhort, enlighten, curse, bless, or make promises to me, you are beyond me, speaking from a hope and clarity—or damnation and darkness—which is not mine and which your words open. And most remarkably, in that I also have myself as my object, I transcend *myself*, I am beyond myself as a describable object in the world; and so am not merely a describable object.

What I then am, is a specifically theological question. I may transcend myself in two opposed ways. There is a transcendence which is the unalterability of the past; and there is a transcendence which is the freedom of the future. As non-object, I may be the one I *was* in the beginning, and still "really" am in an eternity which is the persistence of the beginning; or I may be the one I am not yet but will be in that eternity which is the triumph of the end. If the gospel is true, the true God is the triumph of the last future. Then the self-transcendence which leads to life must be so described: you speak to me from a hope and clarity which is *not yet* mine, and I am *future* to myself as an object in the world.

Just so, the body, which is thus transcended, mediates the past. In that I give myself as body, I give the one I already am, I give the product of my deeds and sufferings to date. The only available self is the so-far-achieved self. The body is the possibility of *re*cognition, the availability of continuity with the past.

Fourth, in that the body is the available person and mediates the past person, it is the person's *identifiability*. To address myself to one addressing me, I must be able to pick him out from the maelstrom of actuality. I may do this by merely pointing—to his body, not his spirit. Insofar as the act of identification becomes linguistic, it occurs by, or depends upon, "definite descriptions": "the one who . . . and who . . . and who . . ." and so on until the "Oh, that one" falls. The clauses after "who" will either be descriptions of the person's bodily appearance or location, or biographical items, items of that past which the body mediates. Identification depends entirely on the body; a pure spirit would be—at least for all others—no one in particular and everyone in general.

Fifth, it is insofar as the possibilities of object-presence, which are the body, are realized, that there occur *visible words*. A person who was present only by utterances of language would withhold his objectivity. It is insofar as in our communication we grant ourselves as objects that we make words not governed by grammar, and so not replaceable in their givenness as objects in the world. The totality of my visible addresses is my body's realization, its gesture, its act.

IV

Personal life occurs only in community. Just so, it can fail, according to either of its aspects, spirit or body.

Were I a fundamentally self-contained entity, I would not be spirit. I might perhaps still be a sort of abstract mind, perceiving reality beyond myself. But since I would not be drawn or shaken by that reality, I would not be drawn or shaken by what is beyond what I at any moment am. I would be changeless—which were I God, would be fine for me and disastrous for all else, and since I am not God, would be irrelevant to all else and disastrous for me. Were I a fundamentally self-contained entity, I would not be self-transcendent in time.

Insofar as late-modern ambition is that each of us shall be sole subject in his "own" life, the possibility of spirit is attacked, and must be fought for with increasing explicitness and tenacity. To the exact extent that marriage indeed becomes a revocable arrangement between permanently "independent" individuals, religion becomes self-realization, politics retreat to the "privacy of the voting booth," and in short the consumer ethic generally triumphs, our life is in the most primitive sense *dispirited*. Simultaneous lethargy and frenzy is the dominant characteristic of all those persons and groups in which late-modern abstract individualism is most consistently achieved. It is our society's trick to make egocentricity a virtue; but it will not work, for my alienation from you is my alienation also from myself.

Our reality as spirit for one another is not self-sustaining. It can fail, regularly has, and now often does. If there is spirit that will not fail, we call such spirit *God*. God's presence is the coming of such Spirit.

Were I a fundamentally self-contained entity, I would not be body. I would undoubtedly be an organism, and subject to Newton's laws about masses in space. And we would impinge on each other, in the way of the celebrated billiard balls. But I would not be *available to* you, nor even to myself; there would just be this organic mass, fundamentally interchangeable with any other, and precisely as incomprehensibly and externally identified with a particular mind as Descartes found it. Were I a fundamentally self-contained entity, I would not be available through time.

Our reality as bodies also can fail. The progressive disembodiment of late-modern civilization is full of ironies—as that Christianity is routinely attacked for, of all things, enmity against the body, often by persons visibly at war even with the organic condition of their own embodiment. Who devalues the body? Those for whom its gestures make no commitments, or those for whom they can make irrevocable commitment? Those who find freedom in casual nakedness, or those who reserve this most visible word for those to whom they have something extraordinary to say? Our society's frenzy for the body is precisely frenzy for what we lack. Those who refuse all decisive commitment and so withdraw from availability, who have no grasp on the past, who wear instant clothes and make instant love and eat instant food, who forever are seeking identity, flit as wraiths through time, hungering for embodiment.

Body and spirit fail together. Were you pure spirit in my life, you would be nobody in particular, but a nobody who yet gave me orders. That is, you would belong to one of those impersonal but ruling collectives—bureaucratized corporations, militarized government, or the "media"—that do in fact now determine so much of life. Were *all* others pure spirit in my life, these collectivities would appear to and in me as one and absolute, the dream of totalitarians would be fulfilled—and freedom and spirit too would cease.

The obvious outcome of the last paragraphs must be the proposition: if there is body that does not fail, we call such body *God*. Therewith we have the great offense of Christian discourse about God. And therewith we have the subject of the next chapter and the foundation of Christian sacramentology. For indeed, God is a person; and that means that he is Spirit *and* Body.

PART TWO

SACRAMENTAL PRESENCE

4

The Body of God

I

The fundamental proposition we must grasp, to understand the Christian sacraments, is this: there is at least one matter we have to communicate with each other, to the saying of which the embodiment of discourse is essential, and that matter is God. Whatever else a disembodied word could be, it could not be a word of or to God. Indeed, the disappearance of ritual and art and physical expression from our ordinary communal life is the heart of our practical atheism. Those who need special "groups" to touch each other, are the ultimate unbelievers.

Since I am a creature, I may attempt to be present to you in some purely "spiritual" and disembodied address. We can also imagine my success, by which I would become for you an ineffable being-in-general, and so make you my slave, my object only, a thing of the past also for yourself. The dialectics of this attempt have been worked out again and again in the modern world: by thinkers[1] in warning or despair and in practice by totalitarian politics and corporate capitalism.

God cannot even be imagined as so revealing himself. The word in which God—for the present, *any* God—communicates himself must be an embodied word, a word "with" some visible reality, a grant of divine objectivity. We must be able to see and touch what we are to apprehend from God; religion cannot do without sacrament.

This is so because the inalienable characteristic of any reality we could call "God" is eternity. What makes God God is that he transcends the discontinuities of time, that he binds the wounds that open between our past and future, that with him what I have been and what I may and must yet be somehow make one life. The address of God—any God—

28

rhymes remembrance with hope, is the possibility that anticipation may vivify the past and recollection give content to the future. God is eternal: in his presence my present embraces and is embraced by the past which is its substance and the future which is its point.

Therefore the address of a God must be spirited *and* embodied, language *and* sacrament. It must open an infinite future, but it must rhyme that future with all the past. Therefore it must be inalienably spirited *and* inalienably embodied. A disembodied, purely linguistic communication, however it might occur and whoever or whatever might be able so to speak, could not reveal God. God's presence must grant an object.

II

I have been describing what must be true of the word of any "God." But, of course, the description was made from the viewpoint of faith in the specific God of the Bible. The observations made are, I claim, true; but they are undoubtedly not those a Buddhist would have made about his own religion. The word of God is indeed necessarily embodied in any religion; but most religions do not make God's word central, nor therefore its embodiment.

In religion untouched by the biblical message, the God's eternity is grasped as his *immunity* to time, as his changelessness. This God is eternal because he has no future, being from the beginning all that he ever will be. Just so, such a God has no past either; for he never was anything he is not now. Plato clearly defined the reality of normal religion's God: he is a "standing present," an infinite present moment unbounded by anything yet to come or no more here.

Vice versa, the present moment of normal religion's God is in no way like our present moment, bounded by past and future. This God's present is neither the palpable stretch of time, itself an arena of change and action, that we ordinarily mean by "the present," nor is it the moving line between past and future which we may conceive if we turn to speculation. This God's present is pure changelessness, a single moment that swallows up all memory and all expectation—and *so* rhymes them. This God's present can therefore at best only be *imitated* by the presentness of any body of the world; no reality of this world can truly *be* his body. For all realities of the world are temporal and subject to change. If the word that rhymes our past and future does so by abolishing time, a body in the world can only momentarily be that word's embodiment. In normal religion, no visible word can more than momentarily speak the coherence of past and future; then it must be left behind.

The embodiments of the word of normal religion's God can only momentarily imitate God's present to us. If, then, religion's profoundest movement, the longing for God *himself*, comes alive in such religion, this longing must soon leave all embodiment behind. At the highest stages of non-biblical religion, there are no more sacraments. If such religion is open to mystical experience, the mystic ascent will soon see all embodiment as a barrier between God and the self that must be pierced, and see all sacraments as crutches for beginners. If such religion is open to philosophical sublimation, its philosophers will soon talk of its sacraments as mere "symbols," no longer needed by those who achieve the higher knowledge. If such religion is a source of moral energy, its activists will soon contrast "outward forms" with a true religion of love for the neighbor.

We have arrived at a paradox. That God—any God—speaks, requires embodied words. Yet for normal religion, embodiment is to be overcome. There is, however, no contradiction. For in normal religion, God's speech is itself a phenomenon of the lower levels. The ascent away from the embodiment of God's word leads to God's silence; but the God of normal religion is, in his own true reality, silent. The apprehension of God by his self-communication is, outside biblical faith, a mere starting point toward his more passionate or more true or more active apprehension.

The paradox of normal religion is yet more drastic. Insofar as we are personal beings, and therefore live only by communication, we may well think that a silent God would be for us the same as no God at all. At normal religion's last heights of mystical illumination or philosophical penetration or moral urgency, it agrees—and does not shrink from the consequence. Thus Buddhism and German idealism and American activism agree in one thing, that worry about God belongs to an inferior level of religious experience. The most highly developed forms of normal religion either drop the word *God* altogether, or use it as a cipher for realities that could be described without it, or use it for the absence of specific reality, for everything-in-general and nothing-in-particular, for Silence and Nothingness.

Just at this point, Christianity is an abnormal religion. If Christianity makes religiously odd claims about its sacraments—e.g., that God is "really" present in them—it does so because its God is a religiously odd God: he refuses to fall silent. The very first doctrine to be fully worked out in all the history of the faith, and the doctrine by which Christianity once and for all grasped its own individuality among the religions of mankind, is that with the gospel's God there is *no* "silence of eternity," that this God's word is eternally spoken, that this God *is* his word.

Though often tempted, Christianity has at every turn refused to share the great religious quest for God above and beyond his communication with us. In the Arian controversy of the fourth century, it was tempted to the mystical form of the quest: to seek direct experience of God transcending the experience of the story about Jesus. The temptation was overcome when Gregory of Nyssa at last said clearly: of the God we worship, there *is* no such experience. He is wholly in Jesus his Word; there is nothing of him left over to be otherwise experienced. In the Pelagian controversy of the next century, the church was tempted to the ethical form of the quest: to achieve goodness with merely the *help* of the gospel. The temptation was overcome when Augustine at last said clearly: apart from what hearing the gospel does for us, we have no goodness to be helped. By the systematics of late medieval theology, the church was tempted to the intellectual form of the quest: to define the reality of God by what we see and deduce of him rather than by what he says to us. The temptation was overcome when Luther at last said clearly: true theology begins and ends as interpretation of God's reality by what the gospel says about the Crucified.

As the gospel's God refuses to fall silent, so he refuses to fade away at the heights of our religion. Of course, what Christians *call* "God" is often in fact the God of some more usual form of religion; then movements such as the late "Christian atheism" are a necessary protest.[2] But strictly speaking, the proprium of the religions of the Bible is that they are never atheistic. Christianity—like Judaism and Islam[3]—is and remains proclamation and worship of God, at all possible levels of sophistication or naiveté.

Therefore: while sacraments have precarious or penultimate status in religion by and large, it is a distinguishing mark of Christianity that it is decidedly and finally sacramental. If God is one thing humans have to communicate with one another, to the saying of which the word's embodiment is essential, God is the one thing Christians cannot cease to communicate. Insofar as our communities remain faithful to the specific gospel, we are bound to embodied discourse. All anti-sacramentalism in the church is forgetfulness of which God we worship; it is idolatry. The gospel wants to be as visible as possible.

III

The gospel's insistence on embodiment has radical consequences for the life of the gospel's community. It has even more remarkable consequences for our understanding of God.

The God of the gospel does not merely happen, given certain conditions, to reveal himself; so that if the revelation succeeds and we know God, we find some other reality than the revelation that led us to him. The God of the gospel so reveals himself in Jesus Christ that when we know God, what we know about him is just that he is the one who reveals himself in Jesus Christ.[4] And in knowing this, we know all there is to know about God. The God of the gospel does not merely have a word for us; he *is* his Word. The event that God is and the event that we are addressed in Christ are but one occurrence; God's act of self-communication is the act of his reality as God.

Once it is given that there is God, and that there are also we who are other than God, all religion admits that an act of divine self-communication must occur if we are to know and will God. But the gospel says of its God that he *is* his self-communication. Therefore the gospel must say that God would communicate himself even if there were no others than God, or if he had cut us off from himself and spoke no more to us. This assertion that God would be in communication even if not with creatures, is the doctrine of the Trinity: the reality of relation and communication is given in God himself, prior to all relation and communion of God with any who are not God. And indeed it is that doctrine which finally interprets all Christianity's claims about its verbal proclamation and sacraments.

If the God of the gospel does not merely penultimately and for certain purposes communicate himself, and if divine self-communication is essentially embodied, it follows that the God of the gospel does not merely penultimately and for certain purposes embody himself. God *is* the Word he speaks; and the word he speaks is an embodied Word.

Which is what was to be demonstrated: God has a body, in at least all the five ways described in the last chapter.

To assert that God has a body is mightily to offend our entire inherited way of thinking about reality, and to ally oneself verbally with a rag-tag of Christian theological history's conceptual incompetents. But it is also to ally oneself with the whole tendency of Christianity's spiritual and liturgical language, and with the deeper and less inhibited thrusts of its theology. The whole of our theological language and education is shaped by the teaching of late pagan antiquity, that body and spirit, object and subject, are two radically distinct sorts of realities, and that if God is—as Scripture indeed teaches—true Spirit, he therefore cannot be body at all. But that this way of thinking is inevitably our initial way, does not make it true. My venture in this chapter, which is the conceptual heart of this book, is simply to take seriously the *special* ways in which the gospel talks of God, despite the offenses to which that first leads.

Christianity must assert the embodiment of God, and has always done so, however half-heartedly. Traditional theology, at least in its popular versions, has handled the matter by describing a series of what one can only call metaphysical additions. First there is God, who as such is permanently disembodied. But this God is also, in a second place, triune, which enables his right hypostasis not to know what his left hypostasis is doing: the Son can involve himself with bodies while the Father maintains the divine immateriality unsullied. The Son's involvement with bodies is required by God's grace; for we, to whom he wishes to be present, can apprehend no presence that is not a bodily presence. Therefore the Son was united with the man Jesus, who does have a body; thus embodiment was added to God. On returning to God, the Son took this body with him. But in the sacramental side of the gospel-proclamation, and especially in the bread and cup, God provided a substitute. Now there are, on the one hand, the sacramental objects present to us, and on the other hand, the body of Christ. The task of sacramental theology is to explain yet another addition: how Christ's body gets joined to the bodies at the table, or perhaps vice versa.

What is proposed in this chapter is quite a different doctrine of God's embodiment, a doctrine of God as embodied in and of himself, and not only by additive adaptation to us. I will assert of God as such all the descriptions by which the previous chapter specified the phenomenon of the personal body.

IV

The embodiment of God can be described in three steps. The first is to note that if God indeed is word eternally in himself, then God eternally *addresses* God. God intends God, God has God as an object of will and knowledge, God has God as what he can describe and specify. God has himself as his own *object*.

Just and only so, God can if he wills be an object also of others than himself. If that as which God intends himself and some object presented to our intention, are the same, then we know and will God. That God "reveals" himself means that the following occurs: God speaks promise to us; we seek to reply; and an object which we intend as we seek to reply, an object to which we address ourselves as in speaking to you I address your body, is the same object that God intends in the eternal conversation that is his own life. This event can be. God is, also in his self-intention and self-possession, utterly free. If he chooses to have himself as an object that is also our object, that is how it is.

And in fact, relevation occurs. "The gospel," an unconditional promise of every human fulfillment, that only God could legitimately make, does in fact sound through our times; we do in fact apprehend a call that claims to be from God. This promise is made "in Jesus' name," in the name of an historic person who can be and is our object, and, at least to begin with, in the most straightforward sense. It is precisely in that the promise is made in such a person's name, that the promise is not the intrusion of some ineffable "pure" spirit, to reduce us to slavery.

When we believe the promise, this Jesus is the object of our intention: it is he that we know and turn to. But if the promise is *true,* if it does communicate unconditional final creaturely fulfillment, if it is the insurpassable word of God, then this same object Jesus must be the object also of God's intention of himself. As God turns to himself, to what he knows and wills for and of himself, he turns to Jesus, the man from Nazareth. It is in knowing and willing what happened with Jesus and what is promised by these events, that God knows and wills who and what he is. He might have turned to himself as to some other personal object; but in marvellous fact he does not. Just so, straightforwardly and without construction of any metaphysical layer cake, Jesus, the body who dwelt in Palestine, is "one of the Trinity."

Of course, the above is true only by Jesus' resurrection. If Jesus were our object *only* as an item of history, only as Caesar or great-grandfather are our objects, he would not be the revelation of God. For God is God of the living: his body is not a corpse. To be the revelation of God Jesus must be now a living man; and to be that he must *now* speak ever new and surprisingly to us. Also this speaking must be embodied, and he be a body in it. We arrive again at the sacraments.

The body that is the church, and the sacramental bodies around which it gathers, are said in Scripture to be the body of the living Jesus Christ. What this can mean and how it can be true, are the matter of the next chapter. Here we are concerned with the gospel's sacramental embodiment as the embodiment of *God* only. Moving from the historic Jesus' embodiment to the sacramental embodiment of the gospel proclamation, I may to this concern simply repeat myself: if God chooses to intend himself as our washing, bread, cup, gestures, and touchings, as those objects that make the present-tense body of Christ, then he so chooses and the ensemble of all these is in fact his body. As God turns to himself, he turns to the shared loaf and cup, to the bath, to our sheer visible and tangible presence to one another, and in general to all our community's objectivity in the gospel. In all this, he sees himself. That he does so, is our salvation.

The second step: to say that God has a body is to say that God *transcends* himself, that he has history. The true God is eternal not because he *lacks* time, but because he always *has* time. There is in God beginning and goal, what is left behind and what is set ahead, what is past and what is future. God possesses himself as a body-self he transcends, as what he frees himself from and for. The body of the historic Jesus ended on the cross; and each sacramental embodiment of the gospel ceases. It is precisely in that God at once moves beyond these endings, and yet defines his life by faithfulness to them, that he is—in his own particular way—eternal God.

In transcending himself, in having beginning and end, God is like us. This need cause no embarrassment, if once we are over the inherited

notions of "pure" spirit and its time*less* sort of eternity. That the
dialectics of personal life operate both for God and for us simply means
that he lives as a person and involves us in that life. What happens
with Jesus is the involving.

God leaves himself behind, and just so chooses and wins himself, for
the goal that is his own purpose and our fulfillment. The event of this
is the crucifixion and resurrection of Jesus. Self-transcendence is not
so simple as loose talk about "self-realization" and its banal like suggests. Really to leave one's old self behind is to die: it is have one's
body as the corpse kind of body—all serious religious and political
commitment has known that. To be beyond oneself *then,* to look back
then, is either to be deathless disembodied spirit, to have fully *escaped*
from the body, or it is to *rise* from the dead. To do either by oneself
is to be God; the thing once done, others can be included. There are
really only two candidates to be the true God; and they are mutually
exclusive. To be deathless disembodied spirit, is to be Brahman-
Atman; to bring off death and new life in one personal embodied life,
is to be the Trinity.

In the doctrine of the Trinity, the "Father" is God as the beginning
of an infinite self-transcendence. The Father is precisely a *hope* that
always calls for what is not yet—who longs for the joy and mutuality
we yet do not realize, and just so creates them, who when there was
nothing but himself evoked what was not yet from that nothing. It is
precisely the accomplishing of the hope that is the Father, that is the
being of God.

The Father knows himself in Jesus' body that walked to the cross,
and in the objects that are used and used up in the gospel-communication. That is, he knows them as visible *words*: he knows the future
they open, the possibility they promise. We know God in that these
very same objects are given to our faithful intention, to all our listening
and looking for the hope God is for us. Just so, the Father is the
object of our faith: the one to whom we address our prayer and praise.

We learned to call God "Father" from the Gospels' record of Jesus'
usage. "Father" was Jesus' address to God as embodied in the history and religious practice of Israel. That address so directed actually
reaches God, that this embodiment is actually of God, is finally achieved
in Jesus' own life, death, and resurrection. Following Jesus, and
enabled by what happened with him, we too say "Father," we too turn

to God and talk to him and bring our gifts: we too make him our object.

When Protestantism becomes abstract or a touch bitter, it sometimes supposes that we are always and only God's object and he never ours, that the whole of our religious and liturgical turning to God, the whole reality of prayer and sacrifice and praise ought really to be eliminated, that it is at best God's concession to our weakness. And indeed, we have seen that Christianity is a very peculiar religion, that its prayer and obedience have a foundation and place different from those of other religion: God, according to the gospel, has communion with us solely by his address to us and not at all as a result of our quest for him. But God does not maintain his exclusive initiative by *hiding* from our prayer and obedience, by de-objectifying himself from before us. Rather, he maintains his exclusive initiative precisely by intruding himself embodied into our lives and refusing to let us escape from or transcend this embodiment. God is utterly sovereign precisely in persisting as our religious object, in letting us turn to him as "Father" with our prayers and songs and offerings, and never letting us turn to him in any other way.

It has regularly been asked: Would God really let his body be pushed about on the Supper's table, or given over to all and sundry who come? The question is logically ironic and poses Christianity on its knife edge. For to answer "No" is to confess the sort of God who could have no body anyway. It is precisely in that the Supper, and all the sacramental reality of the gospel, enact God's giving of himself over to us and his lordship just *thereby* established, that it can be God's true embodiment.

Third, God *identifies* himself by Jesus. This is the deepest yet most quickly made statement of God's embodiment. In that God is self-transcendent person, the question "Who am I?" is his question as it is ours, though the threat of puzzlement and failure is not. And in the inner converse of his life, he answers, "I am the one who raised the man Jesus from the dead." That this is so, is the saving fact. That it has come to be so, is the saving work. This inner self-identification is God's very being. He might have been other than this affirmation of the man of our hope; that he is what he is, is the accomplishment of Jesus' life, death, and resurrection.

If there has been the resurrection of Jesus, then to the question "Who is God?" we must answer, "Whoever did that." When we are being religiously usual, we identify God by our religious needs, e.g., "God is whoever is omnipotent, as I—I have just again discovered—am not." Then we seek additional information, e.g., on what terms he will share his omnipotence, from revelation. The gospel has a different logic. The truth of its knowledge of God occurs in that God freely identifies himself in the same way that he lets us identify him. The fact of revelation is the fact of freely granted coincidence of the way we pick God out and the way he picks himself out.

In The Great Thanksgiving of the Supper, according to most ancient orders, the prayer called the Anamnesis turns to God to recall before him the life, death, and resurrection of the Lord, and to plead for fulfillment of the promises to which God by these events committed himself. At this place in the service, this reminding of God is done not only with the words, but with the bread and cup to which the Narrative of Institution has just turned all our intention. Thus we propose these objects to God, as those by which he shall remember his past acts and the commitments thereby entered, i.e., as those by which he shall identify himself. Just so, the sacramental objects are, in this third way, the body of God.

V

I must return briefly to an earlier concern of this chapter. I can now say *why* Christian faith is essentially a communal reality and not an individual possession: the sacramental presence of the gospel's particular God is not separable from the community it creates.

The presence of a "pure" spirit would reduce me to slavery. Just so, it could not be the presence of God, who must be precisely the meaning of my life. Yet normal religion at its higher levels seeks precisely the presence of pure spirit. Here is a second paradox to be resolved.

On one condition, a present pure spirit would not enslave me: if that spirit turned out ultimately to be identical with me, so that he did not at all stand over against me. And just that is the assertion and aspiration of normal religion at its higher levels: "Brahman is Atman," the Absolute without and the Deep within are identical, God is always already in me as my own true self. But this has a drastic consequence: since the same must be true for you, and since there can be only one pure spirit, your deep self and mine must also be identical. For high normal religion, there is finally no plurality of persons, and community, the mutuality of persons, is a phenomenon only of lower levels of spiritual progress. At the summit, I am absolutely alone.

For biblical faith, on the other hand, God's presence is never pure spirit; he is always embodied. Thus he is and remains *available* to me, and just so another person than I; and his self-communication is always an address to me from outside. But it is my fellow humans that are out there talking. Thus the address of the gospel's God is always also the address of my fellows; and the presence of the gospel's God is always also their presence, and just in their available externality to me, in their embodiment. It takes at least two to gospel, one to speak and one to hear and turn-about.

The embodiment of God's word is permanent. In all eternity, therefore, there will be no community with God that is not also our community with each other. The verbal and more-than-verbal speakings of this God's word are always also rites of community: e.g., baptism is at once initiation into God's fellowship and into ours. This simultaneity obtains for the communal rites of all religions, at the lower stages—that is where the word *sacrament* came from in the first place. But in Christian faith, the communal rites will not fade away, nor can they be transformed into symbols or means of a private relation to God. And this too holds for all eternity.

NOTES

1. The greatest treatment is still the first, the "Slavery and Lordship" section of Hegel's *Phenomenology of Spirit*.

2. It should be noted that Thomas Altizer is *not* an atheist, even in this sense. For him "death of God" belongs to the rhetoric of a specific, and intensively Christian, doctrine of *God*.

3. In Judaism, the nation is the sacrament. In Islam, no sacraments are needed since nothing is in fact said about God save that he is.

4. To have worked this out in every thinkable detail is the permanent historical achievement of Karl Barth's *Church Dogmatics*.

5

The Present Christ

Every existential address is someone's presence. If I hear a word that in any way opens or closes my future, I have to do with some person; the only question is, with whom. The audible and visible gospel is an address to me, and so is someone's presence to me. It is only a vice versa of much of the previous chapter to say: and that someone is God.

The gospel is a community-creating existential address. When and where its speaking occurs, we are in some person's presence and not only in the presence of the churchly collective. The question is: in *whose* presence? Since every believer contributes to the speaking of the gospel, and does not merely hear or recite it, part of the answer must in each case be that we are in the presence of a creative believing witness. But that cannot be the whole answer. For there is a further proposition to be reckoned with: every existential address that creates *eschatological* community is *God's* personal presence.

Given what is already established, the just-stated proposition is analytical. What we *mean* by "God" is whoever or whatever has all the future there is, so that his community can never fail. If there is community against which the gates of hell will not prevail, if there is fellowship open to eternal fellowship, the word that supports such community must be God's personal self-communication. If a promise is spoken that promises the final accomplishment of the human enterprise, the occurrence of this speaking is the presence of God—if, of course, the promise is true.

In an authentic family, mother and father create a community by the aspirations they state for the group; just so, they are inevitably somewhat more than human, the inevitable originals of the childrens' inner ikons. Yet Mother and Father move to death, and so can honestly make only conditional promises: "If I can . . . I will. . . ." The first time their conditions are called and they cannot do what was promised, Mother and Father lose their capital letters, rejoin the rest of the family in merely conditional possession of value—and the family knows its mortality.

Every personal address grants new human possibility, and just so sustains the life of some community. But within any community to which I contribute, I am dependent on its continuing moral discourse for my very ability to address it. Just so, my word can open no certainly triumphant hope, no hope in utter defiance of the community's own possible failure. There is, e.g., no way for me to say to America in my own competence: "American liberty will come to all nations and to all corners of life—if need be, in despite of America." If there is in any community a word that sounds so, and is not mere hybris and illusion, its event is God's presence. If the gospel is not hybris and illusion, then where it happens God is.

But now we must consider that the gospel, the audible and visible speaking of which is the presence of God, has a narrative content. It is not an abstract declaration of God's good will for us. It is an account of human events past and future, the story of Israel and Jesus the Israelite.

My discussion of God's presence has been in fact christological at every step. I must now make this explicit. The presence of God was understood as his presence in the story about Israel's Christ; it is what this says about *Christ* that we have now to consider. The presence of God in the audible and visible gospel was explicated by God's identity as the Trinity; it is what trinitarian talk about God says about *Christ's* presence in the gospel that is our next matter. How may we describe the sacraments as events of Jesus' human presence? In particular, as the sacraments are *embodied* words, how may we describe them as his *bodily* presence?

There is a short way with this question, if the assertions of the previous chapter are accepted. The presence of God as "pure" spirit would destroy us. It is the promise of the gospel that the true God is our God for good and not for ill; if this is so, then—at least in the gospel itself—God is never present except embodied. God's body is Jesus Christ. Therefore the sacramental presence of God is always also the presence of this man; the body that lived in Palestine and hung on a cross, and the embodiment of the church's gospel-proclamation are but one reality. But these dialectics, though they are true and say all there is to say about the reality of Christ's bodily presence in proclamation and sacrament, are too compressed for our present purpose. We must examine more concretely the gospel and its assertions about Christ.

II

The most concise statement of the gospel is: "Jesus is risen." There is no strand or stratum of New Testament witness which can not be derived from this sentence. This is the news with which the first witnesses crisscrossed the Mediterranean world to create the church. The news can be unpacked in many ways; e.g., in the Hellenistic mission it was unpacked to meet late antiquity's longing for a true monotheism: by conquering even death, the God of Israel—the missionaries said—had established that he is the single and only power with which we must reckon. The gospel occurs always as an act of interpretation: the moving hopes and fears of those who at a time speak and hear, and the claimed fact of Jesus' resurrection are brought to interpret one another. The event of this confrontation is the speaking of the gospel. Yet to whatever unexpected proclamations the history of this interpretation may bring us, the one pole is always "Jesus is risen."

". . . is risen" is a predicate meaningful only within the tradition of Israel's history and faith. Alone among religions, Israel made no compromises with death. Death was not for Israel the gateway to other life, not even in the form of lasting fame and glory as among the early Greeks. "In the grave, there is no praise of JHWH," was Israels' last word on the subject. Therefore Israel's God, uniquely among gods, bore nothing of Beneficent Death or of polar and supplementary Decay and Growth about him; he and death were simply opposites. "God is the God of the living and not of the dead," said Jesus. Death was and remained "the last enemy," in whom all enemies of human fulfillment— sin, evil, or meaninglessness—are comprehended, the reality which transforms all future into might-have-been. And JHWH's claim to be the one true God could finally be established only by conquest of death. The question addressed to Ezekiel was Israel's one great question: "Son of a man, can these bones live?"

In Israel the claim that one "had risen from the dead" was thus a claim that Israel's God at last had fully verified his godhead, and that just so mankind's way to fulfillment was open. ". . . is risen" has therefore nothing to do with resuscitation, with a merely temporal and temporary benefit to someone who will yet die. If one is "risen," then death is *behind* him; and then neither death nor guilt or impersonal evil can close his future. But then nothing can any longer defeat the hope by which his life has been moved, by which his choices have been made, and his sufferings endured. What this may mean for others than the risen one depends on what his desires and decisions in fact have been. However the risen one's will has been defined, that will must triumph. In the New Testament, "Jesus is risen," unpacks to "Jesus rules" or "Jesus is Lord." The well-known ambiguity of "Lord" in the New Testament, as title of a man with disciples and as divine title, perfectly reflects the dialectic in which God's own deity is achieved in and as the triumph of one man's hopes and choices.

If indeed one is risen, then the question for all others is: "*Who* is risen?" It is the *identity* of the risen one that determines the meaning of a resurrection. Were the message that Hitler was risen, this would be no good news. It is to the question of identity that "Jesus . . ." gives answer; the proper name identifies the subject of whom the resurrection claim is made. It is because *this* one is risen, the last prophet of Israel and the friend of publicans and sinners, because *his* hope is now the rule of reality, that the witness of the resurrection was good news for the world. Once, the mere name "Jesus" sufficed for most hearers; and specific remembrances of his life served other purposes: encouragement, validation of community rules, etc. But increasingly the response to "Jesus is risen" had to be "And who is that?" Then remembrances of Jesus had to be used to back up the name, to identify the one of whom ". . . is risen" is true. These remembrances became identifying descriptions to say, "Jesus is the one who . . . and who . . ." We see this in the sermon attributed to Peter at Pentecost: "Jesus of Nazareth—a man attested to you by God with mighty works and wonders and signs . . . whom you crucified. . . ." The end product of this development was a new literary form, the canonical and extra-canonical Gospels.

Jesus was a preacher of Israel's hope, of the kingdom that will be the fulfillment of justice and freedom and love between all creatures. He so preached the kingdom as to invest his own life entirely in this hope for his fellows, and thus himself to be freed and just and loving for them. And this he did with a radicality that violated all the restrictions we must yet place on our mutuality and that turned upside down all the values based on those restrictions. "Blessed are you poor," he said, but "alas for you who are rich!" Such a self-investment, at any time prior to the kingdom's very coming, had to be fatal. Thus Jesus accepted death as the last and completing act of his mission. That *this* man, defined in his personhood by *these* choices and sufferings, has death behind him and must therefore triumph, is the news called the "gospel."

Now suppose I say all this to you, say that Jesus is risen, in some words that carry the force just explicated—what then? Then I make you a promise: that the hope of your life will be fulfilled by Jesus' victory. It is an unconditional promise; all your failure and rejection that might frustrate other love are this love's mere occasions. That is, it is an eschatological promise, of the fulfillment of history, overcoming all the impediments that frustrate inner-historical fulfillments.

The question is: do I have the *right* to make this promise? The one who makes a promise undertakes the conditions of the promised future's realization. In the eschatological case, I cannot do that; only the one man who has death behind him can. If the gospel-utterance is anyone's promise—and were it no one's, it could be no promise—it is Jesus' promise. Its making must be *his* act, *his* presence. "Where two or three are gathered in my name, there I am between you."

And then the gospel must be Jesus' *embodied* presence. For the body is the identifiability of personal presence. We know who the Jesus who walked in Palestine was. But if now there is a disembodied "Jesus" among us, we cannot know who he is; and then we cannot know whether to seek or flee from his presence, and his word can be no gospel. If the gospel is indeed gospel, its speaking is Jesus' presence as *himself*: in the same body that Mary bore.

Therefore, we must assert: the body Pilate hanged, and the embodiment of gospel-speaking among us, the ensemble of the gospel's sacramental reality, *are one thing*. The speaking of the gospel does not occur as a sheer transfer of what sentences could say, but as the complexly embodied discourse of the Christian community. This "body of Christ" is all the body the risen Lord has or needs, and is for him as for us not other than the body at Mary's breast.

If the assertion of the last paragraph is false, the gospel is false. My next two tasks are to unpack it a bit more—III and IV below—and to show how it is possible for it to be true—V below.

III

The body is the object-presence of a person to other persons. So far, there is no difficulty in seeing what is claimed about the sacramental presence of Christ. If indeed the speaking of the gospel is the personal address of Jesus Christ, then the objects by which this address is available to us, the whole of what we may intend with eyes and hands and all our senses as we listen and answer, must be his body. If we stick strictly to what the previous sentence *says*, its sense is not esoteric: what is said is what may be said about *any* event of one human's presence to another.

Believers pray to God in Christ, or to the Father by the Son's mediation, or sometimes explicitly to the Lord Jesus, as in the ancient cry at the Supper, "Come, Lord!" Where do they talk to when they talk so? Believers are gathered by Christ. What is the common focus of their attention when they gather so? The point is as simple and crude as that. Where do believers look when they try to hearken to the gospel and when they pray and sing praises? More bluntly yet, but the very same question: what do they look at? If I speak to you and you hear and answer, the event presents objects to which you may attend, to which indeed I will expect and demand that you attend: "my" eyes, "my" mouth, this diagram I show you. What when Christ speaks? It is not possible to be addressed and respond without attending to somewhere. When Christ addresses us, where is that?

In the sort of religion which will ultimately disembody God, which will lead out of the world of objects, revelation creates the exits. The necessarily bodily events by which the divine penetrates our world to call us to itself make special places and forms transparent to divinity beyond. At the lower stages of such religion, these holy places and images are straightforwardly the objects of worshipers' intention: they are shrines and idols. But at the higher stages, all spiritual technique is used to escape *through* these embodiments, and so to look to nowhere and at nothing—and just so to commune with God. True adepts of Indian or shamanistic religions have preternaturally refined and potent means to this end. Christians who by mistake conceive God as disembodied usually get no farther than closing their eyes, or peering downward and backward through the navel, trying to see into themselves and away from out there.

Hearing and responding to the gospel works altogether differently. We are to turn neither to shrines and idols nor to nowhere. The whole object-reality of our community is the body of Christ. When we pray, we properly look right at each other. When we gather, we gather around the bread and cup. When we meditate, it is on the gifts of the water. When we seek Christ's peace, it is in the kiss of a fellow believer.

IV

The body is the person's objectivity also to himself. So the embodiment of the gospel must be Christ's objectivity also to himself. This is the pivotal assertion of this chapter, in two ways.

First, it poses the *truth* of Christ's embodiment for us. The embodiment of the gospel, presented to us as the body of Christ, is *truly* his body for us if and only if it is that also for him. How this can be so is the matter of the next section.

Second, it opens the *differences* between Jesus' resurrected life and our life with death still before us. The determinants of bodily reality are all given in the life of the risen Christ; but clearly they work differently together. And—fantastic as the enterprise is—it must be possible to say something about the differences. What these may be is the matter of this section.

The risen Jesus identifies himself by the body born of Mary and ended on the cross. He is for himself the one who so preached the kingdom to his fellows as to leave no more time for evasion or works-righteous preparation, the one who was friend of Publicans and sinners, the one who was crucified. These identifications are all in the past tense. The accumulation of such identifications did not simply resume with the resurrection. For the resurrection was not the cancellation of Jesus' death, a mere resuscitation. The defining of what it means to be the particular individual Jesus was concluded by his death as it will be for each of us. Through all eternity, Jesus the Christ is the one who in Palestine hoped for his fellows, to the death.

In that he now lives, Jesus identifies himself also in the present tense, by all that objectively makes the community of his disciples. He identifies himself for himself by the washing, by the eating and drinking, by our mere looking and hearkening to each other. He is for himself the one who brings John Schmidt and Peter Harkins together in a touch of peace at 11:14, July 13, 1977 at St. Peter's Church, Middleville, the one by the seeing and taking of whom the people of St. Peter's are gathered in the Supper later that same morning, the one who. . . . This self-identifying is in itself like that before Jesus' death or in our lives now; but it is separated from Jesus' pre-crucifixion life by death. The Lord's self-identifications by what now happens in his disciples' gatherings *add* nothing to his individuality; they do not enter his past-tense accumulation of identifications. The Lord has nothing more *to get of himself from them*; in the present tense, Jesus' body is wholly constituted in the availabilities by which he gives himself to others.

Just so, the Lord's past in Palestine and his present in the congregations make one coherent life, and the body in Palestine and the body in the congregations one body. For that Jesus now bodily *is* only in the achieving of hope and mutuality among his fellows, is precisely the only appropriate conclusion of what in fact particularly happened in that life between Nazareth and Golgotha. Just so also, Jesus' life *has* its appropriate conclusion, and death is defeated for him. For that is death's power: to deprive our lives of their conclusion.

Now we are in position to evoke the particular *self-transcendence* of risen life. Jesus is always beyond the body that arrived at the cross, and beyond what on any occasion happens with the bread and cup and water. But he is beyond them in the particular self-transcendence we call "love." The risen Lord lives in his affirming of his disciples' freedom, in that he finds the possibilities of humanity given by each and all of our life-and-death-defined selves. And to this finding there can be no end. Even though what it means to be Jesus was settled at the crucifixion, there is for Jesus no possible end to creation. His life—so defined at his death—is love which is endless.

I return to the starting point. Jesus' past self is available to him in such a way that the possibility of aggrandizing himself, of having himself as an object to be built up, is excluded; for death intervenes. In the present tense, Jesus has himself only as the object of *our* hope, our building-up, even our self-aggrandizing. And just so, Jesus is available to himself as but one united object–self; for precisely and only *this* present and *this* relation to the past are coherent with that past which Jesus in fact lived.

V

Finally, I have to consider how the embodiment of the gospel *can* be Jesus' same body that Mary bore and Pilate killed. I could and perhaps should simply declare the mystery: if the gospel is true, then our situation in time is simply very and oddly different from what we would otherwise conceive, then we simply are embraced in time by the human person of Jesus, in spirit and body.

All aspects of Jesus' presence to us are the same as of any other person; but they work together very differently. When I hear the gospel, I am addressed with the implicit or explicit claim that it is Jesus with whom I have to do. When I say I do not see him, that our communion lacks an object on one side, I am referred to the objectivity of the speaking and hearing community. If I then suppose that "Jesus" is here just a label for the community he founded, I am corrected and referred to the historical personage. And when I then ask how these two—the objectivity of the community and the historically objective Jesus—can be the same, the answer is that the gospel address, in which all these realities appear, is an eschatological promise and therefore beyond the divisions and incompletions of time.

Nothing, I claim, is wrong at any step of this chase. And perhaps it would be best just to affirm the oddity about reality which the chase delineates: that Jesus' personal presence definitively brackets us in time, and that Jesus' personal presence is bodily as is every personal presence. Our location in time between past and future is in any case our great mystery; it is simply the gospel's version of this mystery that what encloses us is Jesus' life. That his word's embodiment is his body-presence to us is then no additional mystery. If Jesus is indeed risen, then all the last section's assertions about his life and presence are mere tautological analyses—and we might leave the mystery as the mystery of the resurrection itself.

But the oddity about time thus acknowledged is God. Perhaps, therefore, understanding may be served by some additional dialectical hovering about the mystery of God, that is, his Trinity. Or, what is the same, by asking how the embodiment of the gospel *can* be Jesus' bodily availability also to Jesus himself. Or, what is again the same, by asking how, if the objectivity of our community is all the body of Jesus there now is, Jesus can now be at all a subject to own this body.

When God's embodiment is conceived as a process of metaphysical joinings, the problem of Christ's sacramental presence is posed correspondingly: there is the risen Jesus with his own body at one place—the "right hand of God"; there are sacramental occurrences and in general the objectivity of the church at other places; and the question is how Christ can, from his place, possess those distant occurrences as his own embodiment. I have already generally denounced this conception. Where *is* the "right hand of God," if it is a place somehow separated from the places where the sacraments can be celebrated?

God knows and wills himself only as the one who raised Jesus: he has the man Jesus as his object-self, his body. But the man Jesus is—objectively!—a person, subject and object, spirit and body. It is this *person* who is the body as which God possesses himself. Just so, this person, body *and* spirit, has all time and space for his life, he is when and where God knows himself. And if then God knows the embodiment of the gospel-proclamation as his own embodiment in our communities, it is the person Jesus Christ who is thereby real in our midst: as object *and* subject, in body and spirit, *and* in that self-possession of the object by the subject, of the body in the spirit, which makes the reality of every personal life. So does the risen Lord possess the object-reality of the gospel as his own bodily self.

The mystery is not esoteric. *All* things are, and are in the way they are, in that God intends them—that is the doctrine of creation, the Christian version of the inescapable wonder that there is anything at all. If God by the resurrection intends the person Jesus as the body who is where he sees himself, that is the real case. The mystery of Jesus' bodily envelopment of all things is the last mystery. But it adds no additional mysteries to those of creation and resurrection, to the mystery of our own and all creatures' being by the intention of God, and the mystery of God's achieving of his own deity by one creature's victory over death.

VI

Rudolf Bultmann said: "Christ rose into the proclamation of the gospel." That is the whole truth of the matter—if we sharply stipulate two things which Bultmann perhaps did not quite. First, the proclamation of the gospel is intrinsically embodied; had it no sacraments, it would not be a proclamation into which anyone could be risen. Second, this fact of the proclamation and of Christ's vivacity in it, is a fact not only of our lives but of God's.

Christ is wherever "two or three are gathered" by right talk on his behalf. Christ is where you and I are face to face and I say, e.g., "Because Jesus lives, your fear of permanent commitment is groundless." Then and there you can *intend* him, intending to the very sound of my voice and to the spatial patterns we make together. If I say it with bread and wine, you can also taste and touch and swallow, and just so intend the Lord. You can do this and be in concord with reality—your intention can have its intended object—because you are in concord with God's triune intention by which all reality is determined.

6

The Gift of the Spirit

I

Jesus can be body in the church's sacramental community because his life encompasses us in time. That he is behind us, so that we can remember him, is unproblematic, and by itself would be no use: to live in mere recollection of one whose life was in historic fact a summons to live in anticipation would be a remarkable contradiction. A Christianity that did not remember Jesus precisely by expecting him, would be either fantastically absent-minded or pretended. It is decisive that Jesus is also *before* us, to speak promise that *calls* us to him. Only so can he be present for us now.

Jesus is present as a subject of our communal life, *in that* the word that lets us remember him is itself a promise of the last future. Precisely our memory of him is our knowledge of that to which all our life will be brought; he is not merely a transcended item in time but the one who transcends. Just so he has all time and is free in time; just so he is body and spirit for all times, a present person for us.

Thus it is because the gospel is an *eschatological promise,* that its embodied speaking can be Christ's presence. The gospel promises Jesus' final triumph, the outcome of all Israel's history. To the oppressed and the oppressors it speaks liberation of all from all kinds of bondage. To the loving it speaks the expansion of love to embrace mankind and the opening of love to endlessly innovative affirmation of the beloved. To the curious it speaks the vision of God, in whom truth is given to infinite exploration. To whatever fears and whatever hopes it promises their *fulfillment,* as interpreted by the story of the Lord and his crucifixion.

There is again a short way, if earlier positions are accepted. That the gospel is an eschatological promise, and that it is the word of God, come to the same thing; for what makes God God is just that he has all the future, that no occurrence of history can impede or limit his hope for us. And it was in the gospel's being the self-communication of the triune God that we found the possibility of Christ's embodied presence when the gospel is spoken. But it will be better if I take a slightly longer way also here.

We have seen that and why the making of a promise is, if the promise is true, the coming of a person. But the promises we usually make are fragile. They have hidden conditions. Suppose I promise to explain the sacraments to you. If the promised future understanding is in fact to come, all manner of things must first be done; the content of my promise is precisely that I will see to these and not load them on you. But, of course, I cannot guarantee performance under all circumstances; for the future in which to perform is not without limit mine. There are proper limits to what I will do to achieve your knowledge of sacraments, limits set by my mortality. It may turn out to be unexpectedly hard to explain the sacraments to you; as the time devoted to the task lengthens, I may yet have to give up—perhaps precisely to keep other promises. At some point I will after all say, "You will only understand the sacraments if you . . ." whereupon my promising turns after all into the laying down of a law.

When my promise turns to law, my personal availability to you is withdrawn. Then either I live on in your life as a destructive "pure" spirit, or my voice merges with that of some collective of which you and I are members. The latter is the good and usual case. Continuing my example, my voice will be replaced in your life by a general agreement in the church, "One should know about sacraments; let us arrange to study them." And my presence to you will cease.

All other things being equal, Jesus' presence to us ceased at least nineteen hundred and some odd years before this writing, when the condition behind all conditions, death, was called for him. It can be otherwise only if his promise to us transcends all possible conditions, and, of course, if it is true. A promise that is eschatological and true would bring a presence that can not be made to withdraw by the calling of any conditions. Only such a promise could be the presence of one who has died. The gospel claims to be such a promise: it is eschatological and it claims to be true.

To be sure, we do often speak of a certain presence of remembered persons in the communities that remember them, also when the word that reminds of them is not a word of final promise. In a way, Socrates is indeed present in the Western moral and intellectual community, and Mary Baker Eddy among the Christian Scientists. But so long as the utterances by which an historical figure is present are conditional—"As Socrates said, you must know yourself to know anything"—this presence poses no other challenge than those posed by the community itself. Socrates himself does not stand out free over against the community, speaking promises that sustain and judge and create the community. This presence is not *personal*.

All this is to say that Jesus is present—if at all—as the ultimately *coming* one, that his reality among us is the reality of the present communication of the last future, the promissory present granting of what will not be until the end. His presence is, like every personal presence, spirit; since he has died, he can only be present in the spirit that blows from the *last* future, the Spirit that God is. Where Jesus is, if he is anywhere, there is the "Holy" Spirit.

II

There is spirit wherever there is community. If a community has identity, if it is gathered around and as a specific body, then it has *a* spirit, an identifiable particular freedom that moves the community and moves those who encounter the community. We are unmysteriously familiar with the phenomenon: "What sort of spirit did the meeting have?" we ask.

There is spirit wherever there is personal presence. If a person addresses me in the hopes and fears of my life, and so as to identify himself and grant his hopes and fears as new possibility for me, there is a spirit. We are familiar with the phenomenon: "the spirit of Lincoln" once ruled this country.

All Christianity's talk of the Spirit unpacks one simple but drastic experience and claim: the spirit of the Christian community and the personal spirit of Jesus of Nazareth are the same. To be free by Jesus' presence is to be free for one another; to be free by one another's presence is to be free for the Lord. But if this is true, then this spirit spans time's discontinuities; in this spirit, Jesus then in Palestine and we here now are together before the future. That is, this spirit is *eternal*, is God, is the Holy Spirit. The spirit that is our freedom for one another, and the spirit that is the risen Jesus' freedom for us and our freedom for him, and the Spirit that is the Father's and the Son's freedom for one another, are all one. "God is spirit, and they that worship him worship in spirit," is the Bible's only ontological proposition about God.

In the Bible generally, the Spirit is God as the power of the future to break the present open, to overcome the present's immobility under the dead hand of the past, and just so to fulfill all the past's promises. The Spirit is always the Creator Spirit, who calls forth what is not yet, whether from nothing or from the limits and perversions of what already is. The Spirit came upon the prophets to call them out of themselves into audible and visible words that summoned the future. The fetus in Mary's uterus was there "by the Holy Spirit" exactly insofar as it was surprisingly and way-breakingly there. The Spirit is the giver of the gifts needed by the congregation of believers just insofar as those gifts are anticipations of the characteristics of life in the kingdom.

The Spirit is a presence. But the present fact that is the fact of his presence is the fact that we do have a conclusion, an outcome of our hopes and sufferings, and that we are now therefore free to live for what is not yet present. The Spirit is the power of the end, now to be at once the judgment and the goal of every status quo.

God the Spirit, the "third" divine "hypostasis" of classical trinitarian theology, is God as the power of his own future, God as beyond himself to be life and act, God as his own goal. That God is absolute and has no purposes that come to him from beyond himself, does not in Christian theology mean that he has no purpose and is captive in himself; it means that he is his own goal, that he himself is the spiritual freedom in which he lives and acts. It means that God needs no other than God for the mutual life and communication in which his freedom occurs. God *is* Spirit: the creative freedom and longing in which he is his own future is his very being.

In that God is future to himself, he *has* future. In that God as future to himself is indeed *God,* he has *final* future, future in which all the hopes of time can be achieved. In that God has final future, he is able to be the goal also of others than himself. The Spirit is God as the present power of his fulfillment and ours. The Spirit is eschatological possibility.

III

It has been debated whether the Spirit's role in the church's sacramental life is to create the Lord's embodied presence or to be brought and given by the present Lord. If that is the question, the answer must be both. But there is something wrong with this answer and so with the question. For the Lord is present as *person*; and personal presence just *is* body and spirit, neither of which is instrumental to the other. The Lord Christ, in his freedom from death and all hindrances to love, is present to free us from enclosure in our present selves. The Lord is present to give himself into community with us; his freedom to do this, and the freedom he thereby gives, *are* the Spirit; and his self-giving is the gift of the Spirit.

Spirit is always spirit *of* someone. The Holy Spirit is the spirit of Jesus; he is the spirit of our gathering; and it is in that he is both at once that he is *God* the Spirit. The Spirit's reality as God cannot therefore be abstracted from his reality as the spirit of our gathering. If God the Father is the object of our faith and service, God the Spirit is the communal freedom in which faith is possible. The question about the Spirit and any of the sacraments is therefore not so much a question of particular rites, prayers, or other events as of the spiritedness of the entire occasion.

Our sacramental action is something we perform in the present: sounds and gestures given as artifacts of the present-tense world, called forth and determined by a tradition continuous through and immanent within time. But the actual import of this tradition means that our action is also promise and anticipation of the fulfillment that is not yet, and that will be a transcending transformation of all the immanent continuities of time. That we eat bread and drink wine in remembrance of Jesus is the sort of ceremony that epochal events often trail in their temporal shadow. But we claim to do it as proclamation of his present aliveness, "until he comes." The truth of the claim just made, is the sacramental reality of the Spirit.

I dislike the word *tension,* but cannot find a better for what has here to be said. The Spirit occurs in the church's audible and visible gospel-speaking in that the sequence and rhythm of the whole declamation and performance make an *eschatological tension.* In The Great Thanksgiving, e.g., of many eastern orders for the Supper, the Narrative of Institution concludes: "For as often as you eat this bread, and drink this cup, you proclaim my death and confess my resurrection and ascension, until I come." To this the people respond: "We proclaim and confess." It is an advent of the Spirit insofar as any sacramental act, in its dramatic structure as a sequence of actions, hangs between what was and what is at last to come. The eschatological tension *is* the Spirit.

IV

In the theological tradition, a recurrent disaster has been that Christ's presence as embodied word, as audible and visible address, and the coming of the Spirit, have been separated and even played off against each other: "I have heard and been baptized and believe." "Yes, but have you got the Spirit as well?" Thereby the Spirit is misapprehended as a free-floating dynamism; such phenomena are real enough in religious and other experience, but are neither the Spirit nor favored manifestations of the Spirit.

It cannot be too emphatically insisted that the *Holy* Spirit has nothing to do with esoteric experiences, preternatural phenomena, or suspensions of rationality—or rather, precisely as much as with ordinary experiences, explicable phenomena, and cultivation of rationality. The Spirit is nothing other than the eschatological spiritedness of the audible and visible address by which Christ presents himself to us and by which we live in his presence. It is precisely in that we speak sentences that our fellowship may be spirited, and in that we speak gospel-sentences that it is Spirited: we may not conceive the Spirit apart from the word. What we can do, however, is more sharply conceive the Spirit by an appropriate analysis of the word.

On the one hand, our discourse with each other is the location of our determination by the *past*. In the grammar and vocabulary of the language we are taught, the whole history of our culture imposes itself on the ways in which we are able to deal with reality, to see possibilities, and define fears and have goals. But on the other hand, language is the location of our openness to the *future*. It is only because reality is not there for us in its brute self merely, but is there for us in our words to each other about it, is there interpreted and so interpretable, that the world as it has come to be is not final for us, that we are able to will and evoke what is not yet.

The articulation by which sound becomes language is of many kinds.

In any actual language, some sorts of articulation have semantic function: they are coordinated by rules of usage to the articulation of the world. Thus they enable our utterance to be *about* something. Other sorts of articulation lack semantic function, or have it only incidentally; we label these "rhetoric," "music," "style," etc.

The semantic articulations of utterance enable it to mean the world deposited by the past, to seize hold of what is. By the semantic articulations of utterance we can communicate the facts, we can have a world in common. What then do we communicate by the nonsemantic articulation of our utterances? By its music, rhetoric, rhythm, etc.? I suggest that we thereby bespeak to each other the openness of the future merely as such, the sheer possibility of things being the way things are not, the sheer hope of somehow overcoming the facts. By the music and rhetoric of utterance, our world-sharing moves, we communicate freedom, we share spirit.

Perhaps this explains why at various crisis times "speaking in tongues" has been treasured as *the* gift of the Spirit. One speaks in tongues by deranging the semantic rules of language so that no world-coordinated articulation can occur; then the only thing communicated is openness to the future merely as such, abstract spiritedness. Purely instrumental music is the sophisticated church's tongue speaking. The notorious danger of this communication is that within it there is no way of identifying which spirit is invoked. But in most churches the danger is surely still the opposite: unmusical, halting, rhetorically feeble utterance, by which we do not move, by which we share all too conclusively the world that already is.

Insofar as the gospel is a verbal event, it is fundamentally by the *motion* of its utterance, by clear and springing rhythm, lifting music, precise rhetoric, that we are specifically grasped by the Spirit. What we mostly can speak *about* is the world that is. It is by the ways in which speech itself moves that the eschatological tension of what is with what is not yet comes to utterance.

I can most easily make the point negatively. If the language of our gospel-address is broken and unnatural in its speech rhythms, if we read texts that set us glumly aback just as we are well launched into declamation, if "free" prayer simply means clumsy and repetitious prayer, this is not merely an aesthetic misfortune; it is quenching of the Spirit. If music provides no way for the congregation to move singingly together,

it is quenching of the Spirit. If our speech has no grandeur, it is quenching of the Spirit. The American black church knows this. So does the
white church—but it *wants* the Spirit quenched.

In that the gospel is embodied, these considerations apply even more
urgently. What our mere static body-presence to each other would communicate would be our sheer givenness as items of the objective world,
the sheer availability of realities created by past history and now deposited in the present. Our body-presence to each other will precisely
not communicate hope and freedom, unless it is the embodiment of a
word that does, unless a promise "comes to" it. And what happens to
our bodies when they become the embodiment of *promise*, is that they
move. As sheer static objects, our bodies speak the status quo. They
speak freedom precisely in that they are broken out of their stability. It
is as gesture, as meaningful action, that our bodies become part of a
word of promise.

Eschatological tension occurs in our gatherings in that our bodies are
set moving: in that they stand, sit, parade, reach out, make signs. If
music and rhetoric are the Spirit's home in the gospel's sentences, *choreography* is the Spirit's home in the gospel's embodiment. Every sacramental performance is, in one respect, a dance. In the Supper, for
instance, the inevitable distinction between host and diners, the necessary
actions of giving thanks *with* the bread and cup, and the essential
actions of distributing and taking the bread and cup, necessitate a flow
of motions and spatial patterns which only terminological prejudice can
refuse to call choreography. The dance may be very simple indeed,
when the Supper is around someone's kitchen table; or in a great eucharistic assembly it may approach the formalization, and even require
some of the training, of ballet. Whichever—our bodies share the eschatological tension of the Spirit in that they move together through space
with dramatic intent.

V

The Spirit is not primarily the *object* of our faithful intention; the Father
is that. Nor is the Spirit primarily the *presence* of God to address us
and be our object; that presence is the risen Jesus Christ. The Spirit is
the *freedom* in which all this happens. Nevertheless, God's freedom is
not other than God; and therefore it rightly also happens in our gatherings that the Spirit becomes the object of our faithful intention, just as

the Father, and that we speak of the Spirit's presence, just as of the Son. There are special rites and invocations of the Spirit in all parts of the church's sacramental life. But even when the Spirit becomes the object of our direct address, the rites should and usually do remain appropriate to the Spirit's reality as the freedom in which all our rites take place: the Spirit is not just there, the Spirit is invoked and given. The Spirit *comes.*

Every sacrament is a coming of the Spirit. Insofar as sacramental action includes also our prayers and praises to God, the Spirit form of prayer is *invocation*: "Come Holy Spirit!" In the ecumenical tradition, such cries, *Epiclesis,* are at the heart of both the Supper and Baptism, as in the great Antiochene liturgy "of the Twelve Apostles": "we pray, Father omnipotent. . . . that you will send your Holy Spirit over these gifts . . . and thus show forth this bread as the adorable body of our Lord Jesus Christ and this cup as his blood, that they may bring all who partake to life and resurrection. . . ." *Epiclesis,* the prayer for the Spirit's coming, is the word precisely appropriate to the particular way in which the Spirit is there sacramentally.

In that God lets our words be the gospel, they are address not to God but to one another. The Spirit's reality in our sacramental address to one another is that the Spirit is *given.* Whenever in the church's sacramental life the Spirit's coming becomes thematic, there are special embodied blessings to bestow the Spirit. So at ordination, the ordaining minister lays hands on the candidate, and either prays for the gift of the Spirit or declares it directly. The formula in the Book of Common Prayer is as drastic as could be: "Receive the Holy Ghost for the office and work of a priest in the church of God. . . ."

There is nothing esoteric about the sacramental invocation and giving of the Spirit. We should not think of the Spirit as a weird force or invisible fluid to be gathered and channelled. When you and I are present to each other in mutual speaking, there is body and spirit. When Christ is embodied among us, present as the gospel speaking, there too is spirit, the Holy Spirit. If in a community's freedom that freedom itself becomes the matter of our communication, it creates words of invitation and gift. Just so, when the reality of the Spirit becomes itself thematic in the community of the gospel, invocation and bestowal are the forms answering to the Spirit's mode of being.

If you, authorized to speak for the community of the gospel, say to me by word and gesture, "Receive the Holy Spirit," then I do. This is not because you possess some esoteric ability to channel divine force. Life in the believing community and possession of the Spirit are exactly the same thing; for life in any community is life by the specific freedom maintained by that community's mutual addresses, and if the gospel is true, the specific freedom of the believing community is God the Spirit himself. If you are able to take me into the church, you can and do grant the Spirit. And the community's permission to fill specific roles in its life, and possession of the Spirit "for the office and work of . . ." are exactly the same thing. If I am granted a special freedom in the community, I am granted a special gift of the Spirit.

The assertions of the last paragraph do not debunk the giving of the Spirit. They do not say that possession of the Spirit is "merely" life in the church. Rather they praise life in the church. They say that the spirit that comes when two or three are gathered by the gospel is nothing less than God's own freedom, nothing less than present invigoration by the last goal of all things.

PART THREE

THE INSTITUTION OF THE SUPPER

7

Mandate

I

As it happens, the church has only one fully developed, clearly contoured and solidly instituted visible word of the gospel simply as such
and as a whole. Just so, the same rite is also the great embodiment of
the church's response to the gospel, the church's chief embodied prayer.
Its dominance has given it many names: "Eucharist," "Lord's Supper,"
"Communion," "Mass," and even just "The Liturgy." It is exactly as
old as the gospel itself, and its centrality in the church's life is uninter-
rupted. There would be reason to identify a Christian as someone who
regularly joins a meal-fellowship of bread and loving-cup, to give thanks
for Jesus.

II

The origin of the Supper seems to have been not one event but several,
the exact history of whose concurrence cannot now surely be recon-
structed.[1] First was Jesus' meal-fellowship with his disciples, during his
ministry.[2] After the resurrection, the disciples resumed the fellowship
which had been theirs before their Lord was crucified. If he was indeed
risen, by his renewed presence to constitute their community anew, there
was no reason any longer to forego the fellowship. And there was then
every reason to resume it; for the meal-fellowship they had as disciples
of Jesus was laden with the whole content of their relation to him.

Jewish meal-fellowship was and is in any case religiously charged. In
this, Judaism has been in no way unusual. It is universal among humankind that, second to sexual intercourse, eating together is the most
binding communal act. In integral cultures, this fellowship is cultivated
for its own sake, and has its own visible words: e.g., a common bowl or

62

a system of toasts. Moreover, in religiously vital cultures, the fellowship essentially involves God; every right meal is a sacrifice. For to eat we must kill (if someone thinks that killing only plant life avoids this, he only betrays an anthropocentrism for which most of mankind has anciently been too sophisticated). To eat is to kill in order to give life. And only God can do that. Therefore, to eat is to blaspheme—unless we pray God to join the act. If we do, the meal is a sacrifice.

Among the Jews, the fellowship and its sanctification by God was and is ritualized above all in rites of *thanksgiving*,[3] appropriately to the character of Israel's religion. I will speak much of these rites; for now I need only describe them so far: one diner praises God for his saving acts, including of course the gift of food, and all others join the praise by some act of table-sharing.

The particular meal-fellowship of Jesus with his disciples seems to have had two special notes, by which it became an embodiment of his proclamation. First, as Jesus proclaimed the coming kingdom of God, he did so in such a way as to make the meeting with himself decisive for the hearers' entry: "Who confesses me before men, the Son of Man will confess before the angels of God . . ." (Luke 12:8). Just so, meal-fellowship with Jesus was a fellowship open to the very fellowship that the kingdom would be—thus the Sons of Zebedee came to Jesus and asked to keep their places of honor at Jesus' table, when the kingdom came (Mark 10:35f., par.). In the primal church's Supper, this same note appears: the church holds its meals "until he comes" (1 Cor. 11:26).

Second, Jesus notoriously "ate with publicans and sinners" (Mark 2:15, par.; Matt. 11:19, par.; Luke 15:1). This may, in fact, have been much of what stirred the fear and hatred that led to his crucifixion—which is hard for us to understand, since we take our meal-fellowship so lightly. The "publicans and sinners" were those genuinely unfit for the kingdom. Meal-fellowship with Jesus somehow transcended their unfitness; the meal was atoning. In the primal church's Supper, this same note appears: the meal is "for forgiveness of sins" (Matt. 26:28).

A second factor in the origin of the Supper was undoubtedly a special instance of Jesus' meal-fellowship with his disciples, "in the night in which he was betrayed." That Jesus then instituted the church's Supper, in the sense of arranging for it in advance, is highly improbable, being utterly inconsistent with what we otherwise know of his relation to the future of and after his death. But Jesus may indeed have that night interpreted the thanksgiving-ceremonies with bread and cup which accompanied the opening and closing of a formal meal, by his death and vice versa. Most scholars find this the most plausible explanation for the origin of the tradition of interpretive sayings: "This is. . . . ." Another explanation will, however, be mentioned later. In any case, the institution-pericope itself, with the interpretive sayings, at first circulated separately from the passion narrative's account of Jesus' last meal, and only later was inserted in its present place.[4] Therefore even if we can argue to earliest forms of the interpretive sayings, this does not necessarily locate them as utterances on the occasion of the Last Supper.

Nor does it seem possible certainly to decide what *sort* of meal the Last Supper was.[5] The synoptic pericopes that label it a Passover (Mark 14:12–16, par.) are themselves secondary in the passion account of a last meal;[6] and Paul's account (1 Cor. 11) lacks all reference to Passover. Joachim Jeremias' material arguments in the famous *Die Abendmahlsworte Jesu*[7] are massive in accumulation; but it appears possible to meet them in detail.[8] If the Last Supper was not a Passover, it was probably no sort of established ceremonially special meal,[9] and differed from other instances of Jesus' eschatologically open meal-fellowship chiefly by its place in Jesus' life. Since the institution-pericopes themselves contain no reference to Passover, except Luke 22:15–18, to which see below, the problem need not be important for exegesis of the Supper's mandate and promises;[10] we must only not propose interpretations that *depend* on the Last Supper having been a Passover.

What in the Last Supper was in any case decisive for the church's Supper, was just its being the last. For later recollection, the Last Supper—Passover or whatever—necessarily figured as a farewell supper, a meal-fellowship correlate of the crucifixion itself. A last supper had to be remembered as the crucifixion of the disciples' fellowship with their Master, and just so as the disciples participation in the crucifixion.

Recollection of the Last Supper probably played a role in the origin of the Supper mostly as interpretation of the renewed celebration of fellowship: "Remember, your joyful fellowship with the triumphant risen Lord is with the triumphant and risen *Crucified* One!" The whole of Paul's address to the church at Corinth, in 1 Corinthians 10 and 11, is a reminder of this sort.[11] To the emergence of a sacrament, just such interpretation is fundamental. To the Supper, it is fundamental in that the whole meaning of a sacrament of fellowship depends on whom the fellowship is with: the memory of the Last Supper served and serves to identify the one who is risen to be with us.

Indeed, this interpretive process may have been the origin of the tradition of interpretive "This is . . ." words. The tradition of Jesus' eschatological promises (Luke 22:16–18; Mark 14:25, par.), and the tradition of the words of interpretation were originally distinct.[12] And from Lukan and Johannine tradition it is possible to reconstruct a complete narrative of the Last Supper around the eschatological sayings, with no place for "the Words of Institution." Thus it may be that at the very first there was only the meal of joy, celebrated in remembrance and fulfillment of eschatological promises made by Jesus at his last supper and before. Then interpretation of these meals by the cross-theology created the Supper as we know it;[13] and the liturgical formulation of this interpretation created the two "This is. . . ." sayings.[14] Since *all* the canonical phrases interpreting the bread and cup cannot simultaneously be attributed to Jesus at the Last Supper, some of them *must* have arisen in some such process;[15] perhaps, then, all of them.

Which brings us, third, to the remarkable circumstance that the resurrection-appearances narrated in the Gospels are disproportionately appearances to eat with the disciples (Luke 24:13–35; Luke 24:36–43; Mark 16:14–18; John 21:1–14). Undoubtedly some of the appearance-experiences were indeed at common meals of the newly revived fellowship of Jesus' followers. And precisely those groups in the primal church at whose meals we hear of eschatological joy (Acts 2:46) reckoned the appearance-meals as foundation-events of the faith and community: the kerygma of Acts 10:38ff. lists God's empowerment of Jesus, his mission, his crucifixion, his resurrection, and his manifestation by chosen witnesses ". . . who ate and drank with him after he rose from the dead."[16] Jesus' pre-Easter meal fellowship was already eschatologically open; but insofar as the Supper was a fellowship *triumphantly* open to the fulfillment, insofar as it was *anticipation* of the eschatological community, this must indeed have been the result of meal fellowship with the Resurrected. The great liturgical cry of the most primal Supper was "Come, Lord!" still kept in Aramaic by otherwise Greek-speaking congregations, "Maranatha!"[17]

In whatever precise ways these three factors may have worked together, what came of them is reasonably clear; the synoptic Gospels' tradition of Institution, 1 Corinthians 10 and 11, the notices in Acts, and the *Didache* give a fair notion of the primal church's Supper. There was a full evening meal.[18]   There were special thanksgivings before—at first—and after, presumably for all God's works but especially for what he had done and was about to do through Jesus.[19]   With the first thanksgiving, bread was shared; with the second, a cup of wine was passed around, though poverty or asceticism may sometimes have compelled its omission.[20]   The bread and cup were interpreted by and made to interpret Jesus' death and the "new covenant" thereby guaranteed.

Very soon, the first blessing with its bread-sharing migrated to join the second with its cup, at the meal's end;[21] this was perhaps caused by a growing feeling for the special holiness of the bread and cup as embodiments of the Lord's presence.[22]   Thus a special rite of the Supper, distinct from the meal for nourishment, began to be established.   1 Corinthians 11 shows us the very event.   Paul uses a version of the Institution that separates the two thanksgivings by a meal; but it is clear that in Corinth they in fact eat the two together at the end of the meal.[23] In the Markan version, all reference to the regular supper has disappeared.   Finally, the ordinary fellowship-meal and the Supper became two distinct observances; it is not clear how soon this happened.[24]

One bit of primal liturgy seems recoverable.[25]   In the *Didache*—from sometime around A.D. 100—we find the following dialogue between minister and congregation, as the holiest part of the rite is about to begin.

MINISTER:	Let grace come and let this world pass away!
PEOPLE:	*Hosanna to the Son of David!*
MINISTER:	If any one is holy, let him come.
	If any one is not, let him repent.
PEOPLE:	*Maranatha! Amen!*

Comparison with the *Didache* makes it clear that the ending of 1 Corinthians is an earlier version of the same action; and indeed, Paul's letter may well have been intended to be read at the Supper just at this point.

> Greet one another with the kiss of peace.
> (This greeting is in my own hand—Paul.)
> If anyone does not love the Lord, let him be cast out.
> Maranatha!   Come, Lord!

The complex of action is thus: Kiss of Peace, Acclamation, Proclamation of the eschatological law of the Supper, "Maranatha!" The best guess seems to me to be that here is opening action of a distinct Supper, separating it from a preceding full meal.

So much for origins. What we have so far achieved is only some explanation of how in fact the church came to have the Supper and some information that can be used later. Such an explanation does not answer the question whether we now must or may continue the celebrations, or the question what they should be like. We must again read the Scriptures, not now looking only for historical evidence, but for an apostolic mandate directed also to us.

III

Paul and Luke are splendidly explicit.[26] To any congregations using their writings, they say, "Do this." The usage is a fixed formula stipulating the repetition of a rite.[27] Mark and Matthew can omit the explicit command, since the order to enact the rite is already made by the very form of the texts: they are rubrics for liturgy,[28] as can be seen in the stylized succession of verbs—"took," "gave thanks," "broke," "gave"— and in such usages as "in the same way."

Rubrics are straightforward instructions for action, which those who at any time have responsibility for some part of the church's life make to those who come to share the responsibility. In the case of the Supper, the process has simply continued through history, now to include us. The literary deposit in Paul and the Gospels of apostolic strata of this tradition establishes that the rubrical instructions we receive from the whole tradition have apostolic authority, and so also provides authoritative versions of them.

Our first exegetical question is therefore also straightforward: Do *what*? And there is no problem here either; since all exegetical possibilities lead to the same set of mandated acts. I will start with the versions of Paul and Luke. We read, "Do this." If we are to ask what can be the referent of "this" within the narrated account of a last supper, the *only* possibility is the ceremonies of thanksgiving before and after the meal which Jesus is depicted as having in each case just performed.[29] It is more likely, however, that "Do this" is to be taken as a gloss on the text, emphasizing the generally rubrical character of the account. In this case, observance is stipulated of the entire set of actions listed:[30]

take bread, give thanks, share the bread, take the cup, give thanks, pass around the cup. If we turn to the versions of Mark and Matthew, exactly this last same list of actions is rubrically specified. Thus there are but two exegetical possibilities; and materially they coincide, for the sharing of bread was part of the opening thanksgiving, and the sharing of the cup part of the closing thanksgiving.[31] Thus either way, the texts mandate thanksgiving, with sharing of bread and cup.[32]

Jewish table-thanksgiving is a verbal act with a clear and well-known character of its own.[33] The root utterance is "Blessed be God!" This is addressed at once to God and those present; it is *both* "Bless you, God!" and "Let us bless God." Thanksgiving is neither "prayer" only nor "proclamation" only; it is a third encompassing both.

Protestant theologians sometimes take alarm at this, insisting that our liturgy must always neatly sort out prayer, which is *our* word, from proclamation of the gospel. But here the Scriptures command otherwise. Moreover, the conception that prayer and proclamation can be sorted into two sorts of verbal acts, each clearly labelled, and these then performed one at a time with no overlapping, is very far from reality. Simultaneous address to auditors of different sorts is one of the commonest and most necessary of linguistic actions. The Bible, close as it is to human reality, is crammed with simultaneous addresses to God and a congregation—for examples, the opening doxologies of the New Testament epistles, or nearly all the psalms, or any confession of faith.

In the table-thanksgivings, God is praised for his goodness as Creator, experienced in the meal: "Blessed be God, King of the world, who brings forth food from the earth!" He is praised for his saving acts in the history of Israel: "Blessed be God . . . who has given us a good and spacious land." Thus the *praise* of God is also a *remembering* of his acts, as must be the case with the faith of Israel. And equally, the remembering of God's past acts must in Israel fulfill itself as *invocation* of his future and final acts: "May he mercifully find us worthy of the days of Messiah and the life of the world to come . . ." Thanksgiving thus has three essential components: doxology, recitation of saving history, and eschatological invocation. There is an indefinity of ways in which we may accomplish these at our Supper; but somehow or other, they are what we are bidden to do.

The bread and cup enter the rite as embodiments of the thanksgiving.[34] With the thanksgiving before the meal, the distribution of pieces of bread constitutes admission to the fellowship of the evening and its thanksgivings, and taking a piece of that bread is a visible "Amen" to the thanksgiving being offered. The opening course of bread is thus the embodiment of the group's community in thanksgiving. With the thanksgiving after the meal, the handed-round loving-cup of wine simply is in itself the meal's concluding act of fellowship, with all present and with the God to whom the thanksgiving is made. Just this whole embodied thanksgiving is what the canonical warrants for the Christian Supper specify also for the church.

We may note three points that are vital and canonically normative for both our practice and understanding of the Supper. All three are something of an affront to much current practice.

First, it is the *rite* with bread and cup, just described, that is mandated. The texts are not at all about bread and wine as substances or foods merely; they are about these specific ritual *uses* of bread and wine. The command is *not* somehow to absorb grain agglutinate and grape extract. It is to share bread and drink together from one cup, as fellowship in the praise of God. Any practice, such as the use of small glasses for the wine, which depends on the notion that what is essential is that some minimum quantity of holy substance get into each worshiper, is unscriptural. Such practice simply does not obey the mandate which creates the Supper in the first place.

Second, the bread and cup are there—thinking now only of the mandate—for the sake of the thanksgiving, not vice versa. If the praise of God, for his mighty acts and in invocation of their fulfillment, does not occupy a central place in our Supper, the canonical mandate is not obeyed, no matter what good and pious things may otherwise be done with the elements. The verbal prayer and praise are not merely the preparation and explanation of holy substances. They are an act of their own, of which all the rest of the Supper is—as mandated action—just the embodiment.

Some have resisted clear statement of this point and even deliberately obscured it in liturgical practice, fearing that the pure mercy of God's gift to us in the Supper will be obscured. Let us not, it is said, make much of thanksgiving, since it is our work over against God, whereas the center of the Supper should be his work over against us. The concern is right; and when we come to speak of what God *promises* in and by the Supper, it will guide all our discussion. But at *this* place, the objection is absurd. Scripture's sacramental promises are about acts we are bidden to do; if we do not do them, there is nothing for the promises to be about; and in the case of the Supper, the commanded acts do centrally include an act of praise over against God.

If God's acts were to be emphasized by de-emphasizing ours, the only sufficient de-emphasis would, after all, be total elimination. We should do no praying or singing—or, indeed, any works of love. Most especially, there would be no sacraments at all. The gift of the Supper is God's unconditional promise of salvation, embodied by the bread and cup, which he makes because he so chooses and which he alone will or can fulfill. But we will not promote understanding of this by trying to pretend that the Supper is not also our act over against God. Just because we cannot at all save ourselves, we may do what we can do with utter freedom and gusto—in the present case, give thanks. Indeed, the Supper is *first* our act of praise to God, which biblical promises then make an embodiment of God's gospel to us. If the way we appropriate the promises compromises our act of praise, it saws off the limb the promises sit on.

Third, our act of thanksgiving to God is done with words and with sharing of bread and cup: we have here an *embodied* word of praise. That is to say, the thanksgiving is a *sacrifice*, for embodied prayer is what "sacrifice" is. Here, of course, we have a large historical stone of stumbling. Let it be said once for all: the Reformation's assault on the medieval and Tridentine "sacrifice of the mass" is entirely justified and necessary. Any practice or text or instruction that suggest in any way that what we do here alters God's attitude toward us, i.e., which makes the thanksgiving-with-bread-and-cup a *propitiatory* sacrifice, is ᵃ visible contradiction to the gospel.

Later Protestantism has, however, mostly worried about the liturgical or theological use of the word *sacrifice*; and often under cover of pious abstention from the word invented practices of its own more reprehensible in this regard than any of the medieval mass. The mere terminological prejudice is anyway insupportable. The thanksgiving *is* embodied prayer; and embodied prayer *is* phenomenologically what is meant by the word *sacrifice*. *Both* the word of proclamation and the word of prayer are words of God—"the Spirit himself intercedes for us . . ." (Romans 8:25)—and so seek embodiment. Some proclamation is wrong—e.g., "God will forgive you if you are sorry enough"—and so is some embodied proclamation—e.g., indulgence selling. Just so, some prayer is wrong—e.g., "Here are my good deeds, O Lord; please reward me"—and so is *some* sacrifice—e.g., any attempt to propitiate God with our act.

It should, I think, now be possible to overcome this particular quarrel between Rome and the Reformation. The Reformation taught that at the Supper we offer a "sacrifice of praise and thanksgiving." Their opponents insisted that we also offer the sacramental elements; the strength of this position is the manifest fact that when the Supper is celebrated we do indeed, willy-nilly, in some sense or other present these objects to God. But medieval and Tridentine theology and liturgy took the offering of the elements as an act distinct from the verbal thanksgiving; the verbal praise of God had, indeed, nearly disappeared from the Roman rite. This other separate offering could then hardly fail to be taken as propitiatory. Now that Roman Catholic liturgy is recovering the act of thanksgiving, Catholic theology should perhaps be open to the understanding that the offering of the elements is but the visibility, the embodiment, of the thanksgiving itself. And if it is once clear that the offering of the elements is no other than the sacrifice of praise and thanksgiving, Reformation theology can have no legitimate further objection. I will return to this matter in a later chapter.

IV

The texts contain two further rubrically significant sets of clauses, beside the main listing of actions. The first is, "This is my body" and "This is the cup of the new covenant" or "This is my blood." What these mean is the matter of the next chapter. But they would not have been included in the rubrics passed on in the primal church, unless they reflected some actual practice intended thereby to be mandated. This must have been some verbalization of the specific gospel-promises attached to the bread and cup. We must reckon, therefore, that we are bidden somehow to verbalize these promises in our celebrations. We now usually do this by reciting these very texts, which *may* have been what the apostolic church also did. Thus Paul's interpretation, "For as often as . . . you proclaim the Lord's death until he comes," (1 Cor. 11:26) probably refers to some specific practice in the Supper.[35]

The second is, in Paul and Luke, "Do this, *for my remembrance*." The source and particular meaning of this phrase are very much disputed, especially between proponents of Hellenistic and Israelite-Jewish backgrounds.[36] Undoubtedly, the phrase partly defined Paul's or earlier tradition's understanding of the basic character of the Supper: it is an *anamnesis,* a "re-collection"—whatever that is. Somehow, the phrase specified for Paul the Supper's relation, as a present event, to the past reality of Jesus. But in view of the obscurity in which time has wrapped the terminology, "for my remembrance" fulfills this function for us only most precariously. It will be better to discuss the temporal relations between present Supper and past life of Jesus by direct consideration of the nature of the mandated actions and of the promises, without depending overmuch on the possible meanings of *anamnesis.*

Fortunately, the *rubrical* force of "for my remembrance" is largely independent of the history-of-religions uncertainties. As we have seen, thanksgiving always is a remembering of God's acts. With "for my remembrance," the Supper's rubrics merely *specify* the remembering: in your thanksgivings at the Supper, give thanks for *Jesus.*[37] The phrase "*for* my remembrance" must have partly final force:[38] remembrance is to be the *outcome* of what we do. We may paraphrase: "to bring me to mind," "to remind . . . . of me."

We inevitably ask: Remind whom? Clearly, the thanksgiving's praises of God for Jesus will remind the assembly of Jesus. But Joachim Jeremias pointed out another possible object of "remind:" God.[39] The suggestion has considerable prima facie plausability. Throughout the Old Testament, a chief theological category for saving changes in Israel's situation is God's "remembering;" e.g., "And God heard their groanings and God remembered his covenant with Abraham . . ." (Exodus 2:24). Moreover, it is the people's prayers that remind God of what he has done by which he is committed to them; e.g., "Remember your mercy, O God, and your steadfast love from of old . . ." (Psalm 25:6). In continuity of this tradition, a Passover table thanksgiving says, "Remind yourself of us and of our fathers and of the Messiah and of Jerusalem . . ."

Jeremias connected his suggestion to an implausible reconstruction of Jesus' eschatology and to his particular theory about the background of *anamnesis.* Thus it has not been generally accepted. But as to *the force of the phrase* merely, this is the only likely suggestion. Those who reject it entire seem mostly to argue from a metaphysical prejudice that God cannot be reminded of anything, a view that cannot co-exist with Scripture. We are, I suggest, so to give thanks as to remind all we address, both God and the company, of what God has done by Jesus and of what he is thereby committed to. In some form we are to pray, "Remember, O God, the sacrifice of our Lord, and quickly bring the salvation for which he died."

Here I must make one more controversial point, important again for our practice and understanding. This remembering, to whomever addressed, is an *embodied* remembering: it is done by the thanksgiving of a meal and by the way we eat two of the courses. That is, it is acted-out remembering, dramatically performed remembering. For we are to remember the story of an historical person; the way we remember such realities is by narration; and embodied narration is acting-out. If we at all obey the "Do this" that creates the Supper, a sort of play will necessarily be performed. With howsoever stark simplicity the Supper may be celebrated, an unprejudiced observer will certainly describe it: they are enacting Jesus and his disciples, and they are acting out an aspect of their history together.

The concept of "representation" is in our present situation equivocal, owing to an unfortunate sense Odo Casel gave the word. But as a matter of mere phenomenological fact, *representing* is exactly what the visible word of a story about the past necessarily does, in the case of the Supper as in any other. The representational relation between what we do in the Supper and events in the life of Jesus, was not invented by Casel but by the canonical Gospels, which cast the rubrics for our present act as an account of Jesus' past act, or perhaps vice versa. The texts do not in fact say only, "Give thanks, with bread and cup;" they say, "Do what Jesus and his first disciples did, which was to give thanks with bread and cup."

This circumstance does not posit a command to imitate whatever facets of Jesus' last supper we can discover. Even if, for example, we could discover whether their bread was leavened or unleavened, this would not bind our practice. The canonical institution-texts narrate the Last Supper only rubrically: we are not to imitate everything Jesus and his disciples may have done, but to obey the rubrical commands in their plainest sense—which will then in fact be an imitating of some things Jesus and his disciples are said to have done.

Moreover, we do indeed have to avoid a disastrous theology which has made the word *representation* its shibboleth. Casel taught that the *truth* of the sacramental promises of Christ's saving presence is grounded in the "mystery" structure of all reality, in which representing, as a particular kind of human action, has an intrinsic power to bring what is re-presented from the past into effective presence.[40] This teaching confuses God's act and ours with a vengeance. It is one thing to recognize, commonsensically, that if we do not do what a sacramental command mandates, the correlated promises have no referent. It is quite another thing to say that the action we perform, because of some particular character it manifests, is the ground of the promises' truth.

The sense in which the Supper is indeed a "representation" is strictly phenomenological; this is simply the *sort* of act we are in fact to perform. Why the Supper effectively "re-presents" Jesus, is another matter and the concern of the next chapter. But whether we use or—on account of Casel—avoid the word *represents,* we must somehow recognize the phenomenon: the Supper is a performance of a past event and events, and if the subject of those events, Jesus, is present in the Supper, it is indeed *as* so represented that he is present. To refuse to admit this simple fact, as some Protestants have, is to submit our practice of the Supper to a destructive dialectic. Such rigorists must try to remove all practices that are play acting—e.g., using red wine because blood is red or ceremoniously breaking the bread because Jesus' body was broken. But every time we remove such a facet of the Supper, we merely uncover new ones; and there is no core to this onion.

The Supper's biblical mandate is rubrically rather detailed, and therefore contains some puzzles. Yet it speaks to us a more than sufficiently clear command, which there is no difficulty in obeying: with words and with bread and cup, we are to join in praising God for what he has done by Jesus and in pressing for the fulfillment of what God has thereby promised. When we do this, an event occurs to which eschatological promises "come," to create a sacrament.

If, of course, we do not do what we are told to, there is nothing more to be said about the Supper, since no Supper occurs. If we do something else instead, there may be something to be said about whatever that is, besides that it is disobedience—perhaps even some promises can be made. But there is no way to anticipate that.

NOTES

1. So Ferdinand Hahn, "Zum Stand der Erforschung des urchristlichen Herrenmahls," *Evangelische Theologie,* 35, pp. 553–63, esp. pp. 553–55. Hahn's essay also contains a concise summary of the options.

2. This aspect was brought to attention above all by Ernst Lohmeyer. See, e.g., his "Das Abendmahl in der Urgemeinde," *Journal of Biblical Literature,* 56, pp. 217–52. Joachim Jeremias, *The Eucharistic Words of Jesus,* trans. Norman Perrin (Philadelphia: Fortress Press, 1977), from which all following citations are taken, regards this as the origin of the *church's* Supper, pp. 32, 66f., 205. Entirely opposite is Hans Conzelmann, *An Outline of the Theology of the New Testament,* trans. John Bowden (New York: Harper & Row, 1969), who does not, however, seem to understand the discussion.

3. To this, and to the whole matter of the Jewish thanksgivings, as discussed through the following, see above all Louis Bouyer, *Eucharist: Theology and Spirituality of The Eucharistic Prayer,* trans. Charles U. Quinn (Notre Dame: University of Notre Dame Press, 1968), where the texts are clearly presented with illuminating comment. See also footnotes 31 and 33 below.

4. Most concisely to the point, Eduard Schweizer, "Das Herrenmahl im Neuen Testament," *Theologische Literaturzeitung,* 79, pp. 571–91, esp. 582f.

5. So Eduard Schweizer, *The Lord's Supper According to the New Testament,* trans. James M. Davis, Facet Books—Biblical Series 18 (Philadelphia: Fortress Press, 1967) who provides a succinct summary of the arguments. See also Reginald Fuller, *The Mission and Achievement of Jesus,* Studies in Biblical Theology 12 (London: SCM Press, 1956), pp. 70ff.; Günter Bornkamm, "Lord's Supper and Church in Paul" *Early Christian Experience,* trans. Paul L. Hammer (New York: Harper & Row, 1969), pp. 123–60, esp. pp. 133–34.

6. In Mark 14:13, Jesus sends two of the twelve to prepare, which they do in v. 16; then in v. 17 he shows up with all twelve.

7. Jeremias, *The Eucharistic Words of Jesus,* pp. 41–84.

8. E.g., Schweizer, "Das Herrenmahl im Neuen Testament," pp. 583f.

9. The kiddusch- and chaburrah-meal ideas are disposed of by Jeremias, op. cit., pp. 26–31. The most interesting other proposals are by Wickmann von Meding, "I Korinther 11:26: vom geschichtlichen Grund des Abendmahls," *Evangelische Theologie,* 35, pp. 544–52 (postulated Jewish mourning-meal), and G. D. Kilpatrick, "The Last Supper," *Expository Times,* 64, pp. 4–8 (otherwise unknown pre-Rabbinic Jewish cult-meal deduced from *Joseph and Asaneth*). Neither proposal is overly convincing.

10. Hahn, "Zum Stand der Erforschung des urchristlichen Herrenmahls," pp. 562f.

11. Hans Conzelmann, *1 Corinthians,* trans. James W. Leitch, Hermenia (Philadelphia: Fortress Press, 1975).

12. Eduard Schweizer, *The Lord's Supper According to the New Testament,* pp. 18ff.

13. So far, Jeremias agrees! *The Eucharistic Words of Jesus,* pp. 101–05.

14. So Schweizer, *The Lord's Supper According to the New Testament,* pp. 23ff. This thesis is a successor to the theses of Hans Lietzmann, *Mass and Lord's Supper: A Study in the History of the Liturgy,* trans. Dorothea

H. G. Reeve (Leiden: Brill, 1953), and Ernst Lohmeyer, "Das Abendmahl in der Urgemeinde," that the Supper originated as the fusion of two distinct celebrations: a fellowship meal of eschatological joy and a meal in repetition of the Last Supper. I think Schweizer is probably right; in any case, it is precisely the *product* of the fusion with which we are concerned.

15. In the transformation of Mark's third person ". . . and they all drank from it," into Matthew's word of Jesus, "All of you, drink from it," we see the process at work before our synopsizing eyes.

16. Attention was drawn to this aspect above all by Oscar Cullmann, who unfortunately exaggerated the matter somewhat. See, e.g., his *Early Christian Worship*, trans. A. Stewart Todd and James B. Torrance, Studies in Biblical Theology 10 (London, SCM Press, 1953), pp. 14–18.

17. 1 Cor. 16:23; Rev. 22:20; *Didache* X, 6.

18. *to deipnēsai, Luke* 22:20; 1 Cor. 11:25; Acts 2:46, "When you are full, make your thanksgivings. . .;" *Didache*, X, 1.

19. To this and the following, see the exegeses in the remainder of this chapter.

20. George Kretschmar in Kurt Galling, *et al*, eds., *Die Religion in Geschichte und Gegenwart*[3] (Tübingen, J. C. B. Mohr [Paul Siebeck], 1957–62), I, col. 40; Jeremias, op. cit., p. 115.

21. The matter is most comprehensively discussed by Jeremias, op. cit., pp. 115–22.

22. 1 Cor. 10:16–17.

23. Günter Bornkamm, *Early Christian Experience,* especially chapters IX, "Lord's Supper and Church in Paul," and X, "On the Understanding of Worship"; Conzelmann, *1 Corinthians,* ad loc.

24. Kretschmar, op. cit., col. 41.

25. To the following cf. Bornkamm, op. cit., pp. 169–76.

26. A marvelously convenient summary of the present state of discussion of all questions about the institution-narratives is provided by Hahn, "Zum Stand der Erforschung des unchristlichen Herrenmahls."

27. Jeremias, op. cit., pp. 249–50, 174–78.

28. E.g., Conzelmann, *An Outline of the Theology of the New Testament,* pp. 50ff.; Bornkamm, op. cit., pp. 138–41; Jeremias, op. cit., pp. 67, 113f.

29. Jeremias, op. cit. pp. 249–50, 174–78, most compendiously lays out what is in any case perfectly clear. There are, of course, an infinity of non-possibilities. One should perhaps be mentioned. The internal referent of "Do this" cannot be "Eat" and "Drink" since in the texts that have "Do this," there is no mention of eating and drinking, and in Paul's text this exegesis would give the absurdity at v. 26, "Drink, whenever you drink . . ."

30. So Conzelmann, *1 Corinthians,* p. 198.

31. To the character of table-thanksgiving, to the role of bread and cup, as discussed throughout the following, and to the character of the rubrical commands in this connection, see above all Jeremias, op. cit., who also provides endless evidences and bibliography: pp. 35, 108–10, 173–78, 232–33.

32. Precisely this set was found in the text by Reformation exegesis. See *Formula of Concord* (Solid Declaration) VII, par. 84; Gerhard, *Loci communes theologici*, XXI, 142.

33. The best is to read the many extant texts. Louis Ligier has collected them in part one of *Prex Eucharistica*, ed. Anton Haenggi and Irmgard Phal (Fribourg: Editions universitaires, 1968).
See also J. P. Audet, "Literary Forms and Contents of a Normal *Eucharistia* in the First Century," *Texte und Untersuchungen zur Geschichte der altchristlichen Literatur*, vol. 73, [v, 18], (Berlin: Akademie Verlag, 1959), pp. 643–662, and Bouyer, op. cit.

34. See Jeremias; also Ferdinand Hahn, "Die altestamentliche Motive in der urchristlichen Abendmahlsüberlieferung," *Evangelische Theologie*, 27, pp. 337–74, esp. pp. 338ff.; also Friedrich Lang, "Abendmahl und Bundesgedanke in Neuen Testament," *Evangelische Theologie*, 35, pp. 524–38, esp. p. 531.

35. Bornkamm, *Early Christian Experience*, pp. 140f., Jeremias, op. cit., pp. 106ff.

36. Jeremias presents the evidence on pp. 238–49, and argues for a Jewish background. For an Hellenistic background, see Bornkamm, op. cit., pp. 140ff., and Conzelmann, *1 Corinthians*, pp. 198f.

37. Bornkamm, op. cit., p. 141–42.

38. *eis*

39. Jeremias, op. cit., pp. 244–55.

40. Odo Casel, *The Mystery of Christian Worship and Other Writings*, trans. I. T. Hale, ed. Burkhard Neunheuser (Westminster, Md.: Newman Press, 1962), pp. 50–62, 109–144, 154–160.

8

Promise

Two sets of sayings in the institution-narratives bring gospel-promises very directly to the mandated Supper. The one set, Mark 14:25 and par. and Luke 22:15–18, are versions of a sort of eschatological oath by Jesus. Mark's version is seemingly older,[1] and probably is indeed a farewell saying of Jesus:[2] "Indeed I tell you, I will not again drink of the vine's fruit, until the day I drink it afresh in the kingdom of God." The original point is clear: not that Jesus is going on the wagon, but that the kingdom is so near that the next festive meal will be there, a messianic banqueting.[3]

Our primary concern here is not, however, with the saying in the context of Jesus' life, but with the force of its attachment to the rubrics for the church's Supper. In this attachment, the saying says, on the one hand, that Jesus' promise is fulfilled when the Supper is celebrated; somehow, this meal is a messianic party "in" the kingdom, in which Jesus joins anew. But on the other hand, so long as the promise needs to be repeated, it says that the kingdom has not yet come; the Supper's meal-fellowship is made provisional to its own still future fulfilled reunion. *Maranatha,* "Come, Lord"—both in the Supper and at the Last.[4]

We have seen how our meal-fellowship, as we are bidden to do it, is *representation* of what happened with Jesus in the past. We may synthesize the assertions of the previous paragraph by saying that in the other temporal direction, the promises make our meal fellowship *anticipation* of the fellowship that is to come with Jesus at the last future. The future is not yet; and if what we do anticipates it, this is strictly God's gift. That clearly stipulated, we may then say that as embodied past-

78

tense narrative is representation, so embodied future-tense narrative, embodied gospel-promise, is anticipation. The Supper is both; but in that it is anticipation it is a *sacrament,* a visible word of the gospel.

Anticipation is acted-out prophecy. Anyone can of course prophecy, but only God can make prophecy true. The accuracy of our representation of what has been is our own responsibility; the truth of our anticipation of what will be, only God can grant. It is, therefore, precisely as anticipation that the reality of what happens in the Supper escapes our work to be sacrament and solely the work of God. Representation of what happened with Christ is what the sacramental law commands us to do; anticipation of the fulfillment achieved by what happened with Christ is what the sacramental promises grant. And that our representation of Christ is an actual re-presenting of him lies in the God-granted anticipation.

The meal-fellowship of the Supper is acted-out promise of the last fellowship. To be brought into the fellowship of this Supper is to anticipate belonging to the fellowship of the kingdom; it is bodily promise of that belonging.

II

The second set of sayings are the interpretations of the bread and cup ceremonies: "This is. . . ."[5] It is worth explicitly noting that just as the mandate is of *uses* of the bread and cup, so it is the mandated uses to which these interpretations apply.[6] Unlike the Passover liturgy's interpretations of the meal courses of lamb and bitter herbs, which ceremonialize the eating of these courses, Jesus' interpretations are of an eating and drinking that are ceremonial acts prior to his interpretation.[7] The "is"-promises we have now to consider are not about bread and wine as substances or foods merely, but about bread and wine as used in specific established ceremonial ways. *Nothing at all* is biblically promised about the bread and wine merely as such.

In Mark and Matthew, the bread-word and the cup-word are parallel, with bread paired to wine and "body" to "blood," so that they make one double saying. In Paul and Luke there is simply one saying for each element, with no such parallelism.[8] We must choose which version to take as historically prior, since this will affect our understanding of both: in the one case, we are dealing with one double saying, in the other, with two independent sayings.[9]

The arguments for the historical priority of the Pauline-Lukan type of text are overwhelming.[10]   The historical development moved from a practice that put the bread-thanksgiving before an ordinary supper and the cup-thanksgiving after, to a practice with both bread and cup immediately adjacent.   A development from independent interpretations of each thanksgiving-course to neatly parallel interpretations matches this development of practice; a development in the opposite direction does not.   I will therefore deal with the bread-interpretation and the cup-interpretation as independent sayings.   For present purposes, it is not necessary to decide on an earliest recoverable form; but my own guess is: "This is my body," "This cup is the new covenant in my blood."[11]

"This is my body."   Since "body" is not originally paired with "blood," we can take it in its ordinary sense.   The "body" is then simply the person, considered as an object in the world, of others' and the person's own apprehension and will.[12]

The sentence states an identity—not of substances merely as such, but of actions with the substances.   We may unpack the assertion, in the language of the first part of this book, so: participation in the fellowship of thanksgiving to God by means of the bread = participation in the fellowship of thanksgiving to God by means of Jesus' body, i.e., his object-presence in the world.   What any such assertion of identity means, depends on which half is felt as obscure, to be interpreted by equation with the other.   Is it the Jesus-fellowship that in these texts is taken to need interpretation, or is it the bread-fellowship?   And that, in turn, depends upon whether the texts are primarily to be taken as an account of Jesus' and his disciples' meal then—which we are to imitate— or primarily as rubrics for our meal now—cast in the form of an account of their meal then.

If we are to take the texts primarily as accounts of Jesus' and his disciples' last supper, there are two appropriate questions about "This is my body."   We must ask first: What could Jesus have meant by the sentence on that occasion, or be represented as having meant by it? And second: What does it mean for us now that Jesus then said and meant what he did?   Reformed exegesis has often been of this sort.[13]   If these are our questions, we must take the saying as explanation of *Jesus* and his fate, not of the bread.   "This is my body," spoken by Jesus sitting there in the body, as explanation of another object, would have been pure mystification.[14]   If we take the texts in this way, we should paraphrase, again in the earlier language of this book: "As the bread mediates your thanksgiving-fellowship in this meal, so my body-presence in the world mediates the eschatological thanksgiving-fellowship."

Or we may consider the texts primarily as rubrics for and interpretation of the *church's* Supper, as command and promise addressed to us. Then, of course, it is the bread the church is to use, the meaning of which needs to be spoken. Lutheran and Roman Catholic exegesis has always begun in this way. If this is the way to take the texts, we may paraphrase: "As my body-presence in the world mediates all your thanksgiving-fellowship, so the shared bread will be the object-center of your continuing thanksgiving-fellowship—and just so, *my* object-presence."

It should be noted that neither paraphrase here offered is intended to explain how the claim, "This is Jesus' body," can be *true*; that will be attempted later. Both are intended only to explicate what it is that is claimed. Neither does the form of my paraphrases commit me to asserting that the interpretive sayings are historical words of Jesus.

Critical study of the nature of the texts tends to confirm that the texts should be taken first as rubrics for and interpretation of what *we* are to do, not as accounts of what Jesus and the disciples did. But if we begin in this "Lutheran" way, we should incorporate also the "Reformed" soteriological point about Jesus. Precisely as interpretation of what we are now to do, "This is my body" will become interpretation also of Jesus: the identity-assertion will run both ways. Whereas if we start in the "Reformed" way, there is no motive to move on to the other sort of claim: the texts tell us what happened then, and what those happenings meant, and we are to imitate the event in view of its meanings. This is a complete understanding in itself. In everything that follows, I work from the Lutheran starting point.

". . . given for you." That Jesus' body-self is said to be "given" is a reference to his death; it is sacrificial terminology.[15] This body is given "for" those sharing the bread on any occasion. We should paraphrase: "My body-self, given to you as the bread, is a body-self sacrificed to create thanksgiving-fellowship." In the institution-texts, it is this phrase which most directly makes the giving and eating of the bread into an embodiment of God's promise, a sacrament in the proper sense.

I said earlier that our celebration of the Supper is inevitably a representation of Jesus' fellowship with his disciples. The way in which

"... given for you" interprets the distribution and eating of the bread greatly expands the Supper's representative reality: the giving and eating come to represent the whole sacrifice of our Lord's life. What the Supper represents is not only the meal-fellowship aspect of Christ's life, but all that happened with him for us. Just so, the giving and eating are embodied promise, anticipation, of all the future gained in Jesus' life; when the bread is given us, God promises all his love, bodily.

III

Next the word about the cup. Taken as a saying for itself, "This cup is the new covenant" presents no obscurities. A thanksgiving-cup is a covenant in every case and in the most obvious sense: sharing it is in itself an act of mutual acceptance and commitment. The point of "This cup is the new covenant," lies in the word *new*; *this* covenant-cup, the cup of the *gospel*-fellowship, is the "new" covenant promised by the prophets.[16] Here the whole biblical eschatology "comes to" the actions of the Supper. The sharing of the cup is anticipation of Israel's entire vision of fulfilled human community; and our liturgical and homiletical explication of the cup-sharing may draw on every page of the Old Testament. Moreover, it is to the cup that also the "eschatological oath" first discussed, attaches. The new covenant is "in my blood." To begin, this too is a simple statement—at least to readers of the Old Testament.[17] Covenant is always established in someone's blood; so the ritual of ancient Israel enacted it, and so our daily experience teaches. Jesus establishes the new covenant between God and us in that he gives up his life at once fully to God's will and to his commitment to us, in that the decision of his life is unrestricted self-commitment at once to God and to us.

The phrase is first to be taken about Jesus, the church, and the kingdom, not about the cup.[18] It is also about the cup by the way in which the giving-over to us of the wine can *mean* the pouring-out of Jesus' life to us. This part of the cup-interpretation thus refers to the cup only by way of the cup's representative function as a visible word. The cup-sharing is both representation, done by us, of Jesus' death, and anticipation, as embodiment of God's word to us, of Jesus' final self-surrender.[19]

"Spilled for you" in Luke and "spilled for all people," and "for forgiveness of sin," in Mark and Matthew, do with the cup-word what "given for you" did with the bread-word in Paul and Luke. They need little further explanation, except again to note the connection between covenant and the spilling of blood.

Of course, if no cup is shared, all this is lost. Protestants who distribute the wine in individual glasses suppose that it is in any case, once "consecrated," the blood of Christ or an effective symbol or whatever they hold it to be. Roman Catholics who withhold the wine altogether argue—by the doctrine of "concommitance"—that the whole Christ, "body and blood," is present where his body is present as the bread. Neither rationalization has any merit. About the wine simply as such, apart from our cup-sharing, there is no canonical promise at all. As for "concomitance," even if one could tolerate so crude a notion, it would still be entirely beside the point. For the presence of Christ merely as such is not the blessing Scripture attaches to the cup specifically, so that the question whether the whole Christ is present as the bread alone helps not at all about the cup, as a separable element. Rather, the cup is the locus of the Supper's *eschatology,* of the future opened by the present Christ. And in fact, practices which suppress the cup seem historically to have arisen within versions of Christianity that have lost the faith's community and hope and transformed the Supper into a supply station of individual and immediate blessings.

IV

Finally, we must look briefly at the type of text found in Mark and Matthew. It represents the development whereby the two courses became a holy meal at the end of the meal for nourishment or entirely separate. With this order, the interpreting words for both bread and cup naturally came to be heard as paired sayings, and then actually to assume parallel form: Thus the cup-word now reads, "This is my blood . . ."

Here "body" and "blood" make one concept together, fundamentally the same as "body" alone in the older form. The notion of a *sacrificed* body-self may now be built into the vocabulary itself: it is a killed body-self that is body *and* blood. Thus "This is my body" and "This is my blood" say together what "This is my body, given for you," said in Luke and Paul. The promise of the new covenant, formerly made by the cup-word, now appears in the addition of "of the covenant" to "blood."

The Markan form is a clear loss of precision and force over against the older form. The disappearance of the regular meal between the thanksgivings, however motivated, was already a loss; but it can hardly be reversed. Our liturgical forms and interpretation nevertheless can and should take the Pauline text as chief model.

V

Outside the narratives of institution, there are three New Testament passages we must briefly consider. I will first discuss John 6, the great "true-bread" discourse.[20]

That John 6:51–59 deals with the Supper is manifest, some older Reformation exegesis to the contrary. But in reading the passage, it is vital to remember that experience of the fully developed Supper, with liturgical and catechetical interpretation of the sort represented in Mark, is presupposed in the actual addressees of the discourse, that is, John's readers. The discourse is not primarily intended to interpret the Supper, but to interpret the revelation in Jesus, which in the discourse's second half is done by means of the readers' experience of the Supper. If verses 51–59 are indeed a later addition to John's text, then it is this added interpretation that we are concerned with.

John's one theme is the revelation which Jesus "*is.*" John 6 brings revelation to word as "bread," that which sustains life. The "true" bread nourishes "eternal" life. All the dialectics of the Johannine gospel of revelation appear. The true nourishment is not of this world, but comes "from heaven." The true nourishment's coming from heaven is an act of self-sacrifice. Interrogators inquire after the availability of this bread, to which the response is the great Johannine assertion, "*I am the bread of life.*" This assertion is made by an objectively present human person, whose father and mother the interrogators know. Therefore it causes offense. The only other possibility is faith, here brought to word as "eating" the true bread. Before actual revelation, mankind divides into two sorts, thus fulfilling divine predestination.

John's addressees belong to those who believe and are not offended. The whole discourse is to clarify faith for the faithful. But where do John's readers *do* this believing; where do they know themselves as belonging to the one humanity rather than the other? One place, suggested directly by the content of the discourse, is the Supper, where bread and wine as objective and earthly as Jesus himself, are presented to be eaten and drunk as true nourishment, food and drink from heaven. Because of the Markan type of cup-interpretation which John presupposes, "flesh" and "blood" make one concept here, perfectly correlated to "true bread" by itself in the earlier part of the discourse. The replacement of "body" by "flesh" merely adjusts the awkwardness of "body" and "blood" where both together only make "body," and probably has occurred in the liturgical tradition before John. Between the use of "flesh" here, and "The flesh does nothing" in the next passage, there is, therefore, no relation at all.

When those gathered for the Supper are presented with bread and wine to be eaten and drunk as a nourishment of God's revelation, the possibility of offense is given: at the Supper, John's readers know very well the reality of the discourse's dialectics. If offense is overcome by God's will, believing is in this case the same act as the eating and drinking—thus John's massive insistence on these physical acts, which has offended so many. There is this difference between the two halves of the discourse: in the first half, faith comes to word as "eating" the "true" bread, in the second, an actual eating of food is identified as the act of faith. But this is only a typically Johannine dialectical play: for precisely the possibility of offense which lies in the object-person Jesus' claim to faith is fulfilled in the identification of faith itself as an act upon objects, the bread and wine. Moreover, from the whole Johannine theology, we can note that the equivalent to the physical eating and drinking of the Supper would be, over against Jesus himself as the "true bread," an equally physical seeing and touching.

Because of the saying in the next pericope, "The flesh does nothing," the whole chapter has been a favorite proof text of anti-sacramentalists —so much so that some Reformation exegesis tried to deny that verses 51–59 were about the Supper at all. This is a great irony, since, in fact, the chapter is a chief biblical witness to the fundamentally sacramental character of Christianity. For the revelation to be revelation of *God,* it must pose the exclusive and exhaustive alternatives of faith and offense; it does so in that it comes as an object in the world; this object is Jesus of Nazareth and, in the situation of the church, the bread and wine; and in this connection, no distinction is made between Jesus and the bread and wine.

In 1 Corinthians 10:14–22,[21] the problem is the notorious question of participation in the festive meals of pagans, insofar as these were sacrificial occasions.   In sacrifices that include a meal, the life of the sacrificed living thing binds the god and his worshipers, its death being at once a return of life to the god and a gift of life to those who eat.   In *this* passage, Paul recommends abstaining from such meals on the grounds that participation in such meals is incompatible with participation in the Supper.   Thus Paul regards the Supper as phenomenologically of the same sort as pagan sacrificial meals; he takes participation in the cup and table of the Lord and in the cup and table of idols as self-evidently alternatives.

On this basis, when Paul wishes to say exactly wherein participation in the Lord's table and idols' tables are incompatible, he must necessarily refer to whatever about the Supper defines for him its particularity as a rite of Christian faith.   It is therefore of the first importance that it is the *community* of believers with Christ and with one another to which he refers.

"The cup of thanksgiving—is it not a communion of the blood of Christ?   The bread which we break—is it not a communion of the body of Christ?"   Paul is clearly familiar with the Markan sort of cup-interpretation; "body" and "blood" together are here just "person."   By the bread and cup we are in a community that is the Lord's.   So far, of course, that community might be with the Lord only.   But the next sentences are: "Because there is one loaf, we many are one body; for we all share the one loaf."   Here the "body" of Christ is not the bread, but the church, which is such a unitary entity in that its members are brought together in the sharing of the bread.   The crucified Jesus—"body and blood"—and the believers all make one body, one object-entity, in the world, by virtue of what happens in the Supper with the bread and cup. And it is this incorporation of the believers which is incompatible with any other incorporation.[22]

In 1 Corinthians 11:17–34,[23] we have the passage in which Paul is moved to cite his version of the institution-narrative.   Paul's theological diagnosis of the Corinthians' behavior is that they eat from the bread and drink from the cup "unworthily," and that since the relations created by Jesus' institution between the bread and cup and his own person and death obtain as they do, this is a failure to "discern" "the body" and a solicitation of divine punishment.

The crime charged against the Corinthians is against Jesus himself; the "body" which they inadequately "discern" is the body of Jesus given as the bread and cup—otherwise it could not be the *narrative of institution* that carried Paul from the behavior of the Corinthians to the guilt with which he charges them. The Corinthians fail to discern the presence of Christ as bread and cup. But wherein does this failure consist? Contrary to long exegetical tradition, still entrenched in the church, it does *not* consist in wrong opinions about or impious behavior toward the bread and cup themselves. Manifestly and explicitly, it consists rather in the Corinthians' selfish and uncomradely behavior toward one another, in connection with the regular supper—that, after all, is what Paul's whole admonition set out to discuss.

We must let ourselves move with the beautiful dialectics of the passage. They depend on the full resonances of Paul's pervasive use of "body of Christ." The bread and cup *are* the present body of Christ; I can intend "the body" in them. But if I fail in this, the failure is not directly in my intention of the bread and cup, but in wrong intention of my fellow-believers, as mere individuals rather than as one entity with me, the church-body of Christ. The body-presence of Christ as the bread and cup is there in any case, by Christ's promise; if I fail in my discernment of it, it is not it but I who am destroyed. The presence of Christ as bread and cup is prior to the community around it; it creates the community. But all this once given, the body-presence of Christ as the bread and cup and as the community are not separable.

NOTES

1. The arguments of Ferdinand Hahn are decisive. See his "Die altestamentliche Motive in der urchristlichen Abendmahlsüberlieferung," pp. 356f.

2. Hahn, "Zum Stand der Erforschung des urchristlichen Herrenmahls," pp. 557f. The Lukan version is one of the perennial hard nuts of scholarship. In my opinion, Hahn, "Die altestamentliche Motive in der urchristlichen Abendmahlsüberlieferung," pp. 352–58, and Jeremias, *The Eucharistic Words of Jesus,* pp. 122–25, have solved it: the whole Lukan text, 22:15–20, gives the rubrics of a Christianized yearly Passover with following Supper, such as we otherwise know to have been celebrated by groups in the earliest church, e.g., the "Quartodecimanians." Jeremias, of course, then takes Luke's account as the correct historical account of Jesus' last supper, which need not follow.

3. E.g., A. J. B. Higgins, *The Lord's Supper in the New Testament,* Studies in Biblical Theology 6 (London: SCM Press, 1952), pp. 41ff.; Hahn,

"Zum Stand der Erforschung des urchristlichen Herrenmahls," pp. 555f. So also, despite utterly different reconstruction, Jeremias, op. cit., pp. 217–18.

4. 1 Cor. 16:22; Rev. 22:20; *Didache* X, 6.

5. The most helpful exegeses of these much-debated sentences are provided by Conzelmann, *1 Corinthians,* ad loc.; Bornkamm, *Early Christian Experience,* pp. 141ff.; E. Schweizer, *The Lord's Supper According to the New Testament,* pp. 10f.; Hahn, "Zum Stand der Erforschung des urchristlichen Herrenmahls," pp. 558ff. For much useful information, but far less help with interpretation, see Jeremias throughout. Since Higgins' book, op. cit., is evidently still used in instruction, it is worthwhile saying that its exegesis of these sentences, pp. 45–55, is valuable mostly as illustrative of the arbitrary expedients to which one may be led if one insists on interpreting the institution-texts by a reconstruction of Jesus' last supper.

6. "The . . . formula is not bread and wine, but bread and cup. Thus the interpretation attaches not to the elements as such, but to the act of administration." Conzelmann, *1 Corinthians,* p. 199. This is the common opinion of the exegetes; e.g., Hahn, "Zum Stand der Erforschung des urchristlichen Herrenmahls," p. 555.

7. Jeremias has missed this! Op. cit., pp. 220–21.

8. To *this* point, what the possibilities in Hebrew or Aramaic may be— Jeremias, pp. 199ff.—is entirely irrelevant!

9. On the exegetical weight of this decision, see Bornkamm, *Early Christian Experience,* pp. 142ff.

10. So Schweizer in *The Lord's Supper According to the New Testament* and "Das Herrenmahl im Neuen Testament;" Bornkamm, *Early Christian Experience,* pp. 123–60, esp. pp. 134–38; Conzelmann, *1 Corinthians,* pp. 200–01 *et passim*; Hahn, "Zum Stand der Erforschung des urchristlichen Herrenmahls," pp. 558ff. With *extremely* careful argumentation, Lang has presented the case in "Abendmahl und Bundesgedanke im Neuen Testament," pp. 525–28. The one ponderable *contra* is Jeremias, op. cit., pp. 160–96.

11. Rudolf Bultmann, *Theology of the New Testament,* trans. Kendrick Grobel, (New York: Charles Scribner's Sons, 1951), I, pp. 144–52, asserts "This is my body. This is my blood," with no argumentation, apparently just *because* he thinks it unlikely to be very ancient. Higgins, op. cit., pp. 24–44, argues for "This is my body. This is my blood, shed for you," on the basis of Aramaic probabilities. Jeremias, op. cit., pp. 164–203, argues for "This is my body. This is my covenant-blood (*to haima mou tēs diathēkēs*)," on the basis of Aramaic probabilities and the assumption we are looking for *ipsissima verba*. The choice made here is with Schweizer and Bornkamm, on form- and tradition-historical grounds—which are, with respect, the only *relevant* grounds for such a decision.

12. Hahn, "Zum Stand der Erforschung des urchristlichen Herrenmahls," pp. 558f.

13. As is the exegesis of Jeremias. It is devoted entirely to discovering what the historical Jesus did on a certain occasion, and what difference it

makes to us, historically, that he did it. See *The Eucharistic Words of Jesus*, pp. 218–31. As exegesis of promises directed to *us*, Jeremias' work is useless.

14. As has often been noted by various sectarians and rationalists, whose common sense should not be discredited by association.

15. E.g., Conzelmann, *1 Corinthians*, p. 198.

16. Jeremiah 31:31. To the whole cup-word, Oswald Bayer, "Tod Gottes und Herrenmahl," *Zeitschrift für Theologie und Kirche*, 70, pp. 346–63, esp. pp. 355ff.

17. Hahn, "Die altestamentliche Motive in der urchristlichen Abendmahls-überlieferung," pp. 358–73.

18. Hahn, "Zum Stand der Erforschung des urchristlichen Herrenmahls," pp. 559f.

19. Jeremias, op. cit., p. 179ff.

20. Rudolf Bultmann, *The Gospel of John*, trans. G. R. Beasley-Murray *et al.* (Philadelphia: Westminster Press, 1971) is still the great John commentary; see ad loc. But on this passage see especially, Eduard Schweizer, "Das johanneische Zeugnis vom Herrenmahl," *Evangelische Theologie*, 7, pp. 263ff.; Conzelmann, *1 Corinthians*, ad loc.; Hahn, "Zum Stand der Erforschung des urchristlichen Herrenmahls," pp. 561f.

21. See Bornkamm, *Early Christian Experience*, pp. 123–25, 143–54; Schweizer, "Das Herrenmahl im Neuen Testament," pp. 588f.; Ernst Käsemann, "The Pauline Doctrine of the Lord's Supper" in *Essays on New Testament Themes*, trans. W. J. Montague, Studies in Biblical Theology 41 (London: SCM Press, 1964), pp. 108ff.; Conzelmann, *1 Corinthians*, ad loc.; Hahn, "Zum Stand der Erforschung des urchristlichen Herrenmahls," pp. 561ff.

22. "Therefore, the specifically Pauline ecclesiological idea of the 'body', (*sōma*) expressed in v. 17, is also characterized by an equally real intention in 'we are' (*esmen*), as the 'he is' (*estin*) of the formula of institution itself clearly was interpreted in the sense of a reality by the terms 'participation' (*koinōnia*) and 'to partake' (*metechein*)." Bornkamm, *Early Christian Experience*, p. 144, Greek added from original German.

23. On this passage, see above all Käsemann, "The Pauline Doctrine of the Lord's Supper," pp. 119ff. Also Bornkamm, *Early Christian Experience*, pp. 125–30, 146–55; Conzelmann, *1 Corinthians*, pp. 194f.

PART FOUR

INTERPRETATION OF THE SUPPER

9

The Offertory and the
Great Thanksgiving

I

By the end of the church's first two centuries its attempts to obey Scripture's mandate had come to display a regular order of events, which has remained standard since. There is no reason why this order must always be followed, but it is the necessary given of such a discussion as this.

In the traditional order,[1] the Supper comes after a service of Scripture reading, preaching, hymnody, and prayer. This service, which in effect has replaced the ordinary courses of the meal, is of a type pervasive in the church's life and inherited directly from the synagogue. The effect of this arrangement is to make the meal begin *during* the total service; the bringing of food and drink and the setting of the table thus becomes itself an act of the service and so a visible word. This action is the *Offertory*.

In the late-patristic Western church, the Offertory was a splendid event. The people brought their gifts in kind: bread, wine, and produce. From these, sufficient bread and wine were taken for the Supper; the rest was later distributed to the poor. A money economy obviously must take some of the fun out of this, but it was not economic development that shrivelled the Offertory to the insignificant affair we now know best. In a mass celebrated by the priest alone there is no one to bring gifts. As private masses became through the Middle Ages the dominant form, their practices were imposed also on the congregational services.[2]

Oddly enough, Protestants sometimes cling rigidly to the minimal practice born from the private mass. We should not, they say, make much of our gift-bringing, lest it compete with God's gift to us. The basic error of this opinion has already been discussed. In this instance the protest cannot be carried out anyway. Since there is no way to avoid having an Offertory and so having it say *something* about and by our gifts, the only sensible concern is to make the Offertory say a right thing. Even if the altar guild just puts the bread and wine on the altar before anyone comes, where they are ignored until half-way through the service, this ignored presence speaks unbiblical volumes: *somebody* must bring or have brought the bread and wine, if not the congregation as a whole, then the clergy and officials.

The Offertory is an audacious act. Do it as ceremoniously *or* unceremoniously as we will, when we bring bread and wine to that table we offer them most daringly to God. For we bring them for him to take as his own body. Such an act must surely be done with prayer. And the appeal must be only to God's promise without reference to the motives or occasion of our gift-bringing. It must be appeal to the future of what God promises to use these gifts for, and not at all to the past of what we have done with them. That is, our prayer must be eschatological invocation. And that is, its most Christianly appropriate form is invocation of the Spirit, of God as the One who brings the future. We should beseech the Father: "Let your Spirit hallow our gifts . . ."

One might indeed speak of a "consecration" of the bread and wine at the Offertory: at this time we bring and devote them to God's purpose.[3] The conception of "consecration" is a tricky one which can be highly misleading and usually has been; but the action or actions traditionally so named are—mostly—essential, and the language of consecration *can* be helpful in speaking of them. Some sorting out is needed.

What must be rigorously avoided is the designation of *any* moment in the Supper that is supposed to mark a metaphysical before-and-after, before which the elements "are" just bread and wine and after which they "are" Christ's presence. There is *no* biblical warrant for supposing that any such transformation takes place or that, if it did, it would coincide with any liturgical act or set of acts. Within the biblically mandated use—which does indeed include acts traditionally labelled "consecration"—the bread and cup simply are Christ's body on the promise that they shall be. *Use* looks temporally forward rather than backward: that the elements are Christ's real presence at any time within the mandated use is not the *consequence* of something that *has* been done to them, but their *openness* to what they *will* be received as, the self-giving of Christ. If we suppose that Christ's presence is the consequence of something done with the bread and wine, we must conceive it as analogous to the presence of a "thing," for that is what a "thing" is, the temporal after-shadow of an event. That is, we must conceive it as analogous to the presence of an *unspeaking* object that would be what it is whether it said anything or not. The biblical God is never present in this way.

If there is a before-and-after, it is in the wholly commonsensical way of the beginning of the mandated action and of the taking of bread and wine to be used in that action. This is the Offertory. And therefore such prayer language as ". . . make now this bread and cup to be the true body . . ." is appropriate precisely at this spot.

II

Next in the traditional order comes the "Anaphora" or "Canon" or "Eucharistic Prayer." Following recent suggestions, I will call it the *Great Thanksgiving*. This is a composition that fulfills at once all the mandated elements of thanksgiving—doxology, narration of saving history, and eschatological invocation—by weaving them all together into one continuous utterance, addressed by the presiding minister at once to God and the congregation. It too is sometimes thought of as the "consecration," and *if* "consecration" is taken in a very different sense than that in which it applies to the Offertory, with some right. For if all thoughts of a metaphysical transformation worked by our action are avoided, then fulfilling the mandate, by which the bread and cup are to be so used as to be the objects of sacramental promises, may indeed be thought of as consecration, and in a traditional order, all the mandated actions except the eating and drinking themselves are brought together in the Great Thanksgiving. The accumulated tradition of texts for the Great Thanksgiving displays a freedom and richness of imagination and a variety of rhetorical forms that are past even suggesting here. But the main theological-rhetorical structure is constant and clear. The structure is trinitarian.[4]

Explicit doxology is addressed to God the Father. This may be as sober as in the first known full text, recorded around A.D. 200 by Hippolytus:[5] "We bring you our praises, God, through . . ." or it may go on for pages, as in the affiliated anaphora of the *Apostolic Constitutions,* from fourth-century Antioch. Sooner or later, the praise of God leaves pure doxology and becomes recitation of his saving acts—in accord with the very nature of thanksgiving. In obedience to "for *my* remembrance," this recitation is christological in whole or part. So Hippolytus: ". . . through your beloved Son Jesus Christ, whom in these last days you sent to be our savior and redeemer and the messenger of your will, who is your inseparable Word through whom you made all things, who . . ." The Great Thanksgiving is praise of the Father for remembrance of the Son.

The remaining element of proper thanksgiving is eschatological invocation. Most texts carry the narrative of God's works through to his concluding work and include petitions for final salvation. But the chief form of eschatological invocation is invocation of God the Spirit. Here a main structure of Christian theology asserts itself. As we have seen, in the Christian identification of God, God the Spirit is God as the transforming power of the eschaton, now to be goal and judgment of what now is. Insofar as thanksgiving is at all points praise of *God,* Christian invocation of the eschaton is therefore intrinsically invocation of the Spirit. Since the explicit acknowledgment of the divinity of the Spirit, only the most absent-minded or heretical celebrations have omitted the petition, "Send, O God, your Spirit . . ."

There is thus a perfect match between the structure of Jewish table-thanksgiving and the trinitarian doctrine of God. This is no accident. It is precisely Israel's special apprehension of God which, impressed with drastic finality by Jesus' resurrection, necessitated the doctrine of the Trinity. And indeed, the trinitarian structure of the Great Thanksgiving apparently resulted from a direct historical development of Christian prayers from existing Jewish prayers.[6] Christian thanksgiving which is not explicitly and clearly trinitarian is poor thanksgiving.

III

To about the same degree as there has been a standard order of the Supper in general, there has been a standard order of the *Great Thanksgiving* in detail.[7] Since the Reformation, the Western church has known many fragmentary and eccentric orders, but also these mostly consist of bits and pieces from the Roman version of the traditional order.

A traditional Great Thanksgiving begins with a dialogue between the presiding minister and the rest of the congregation: "The Lord be with you. And with you. Lift up your hearts." Such dialogue is a regular feature of Christian liturgy; so here at its heart. Dialogue springs from the essential character of our service as speaking and responding to the gospel. The most ancient line of the Dialogue, "Let us give thanks to the Lord our God," is still simply the beginning of Jewish after-table prayer.[8]

Then the praise of God begins. And here there is an historical disaster to record. The Great Thanksgiving of the congregation at Rome, the "canon," developed in an ecumenically odd way,[9] for most occasions limiting the narrative content of praise to the second creedal article. This would have been a local misfortune only, but that Rome's power spread its canon over the whole Western church. And most of the Reformers did no more than remove what they—usually rightly!—disapproved in the canon; but with respect to our *present* concern, mere excision could of course only make a dubious state worse.

Outside the shadow of Rome, the church has praised God for creation, for the redemptive history of Israel, for Christ, and for promised fulfillment. And so it must surely be done. Particularly the recitation of Jesus' life, crucifixion, and resurrection must, to be true to its own meaning, be embedded in Israel's saving history. Bereft of his Israelite identity, "Jesus" becomes a mere unidentified numen whom we will make the servant of whatever self-invented religion we find momentarily convenient. If the church ceases to remember the stories of Abraham and Exodus and the prophets, the isolated remembrance of the one Israelite must soon shrivel.

In the ancient liturgies, this section was often a lengthy declamation. By the fourth century, it was regularly broken by the singing of two short biblical hymns, together called the Sanctus. This has led to some confusion, most disastrously in the Roman Canon. There the part before the Sanctus is a seasonal variable of strictly Second-Article content (the *Preface*, which means just "prayer"); while after the Sanctus the praise of God does not resume at all. Instead there is a conglomerate of petitions and sacrificial formulas. These may once have fitted into the praise of God in an appropriate way, but in the canon known to the Middle Ages and now, the elements of praise have themselves disappeared.[10] Thus left alone, petitions say exactly the opposite of what should here be said.

The mainline Reformers abolished the conglomerate but usually put nothing in its place, not knowing that anything belonged there.[11] This has led to Protestant orders, such as the standard Lutheran order of Dialogue, Preface, Sanctus, and Narrative of Institution, which by the best construction only grudgingly obey Scripture's mandate to praise God, and which therefore perpetuate a real "unitarianism of the Second Article."

Throughout the tradition it is somewhere in the neighborhood of the Sanctus that the church's praises are explicitly integrated into those of the cosmic host. In the West, the traditional Preface ends: "Therefore with angels and archangels, and with all the company of heaven, we praise thy Holy Name . . ." This self-transcendence of our earthly thanksgiving is too prominent in the tradition to be passed by. Who or what are these angels?

Genetically they are the depontentiated divinities of Israel's neighboring peoples. Once Israel had thoroughly learned that all things but the Lord are his creatures, the manifestly subsisting and potent forces of historical existence—the spirits of nations and of earth and of personal inner force—could be understood not as God's rivals but as his created servants, his "messengers." The Judaism of the turn of the millennia had a detailed doctrine of angels by which the clash of historical forces was understood as subject to the final rule of God.

The church inherited this interpretation of reality and maintained it for the same purpose. It supposed that all created reality, insofar as it presses on our communal and individual lives, and especially those created powers to which we sustain a moral relation, describing their work upon us as good and evil, must somehow be susceptible of personal interpretation.

In this, the ancient church was surely correct. There *are* such entities as nations and polities and lands and subconscious selves, and despite all quantifying and predictive knowledge of them, we can and must relate morally to them. If "America" is *only* an impersonal collectivity it cannot play a role between God and us, and then it cannot finally make any moral demands upon us.

At the end, all creation's voices will praise God in chorus, the created historical powers among them. Insofar as we now at the Supper anticipate the end, we anticipate that chorus. But we can do this only as we *let go* of our praises, only as we sing and let our song rule what we say, only as we speak a little bit "in tongues." It is in music that our speech can so transcend itself as to join the voices we cannot translate, and the church has always *sung* with the angels, their liturgical place has always been the hymnic parts. *Said,* ". . . with angels and archangels . . ." is merely mythology; *sung,* it makes perfect sense. Indeed, pursuing the speculation to its limit, it is the very object that our melody is, that is the angels' only availability to us, that is their body in our midst.

In some ancient orders, those of "Alexandrian" type, the Invocation of the Spirit, the "Epiclesis," follows immediately upon the Sanctus, praise having been richly accomplished beforehand. I will consider the Epiclesis rather in its "Antiochene" position at the end of the whole Thanksgiving. Originally at least, no theological significance attached to the divergent practices.

IV

In that the Praise of God is narrative, it is already remembrance of Christ. This climaxes in the next two parts of the Great Thanksgiving: the Narrative of Institution and the "Anamnesis." In some orders, there is a smooth transition from the narrative praise of God to the Narrative of Institution, which thus forms the climax of praise: to the great works of God for which he is praised, the institution of the Supper is here the crown. In other orders, the Anamnesis begins first and incorporates the Narrative. I will follow the first order in my exposition.

In the New Testament church, of course, the Narrative was not handed on as a *part* of the service, but as rubrics *for* the service. And indeed, contrary to much piety and theology, which make the Narrative the one indispensable verbal part of the Supper, there is no strict biblical compulsion to include it at all. Whatever "Do this" may comprehend, it cannot possibly order "Recite the narrative in which Jesus is quoted as saying 'Do this'." We do not know when the Narrative came to be recited as itself a part of the Thanksgiving. Whenever it was, the purpose is clear: the Narrative functions as the *haggadah* of the Supper, the explanatory story that justifies—before God and the company—our performance of the rite and the hopes we attach to it. We dare celebrate the Supper *because* "Our Lord, in the night . . . said 'Do this' . . ."

Given that the Narrative is recited, it fulfills several functions that would have to be fulfilled somehow and are fulfilled with fine economy by the recitation. Classical Reformation theology worked this out with great insight and precision. Since even otherwise knowledgeable theologians sometimes suppose that the Reformation's position here was quite different than in fact it was, I will make my list by reproducing John Gerhard's.[12] By reciting the Narrative, the presiding minister does, according to Gerhard, five things: (1) He declares his intention to obey Jesus' command; (2) He designates this bread and cup as those of which the biblical promises are now to be taken; (3) He "prays that

Christ, present in the sacramental action by the power of his promise, may indeed distribute his body and blood . . . to those present . . ."; (4) He "proclaims that by the power of Christ's . . . institution the blessed bread will be the communion of his body and the blessed wine the communion of his blood . . ."; (5) He calls the congregation to faith in these promises.

By reciting the Narrative, we identify our rite to God as our attempt to obey his command and claim his promises about it. In relation to God, such an identification and claim can only take the form of prayer. By reciting the Narrative we proclaim to the congregation the gospel-promises about and of the Supper. Thus we fulfill the mandate that the promises "This is my body" and "This cup is the new covenant," and that this meal is in general an anticipation of the last fellowship shall somehow come to word in the celebration. In its essential functions the Narrative is thus addressed to God and to the congregation simultaneously and so fits nicely into its traditional place embedded in the Great Thanksgiving, which is in any case addressed to both. As part of the Great Thanksgiving, the Narrative then naturally becomes part also of its remembrance-recital—in some defective orders, the remaining whole thereof.

In Western medieval theology, the recitation of the Narrative, or of Jesus' interpreting words as part of the Narrative, was understood as the moment of "consecration," after which we may reckon with Christ's sacramental presence. I have already shown why there is no such moment within the Supper, here or any other time. Reformation theology sometimes called the Narrative the "consecration" in a different sense, which can be acceptable. In this use, *consecrate* is only a joint label for the simultaneous fulfilling of the five functions listed above. In this use—now the third distinguishable sense—we may indeed speak of the Narrative as "consecration." In my view, however, conceptual clarity will be helped by avoiding the term altogether at this point. Of course, all five functions could be fulfilled otherwise than by reciting the Narrative; then there would not be this "consecration" at all, nor would anything thereby be lost.

V

The "Anamnesis" which either incorporates the Narrative or immediately follows it, is the traditional order's most direct response to the command that the thanksgiving shall be for Jesus' remembrance. It is a

prayer addressed explicitly to God, recalling the divine commitments
made by Jesus' self-sacrifice and beseeching their fulfilling: "Therefore,
O God, we make here a memorial of our Lord's life, death, and resurrection . . . and we pray that you will . . ."

So far back as we have any information such prayer has been the
christological heart of the church's thanksgiving. "For my remembrance" was from the first understood as a command to remind God,
precisely in the Old Testament and Jewish sense. Indeed, it seems to
have been understood as a command to pray on the specific model of
the third blessing of the Jewish after-table thanksgiving, as appointed
for holy days or the Sabbath: ". . . may the remembrance of ourselves
and of our fathers and the remembrance of Jerusalem, thy city, and the
remembrance of the Messiah . . . and the remembrance of thy people
. . . arise and come to pass . . . for good . . . and for mercy on this day.
Remember us, JWHW, our God, on it for good and visit us on it for
blessing and save us on it unto life . . ." Whatever "remembrance"
may have meant before its literary fixation by Paul, the church has from
then on interpreted it against the Jewish background.

The Narrative of Institution has put the bread and cup at the center
of liturgical intention as visible words about and of the crucified Jesus.
A reminder of Jesus that is at this place addressed to God is certainly
made also with these visible words: as the *Book of Common Prayer*
has it, ". . . we . . . make here before thy Divine Majesty, *with these
holy gifts,* which we offer unto Thee, the memorial which thy Son hath
commanded us to make . . ." As we have noted, a prayer offered with
words and such objects is a sacrifice. Thus the Anamnesis is the original
home of the language and experience of sacrifice within the Supper; so
already in the oldest preserved text, of Hippolytus: "Remembering
therefore his death and resurrection, we *offer* to you this bread and cup,
giving thanks . . ." Any phenomenologist of religion, observing the
Anamnesis, would call it a specifically sacrificial act—and nothing is
served by allergy to the word.

Here objects that are visible words to us of Christ's sacrifice are
themselves offered by us: our "sacrifice of thanksgiving," audible and
visible, can have no other content than that relation to God he has himself given us. In the embodied word of the gospel, Christ is a present
body; the content of this particular embodied word is such that, if it is
true, the *sacrificed* Christ is present in our sacrificial act. But this is
only to say that we offer our rite as that by which God shall remember

his promises sealed by Christ's sacrifice: the sacrifice of the Anamnesis is only the Old Testament's concrete and authorized appeal to God, done with visible words.   Indeed, it may be that such language as Hippolytus' ". . . we offer you this bread and cup, giving thanks . . ." emerged only as the nearest Hellenistic approximation to the Jewish idea.[13]

At the Anamnesis, the Supper's reality as sacrifice is at the knife edge. Throughout Christian life, just those points where faith is most drastically itself are those where misunderstanding most threatens; the Anamnesis is just such a point and just therefore has been a matter of major controversy.   The unconditionality of the gospel must of course rule unequivocally: our liturgical representing of Christ's sacrifice is not itself the ground of the presence of the sacrificed Christ nor does it supplement his work, and any texts or gestures or sequences of events that suggest that it is or does are incompatible with the gospel.   It cannot be denied that the church's practice has sometimes—in the Roman West, very often—violated this boundary.   Just because the Anamnesis is the heart of our Thanksgiving, it must be done with full consciousness and precision.   I see three decisive requirements.

First, the Anamnesis must never let its original character fade: it is solely an appeal to God's faithfulness, and never to itself as a "representation" of Christ's sacrifice.   It must always therefore perpetuate the tradition of such great orders as the Byzantine anaphora of Basil, in which the christological recitation goes past what we can *represent* at all, to what is yet to come: "Therefore, O Lord, we bring to memory his saving sufferings, his vivifying cross, his three days in the tomb, his resurrection from the dead, *his ascension to the heavens, his session at your right hand, and his second glorious and terrible Advent.*"   Thereby the Anamnesis turns into confession of faith in the gospel's promises; and our sacrificial act confesses its dependence on the power of God's promise, as the sole ground of its truth.

Second, to be a piece of evangelical liturgy, the Anamnesis must be firmly anchored to the eating and drinking to follow.   In the eating and drinking, it is inescapable that Christ's presence is God's gift to us, not our gift to God.

The ritual connection between the Anamnesis and the eating and drinking can be broken in a variety of ways.   In the medieval and Tridentine church, most present simply did and do not eat and drink. It was precisely at this point that Luther's protest, that the mass as a whole had been changed from God's gift to us into our sacrifice to God, was located: "If they had retained (general communion at every celebration) (the mass) would never have become a sacrifice. . . . But when they substituted for the breaking and distribution of the sacrament the keeping and taking of it by one's self, . . . the sacrifice was invented . . ."[14] In current celebrations, when the Great Thanksgiving is offered at a high altar with large wafer and chalice, and the eating and drinking done with little discs and glasses having no experienced continuity with the business at the altar—the damage is the same.

Third, no previous part of the Great Thanksgiving may have been ceremonialized as a moment of before-and-after metaphysical consecration: with hand-gestures, lowered or raised tones, or whatever. If the bread and wine are presented as *substantially* the body of Christ, we may not offer *this* substance again to God. Those unpersuaded by my analysis of "consecration," but wishing to be faithful to the Reformation, should not offer an Anamnesis—but just this is the reduction of the position to absurdity.

VI

The final main part of the traditional Great Thanksgiving is the *Epiclesis*,[15] an invocation of the Spirit upon the bread and cup and sometimes also upon the congregation. In the earliest examples, such as that in Hippolytus, and not infrequently also in later and more elaborately developed prayers, the only prayed-for effect of the Spirit's coming is his blessed presence. But by the late fourth century, the coming of the Spirit was usually connected with the reality of the bread and wine as the body and blood of the Lord. Three forms of this appear: the Spirit may be invoked to "make" the bread and wine be the Lord's body and blood; or he may be invoked in order that the bread and wine "be for us," or "appear" as, or be the "sharing of" the body and blood;[16] or he may be invoked in order that the Lord's body and blood, whose mere presence is assumed, be "life-giving" or "liberating," food and drink.[17] Finally, and of decisive importance, the invocation of the Spirit is always followed by some telic construction—". . . that we may . . ."—which opens the future of those who eat and drink; and this future stretches to the last fulfillment. Throughout the tradition, the Spirit is invoked as what he indeed is, the presence of the eschaton.

It was apparently in connection with the Epiclesis, and in the Eastern church, that the whole notion of a consecration, in the sense of transformation from "before" to "after," first came into liturgy and theology. The notion once introduced, the Western parts of the church located the moment elsewhere, with the Narrative; and the two halves of the church have been fighting ever since.[18]   The extreme position of this argument is taken by Protestant bodies who refuse to have any Epiclesis at all, being unable to conceive any other function for it than "consecrating," and holding that this has "already" been done by the Narrative of Institution.   The argument is as empty as it is crude; for no *such* consecration occurs at *either* place.

If we once sort out the senses of "consecration," the Epiclesis poses no serious puzzles.   The Invocation of the Spirit, we have seen, is an entirely natural thing for Christians to do at this place, and unless inhibited by extraneous fears, they have always done it.   Of the various ways in which the tradition has made connection between the Spirit's coming and the body-presence of Christ as bread and cup, all are acceptable, once we no longer conceive or ceremonialize a before-and-after consecration.

The Spirit is Jesus' spirit, and the spirit of our gathering, and just so God's Spirit.   It is merely the other side of this relation that the body of Christ is Jesus' body, and the body of our community, and just so God's body.   In the Supper, it is the bread and cup that make the identity of Jesus' body and the church's body.   To invoke God's Spirit on the bread and cup is, therefore, merely to call body and spirit of our relation to the Lord together.   It is to pray that the body of Christ, as it here and now includes us, be a living rather than a dead body.   This indeed happens "without our prayer;" but if that were a reason not to pray, all praise would cease.

VII

A traditional Great Thanksgiving ends with one more grand doxology. In the Roman Canon—for once to quote it favorably—the economy is splendid: "Through him, and with him, and in him, in the unity of the Holy Spirit, be all honor and glory to you, Almighty God and Father, unto ages of ages.   Amen."

Finally, we must mention yet one more section which was generally included by the fourth century, but had a different location in each great family of rites: a group of intercessory petitions for the church and all humanity, living and dead.   Such petitions must be offered at some place in the service, but most modern proposals put them at the end of the synagogue-service, where there should be petitions in any case. Since the matter is currently moot, I will not discuss it further.

VIII

Following the Great Thanksgiving, traditional orders stipulate the Our Father. This is originally congregational preparation for the eating and drinking. In orders where the praise and eschatological invocation of the Thanksgiving have been curtailed, it provides a clumsy recuperation and tends to be assimilated into the Thanksgiving.

The Fraction follows. Breaking the loaf appears in all versions of the canonical rubrics—obviously, if one loaf is to be shared by many worshipers, it must be divided. Insofar as this necessary division of the bread is part of the giving-over of the bread to us, it becomes part of the Supper's representation of Christ's life and death for us, and then inevitably a representation of the breaking of his body. This opportunity for dramatic visible speech is so obvious and compelling that some dramatization of the bread's division is nearly universal in the church's history; even in groups that out of fear of play acting have forbidden it, it always reappears in congregational practice.

Of course, if discs or otherwise prepared bits are used, there is no opportunity for a true Fraction. For the presiding minister ceremonially to break a disc of bread, the parts of which do not make the congregation's food, is a piece of drama independent of the representation that is given with the mandated acts themselves, and therefore intrusive upon them. It should not be done—despite all the centuries in which it has been. Such an inauthentic Fraction is the historically most notable case of the sort of symbolism-mongering which has indeed often shouted down the Supper's mandated visible word.

NOTES

1. For the general history, see first the texts: F. E. Brightman, *Liturgies Eastern and Western* (Oxford: The Clarendon Press, 1896; reprinted 1965); Lucien Deiss, *Early Sources of the Liturgy* (Staten Island: Alba House, 1967). See also Gregory Dix, *The Shape of the Liturgy* (London: Dacre Press, 1945); Yngve Brilioth, *Eucharistic Faith and Practice Evangelical and Catholic,* trans. A. G. Hebert (London: S.P.C.K., 1930); the articles in *Die Religion in Geschichte und Gegenwart*[3] on "Messe" by G. Kretschmar, W. Jannasch, and K. Dienst, Vol. IV, cols. 885–93, on "Gottesdienst" by G. Kretschmar, K. Onasch, K. Dienst, H. Urner, and W. Jannasch, Vol. II, cols.

1763–83, on "Abendmahl" by G. Krestschmar, Vol. I, cols. 40–44; also Josef Jungmann, *The Early Liturgy to the Time of Gregory the Great,* trans. Francis A. Brunner (Notre Dame: University of Notre Dame Press, 1959, pp. 29–73, 200–39, 288–307); Georg Rietschel and Paul Graff, *Lehrbuch der Liturgik* (Göttingen: Vandenhoeck & Ruprecht, 1951), pp. 196–340; and Theodore Klauser, *A Short History of the Western Liturgy,* trans. John Halliburton (Oxford: Oxford University Press, 1969).

2. So Klauser, op. cit., pp. 65–69, 101–13.

3. This conception has a history, in Sweden and elsewhere. See the prayers cited by Louis Bouyer, *Eucharist,* trans. Charles W. Quinn (Notre Dame: University of Notre Dame Press, 1968), p. 405.

4. Prayers structured according to developed trinitarian theology had, of course, to wait the existence of that theology; they appear in the great "Antiochene" liturgies of the fourth century and following. See Bouyer, op. cit., pp. 244–82. Earlier prayers, however, were a chief impetus for the explicit development of the doctrine of the trinity.

5. The critical text of Hippolytus is found in Bernhard Botte, ed., *La Tradition Apostolique de Saint Hippolyte* (Münster: Aschendorff, 1972).

6. Bouyer, op. cit., pp. 91–226, 309f.

7. A magnificent collection of texts is now available: Anton Hänggi and Irmgard Pahl, *Prex Eucharistica* (Fribourg: Editions universitaires, 1968). For a quick survey of the historical situation, see the article "Anaphora" by W. Jardin Brisbrook in *A Dictionary of Liturgy and Worship,* ed. J. G. Davies (London: SCM Press, 1972), pp. 10–17. For a fuller treatment, one book above all, Bouyer.

8. Jeremias, *The Eucharistic Words of Jesus,* p. 115.

9. For a reconstruction of the course of the disaster that is especially convincing in that it is aimed at showing that there was really no disaster, see Bouyer, op. cit., pp. 188–243.

10. To see this, compare the Roman Canon with the Alexandrian family of anaphoras, with which it once seems to have shared a common structure. Bouyer, op. cit., pp. 187–243.

11. For the problem with classical Protestantism at this point, see Robert Jenson, "A Great Thanksgiving for Lutherans," *Response,* XV, 2/3, pp. 52–60.

12. John Gerhard, *Loci communes theologici,* XXI, 149.

13. To the entire question of the essential character of the Anamnesis and Epiclesis, see the remarkable analysis by Bouyer, op. cit., pp. 178–88.

14. Martin Luther, "The Misuse of the Mass," trans. Frederick C. Ahrens, *Luther's Works,* American Edition (Philadelphia: Fortress Press, 1959), Vol. 36, p. 172.

15. E. G. C. F. Atchley, *On the Epiclesis of the Eucharistic Liturgy* (London: Oxford University Press, 1935); Bouyer, op. cit., pp. 310–14.

16. E.g., in the *Apostolic Constitutions.*

17. E.g., in the Armenian *Liturgy of St. James.*

18. Dix, op. cit., pp. 168f.; Atchley, op. cit., *passim.*

10

The Eating and Drinking

I

The eating and drinking are the heart of the Supper as *sacrament*. The presiding minister divides the bread and sees to the circulation of the cup. Some time has elapsed since the proclamation of the Great Thanksgiving; it is therefore generally and rightly customary that the bread and cup are given to each participant with a repetition of the promises: "This is the body of Christ. . . ." It is these words which we must make one more attempt to understand, and here particularly insofar as, in Markan fashion, they all together promise the body-presence of Christ.

Why, to begin with, are these sentences said about the bread and cup specifically? We have seen that in any sacrament it is the entire external event that is the body-presence of the Lord. There is, of course, an odd logical reversal in the question, for we would not have come to speak of the Lord's "bodily" presence at all, except for those words about the bread and cup. Nevertheless, once we have seen that it is the whole external event of a sacrament that is the location of sacramental presence, the narrower specification to the bread and cup requires some explanation. I note three points.

First, the Supper's actions are addressed both to God and the believing participants; but if we look to the Supper's actions strictly in that they are verbal and more-than-verbal addresses of participants to *other participants*, we find that they are all made by or about the bread and cup. It is, of course, addresses of believers to other humans that are the speaking of the gospel. Therefore insofar as the Supper is a speaking of the gospel and so is a sacrament, the shared cup and the shared bread are in fact its visibility.

Second, what the bread and cup as visible words specifically say, is precisely something about the embodiment of Christ in the life of the church. *That* Christ is indeed present as body, that he is not in our midst as a disembodied pure spirit, is itself an essential part of the gospel proclamation. If Christ were not present in the body, every gospel-address would be false. In addressing itself to our hopes and fears, in claiming our lives in all their facets, the gospel claims to be true, and just so claims Christ's embodied presence. "See, I—the real I, body and spirit—am with you," is itself an essential gospel-saying. Insofar as we can at all suggest in a sentence what a visible word says, it is this gospel-saying which is in turn embodied as the bread and cup. In the bread and cup as a visible promise, the *embodiment* of the gospel and of Christ's presence proclaims *itself*.

Third, Christ is not present in the Supper *because* the bread and cup are present and are what they are. He is present in the sacramental action as a whole. We should think, to begin with, of Christ's presence by the whole action of the Supper, and then of how the there-present Christ grants us participation in his reality in the particular way stated by "This is my body . . ."

II

We must next consider what in this situation it is to believe. Confronted by the bread, the cup, and the verbal promises, as a unitary spirited and embodied address, how do we believe *this* word of God? Clearly, by eating and drinking. In this case, therefore, the act of faith and the act of taking, chewing, and swallowing are one act. We believe this particular utterance of the gospel with the mind, to be sure, but also with the mouth and gullet and in our sensory experience of ourselves eating and drinking the bread and cup we have been watching and touching. Given that words are "visible," there is nothing difficult about the notion of such faith; if there seems to be, it is our conception of faith that is faultily intellectual or emotional or otherwise privatized.

Where is Christ "really" present in the Supper? It is often said: "in faith," or "in the heart." And this is the basic truth—but how does he get there? The human heart is not his natural abode, however much it may be Brahman's or a Boddhisatva's; the Christ comes always *to* us. And in this sacrament, his way to the heart—not, of course, to the stomach—is by a uniquely primal and total opening to the external word: the unitary sensory, organic, and mental act of eating and drinking in fellowship.

The act of faith and the act of the mouth are, in the Supper, one act. Thus the object of faith—the present Christ—and the object of eating and drinking—the bread and cup—are, in the Supper, one object. *So are Christ and the elements one in the Supper.*

The sacramental identity is an identity for faith. But lest this assertion be disastrously misleading, we must remember very precisely that faith is hearing, and in each case hearing the word spoken in and by the structure of a particular communication-situation's spiritedness and embodiment. The sacramental identity is not given because we believe it is, but by the structure of the word we here believe.

Our final consideration must be of the *truth* of this identity. But before we proceed to it, we must return to the whole performance of the Supper, and especially to the fellowship that occurs in it, to make certain that the argument just completed does not isolate Christ's presence as bread and cup. Christ is present by the bread and cup, *as* and only as the one represented by the entire action of the Supper. This rule is established by the very nature of Scripture's promises.

The bread and cup are Christ's body *as* his body mediates our fellowship of thanksgiving to God. The bread and cup are in any case, simply as ceremonies, the means of our sharing in thanksgiving; only as such are they the object of sacramental promises. *That this thanksgiving actually is accepted by God and our fellowship in it established for all eternity, and that the bread and cup are the body-presence of Christ, are not two facts but only two descriptions of one fact.* That the bread and cup are the body of Christ, and that we who share them are one body in Christ, are not two facts but only one.

Both Paul and John saw the matter exactly so. The receiving of Christ by eating and drinking is not and cannot be a private act. To a performance calling itself the Supper, which was so shaped that reception of Christ had to be a private act, *no* sacramental presence is canonically promised.

The giving-over to us of the bread and cup represent the entire act of our Lord's life as a sacrifice for us. If indeed Christ is present as the bread and cup, it is the Christ whose life is *this* action, who is present. The giving-over to us of the bread and cup is anticipation of the fulfillment of our Lord's sacrifice in a community eternally bound by his love for all men. Christ's presence as the bread and cup is the truth of this anticipation. The eating and drinking unite us to the fellowship of the cross, whether we will or no.

III

How "This is my body," can be *true* is the matter of the most persistent controversy of Christian history. The solution I propose has been mostly presented in part two, "Sacramental Presence." I need here only elaborate slightly, and make some connections to the history of the controversy.

Among those who have tried to explain the sacramental identity, rather than to explain it away, there have been three types of explanation. Two are based on the assumption that we start with two entities, the body of the risen Christ and the bodies on the table, and then must explain how they come to be one.

Of these, one relies on the power of "consecration"—in the more recent versions fused with the power of "re-presentation"—to effect a metaphysical bond. God can do what he wills, and we are authorized to call on him here to do the inconceivable—to make two entities be one without destroying either. In the most famous version of this explanation, the theory of "trans-substantiation," there are, after the consecration, the "substance" of Christ's body—that is, the self-contained empirically inaccessible doer of all that Christ's body is or does, and the "accidents" of bread and wine, that is, the whole of what about the bread and wine is accessible to empirical observation.

All explanations of this sort are fundamentally misguided, because unnecessary. They rest the truth of the sacramental identity in the power of a liturgical act. As we have seen, whatever potency liturgical acts may have, even grants of God's omnipotence, such potencies are quite irrelevant to the particular claim we have here to understand. The bread and cup, to be for us the body of Christ, do not want to be "made" into anything at all; therefore it is not such a making that we need to explain. And in fact, the historic motive of the doctrine of trans-substantiation has not been to explicate the truth of the Supper—for which it did little—but to establish the power of the priesthood, of those authorized to perform the consecration.

A second sort of explanation relies on the irrelevance of distance for purely "spiritual" entities. The visible words of bread and cup speak to our souls of the bodily risen Christ. If the soul is thereby moved to faith, it is exalted by the Spirit to the supernatural realm, "at the right hand of the Father," where this Christ is. *For the believing soul,* in its transcendence of all distances between the body of Christ and the bodies on the table, the two are one.

The objections to explanation of this sort are even more serious than those to the first sort. According to it, Christ is body-present to us only *if* we are moved to faith by the visible speech of bread and cup. Insofar as what the bread and cup promise is Christ's embodied presence, they are on this interpretation *conditional* visible promises, and so precisely not visible words of the *gospel.*

Moreover, there is no purely spiritual human soul. The human soul has been thought to be essentially pure spirit because it is the image of God. But in Christianity, precisely this last is a fundamental error: the Christian God is essentially embodied. If the soul could indeed leave its body in the assembly to be with Jesus, it would thereby be transformed into the image of a false God, indeed into a demon. In or out of faith, whatever sorts of distance intervene between bodies count also for the soul.

The third historic type of explanation has tried to eliminate precisely the presumption of two separated entities, whose coming together must then be explained. According to this metaphysically revolutionary thinking, in the sense of "location" in which it implies distance to other locations, the risen Christ's body is not located anywhere—affirmatively, he is not separated from any reality. This interpretation was developed by Martin Luther and a few of his more speculative followers. Luther's own statement is blunt: Christ has indeed risen in the body to be where God is, and God is everywhere. If it is promised that the risen Christ is embodied where such-and-such bread and such-and-such a cup are, no miracle is needed for the truth of this promise—no other miracle, that is, than Christ's resurrection itself.

In classical Lutheran theology, Luther's insight was carried through only for narrowly limited topics of Christology and sacramentology. The insight's drastic consequences for the full range of Christian thought, for all understanding of God and of creaturely being, were not developed. It is therefore understandable that ecumenical theology has generally continued to prefer the other explanations of "This is my body," and that even Lutheran theology has tended to mitigate its own case; for a merely partial realization of Luther's insight produces real conceptual grotesqueries. The question, of course, is whether the alternative sorts of reflection are not evangelical grotesqueries.

If *our* bodies—and indeed those of the inkwell and pen—are interpreted basically as "substances," of a "material" sort defined by obedience to Newton's laws, then to say only of Christ's body that it shares God's omnipresence, is disastrous in two ways. First, it makes it impossible to see how Christ's body is any longer a human body like ours. Second, it suggests a sort of christological pantheism: Christ is "really" as much in everything as he is in the bread and cup. But the point is to get over interpreting the body as "substance."

Part 2 of this book contains an attempt to carry Luther's ontological revolution a few turns further, at least for the understanding of God and his works and presence. At no point in my description of God's reality did I make any use of the notion of a "substance" of such-and-such characteristics, nor did I in my more scattered remarks about human reality. In particular, I did not define *bodily* by "material substantiality."

What I have to add here is quickly said. God is omnipresent in his promises: when and where these promises are embodied, then and there God knows himself as an object, then and there God has his body. In that the bread and cup are the center of that rite which embodies the entire gospel, and themselves embody this gospel insofar as it is the promise of God's presence, God is present bodily when and where the bread and cup are. And in that the bread and cup *are for God* the presence also of the man Jesus, also Jesus is body when and where they are—precisely by the omnipresence of God. Jesus has and needs no other body to be risen in full bodily splendor and solidity.

There *is* no other body and blood of Christ, above the clouds or in some other supernatural hiding place, to "enter" or be joined with or "be pointed to by" the bread and cup. Jesus is risen to new spiritual and bodily life; the bread and cup *are* that body. The bread and cup are Jesus' body only, to be sure, for faith; they do not look like his body; his presence is also *hidden* by them. But this does not mean that somewhere metaphysically else it is unveiled; rather, it means that at the last it *will be* unveiled. There is indeed more to Christ's body than now is as bread and cup; but this "more" is precisely the *future* of the bread and cup, the final reunion of the fellowship they mediate, in which all presence of God to us and of us to God and of us to one another, will be like Christ's to us now.

IV

What of any remaining bread and wine after those present have all eaten and drunk? Practice at this point is often a touchstone of what is actually believed about the Supper, peculiar though the question may seem to many.

The saving of bread or wine for any ritual use other than consumption in the current Supper is wholly illegitimate, ancient though the practices are. About bread or wine taken outside the thanksgiving-courses of the particular act of fellowship, nothing whatever is promised by Scripture.

Of course, if the elements' reality as Christ's body were a *consequence* following after a ritual act of "consecration," then that presence would necessarily endure as long as the consecrated elements exist—nobody has yet been so unbiblical as to propose an act of *de*consecration. If the sacramental presence is conceived on such a schema of before-and-after, the "after" clearly can have no limit, and the various sorts of "reservation" are the only rational practice. Protestants who ceremonialize an act of transformation, and then blithely put the remaining elements back in box and bottle, speak a visible word of unbelief in the sacramental presence. But that the conception of ritual transformation makes reasonable and inevitable uses of the bread or wine other than those which Scripture mandates, only refutes the conception; for any theory of Christ's presence is there precisely to explicate Scripture's mandate.

There is, however, one sort of reservation which remains within the mandated use, and which is the oldest of all: carrying bread and wine from the congregation's table to those members of the congregation who cannot be present yet wish to share the Supper. There is no problem about the legitimacy of this practice; it merely extends the geographical limits of a particular Supper and its mandated use of bread and wine. The question is not of legitimacy, but of desirability.

Unless sickness or imprisonment are to amount to excommunication, some way must be found to include the invalid in the congregation's Supper. There are only two possibilities. A celebration of the Supper may be instituted at the invalid's place, or the congregation's bread and wine brought to him. The choice must be made by what the two practices say as visible words, in particular by what they say about the Supper as a fellowship of thanksgiving. If an actual congregation of five or six persons is gathered with the invalid, this may sometimes be desirable. But surely the best usual practice would be for messengers of the congregation to carry—immediately!—the congregation's own Supper to its invalid members.

As to simply left-over bread and wine, there shouldn't be any; and this is easily arranged. Any loving-cup should be finished among those who share it; if the Supper's cup still contains wine when all have drunk, those serving the table must finish it. If bread remains, it can be finished in the same way; or if there is too much, it can be distributed to departing worshipers at the end of the service. And if bread or wine, despite everything, do remain when the service is over, they are just bread and wine and should be treated as such. As for running out, the insoluble dilemma of whether to do anything ritually with new bread or wine brought from the sacristy, is the minister's just punishment for such malfeasance in his or her responsibilities.

V

Disagreement about the interpretation of Christ's presence has been a profound and continuing occasion of the church's disunity, especially at the table itself. There is a terrible irony in this; since in fact Christ's presence as the bread and cup is not separable from the unity it creates of those who share the meal.

Many rationalizations have been attempted, all of them sophistical. The simple case is this: if I and my group celebrate the Supper, and do not admit you, this is excommunication; and if we indeed belong to the body of Christ, as we claim merely by our celebration, it is excommunication from the body of Christ. If you then otherwise celebrate the Supper with a group of your like, we are bound to maintain that this celebration is a mere attempt, in which Christ is not present. If we fail to maintain this, either we are merely being inconsequential, or we revoke our right to exclude you in the first place.

There is no middle ground. If you acknowledge that I belong to the church, you must admit me to your Supper. If you will not admit me to your Supper, you should not then talk about my nevertheless being your "fellow in Christ." In the essentially anomalous situation of a divided church, it may indeed sometimes be necessary to work with degrees of church fellowship, doing some things together and not others. But fellowship at the Supper is the minimum of fellowship in the faith; the only legitimate reason why you and I could not eat it together would be that one of us was a pagan or under sentence of excommunication for notorious wickedness. Differing theories of sacramental presence will hardly suffice. The old question about whether fellowship at the Supper is a means or consequence of fellowship in the faith is an entirely perverse question; fellowship at the Supper *is* fellowship in the faith.

Having delivered myself of these ultimata, I must acknowledge that they are law and not gospel. The divisions of the church are there, and all of us are trapped. We may indeed be unable to do what we know we must do, and this may be nobody's fault. But let us then remember that Nobody is Satan's chief deputy, and that if our separation at the Supper is really intransigent, it is because we have fallen into his hands; and let us rationalize this not at all.

11

Some Liturgical Proposals

I

The theology of the sacraments properly occurs as comment on rites. As the task is not finished in other areas of theology until the theologian suggests what can, in his opinion, be truly said as gospel to the matter in question, so my task of sacramental theology is not finished until I suggest actual texts and ceremonies. Indeed, what propositions of sacramentology *mean,* can only be fully seen in the liturgy they lead to.

I presume the traditional Western general order of service. As the relation between the church's inner life and the world to which it is sent, changes, new situations for the Supper will demand new arrangements. The Supper is being and will be celebrated quite differently than in the traditional order. Particularly, the rest of the meal now often returns; perhaps this will one day become again the norm. But for the present and the foreseeable future, such decisively different patterns will and should be *ad hoc* arrangements for particular situations or occasions, to be guided mostly by the biblical mandate itself. Most celebrations will continue to be those of fairly large established congregations; for them the traditional order cannot be improved.

I thus presume the two-part structure of synagogue-service—"Synaxis"—and Supper, as this is maintained in nearly all denominations; the general content of the Synaxis—Scripture, preaching, hymnody and intercession; and a general pattern of the Supper itself as Offertory, Great Thanksgiving, Fraction, Eating and Drinking, and Closing Service. My proposals will begin with the Offertory. At points where comment in previous chapters suffices, I will not add to it.

II

For the Offertory, the bread, wine, and gifts of money should be brought together from the congregation, both for what this says about the bread and wine and for what it says about the money. Let this be done with the greatest and most general movement and festivity consonant with the particular occasion. The best regular arrangement would be a procession of the entire congregation singing hymns. All bring their gifts of money to an assistant holding the alms basin; and the donors of the bread and wine conclude the procession with their gifts. Such a procession sets the congregation in motion at the Supper's very beginning. The participation of all present is in the Spirit; therefore the physical choreography of processions and gestures must not be restricted to the ministers.

The ministers go to the table, receive the flagon, or bottle of wine, and the loaf of bread and place them on the table. Then the presiding minister offers prayers of consecration and humility. For these prayers, as for those that follow, he or she must if at all possible stand behind the table facing the people. God is not located in a shrine on the church building's far wall and most surely not just the other side of it, but he *is* located where he is body in the midst of those gathered. The prayers may be as follows—throughout this chapter, I give texts only because this is the most expeditious way to suggest content and spirit.

MINISTER: Our Father, accept these gifts.
Use the money to work your good will for the world.
Let your Spirit hallow the bread and wine;
That in the use for which we bring them,
They may be true signs of your gift of new life to us,
And of our offering to you of our bodies and hopes.
As the grain was scattered upon the mountains and is gathered into one loaf,
Gather your church from the corners of earth to your one kingdom.
And as the cup is one cup poured for all, pour us out as one gift for the world.
In his name who is your gift and our hope,
To be one God with you and the Spirit we here invoke, now and forever,
PEOPLE: *Amen.*

PEOPLE: Our Father, we do not presume to come to this feast
                trusting in our own righteousness, but in your great
                mercy.
                We are not worthy to gather the crumbs under your table;
                But you are the God whose nature it is always to have
                mercy.
                Grant us therefore, so to eat the bread of life and share
                the cup of salvation,
                That we may evermore dwell in Christ and he in us,
                Who is one God with you in the Spirit, now and forever,
                Amen.

The reasons for the first of these prayers were given in the previous
chapter. Its text is mostly new, except for the passage for the loaf,
which is from the *Didache.* Reasons for the second, which is adapted
from the *Book of Common Prayer,* will be given in Chapter 12. When
the prayers are finished, the presiding minister and assisting ministers,
if there are such, pour the cup and make any final preparations of the
bread, to establish a break between the Offertory prayer and the Great
Thanksgiving that follows. If custom mandates mixing wine and water,
this is done now, without fuss.

III

The Great Thanksgiving should never be an overfamiliar formula or too
brief. It should always be free and rhetorically lively. And it should
be sufficiently long to have clear internal structure and make an event
through which the congregation passes; otherwise it will inevitably be
experienced as an incantation. The texts I give as examples follow the
pattern of texts suggested to the Lutheran denominations of America
in provisional orders of the Inter-Lutheran Commission on Worship. I
choose this pattern because it handles the traditional parts of the Great
Thanksgiving as discrete units, which makes the structure glaringly clear
and also suggests how any part could be written anew for a season or
occasion. For that would be the ideal: congregations and presiding
ministers who had so firm a grasp on what they were doing that they
could create new language as needed, without confusion. Just such
theological and rhetorical freedom belongs to the specific spirit of the
Great Thanksgiving.

During the entire Great Thanksgiving, the presiding minister faces the congregation, from behind the table if possible. If he must be in front of it, then when he shows the bread and cup to the congregation or raises them in benediction, he turns to the table to take the elements but turns immediately back to the congregation before continuing; if he needs a book, an assistant holds this for him. The very same words spoken at the congregation or spoken away from the congregation, say opposite things. Fully half the danger of the Supper's transformation into a propitiatory sort of sacrifice lies in the mere orientation of the presiding minister, if he speaks the Thanksgiving facing away from the people. What is more, this remains true also with orders sanitized of every other suggestion of sacrifice.

Where it is customary for the presiding minister to sing the prayers, *all* parts of the Great Thanksgiving should be sung, to preserve its unity in the congregation's experience. It should not be necessary to say that all parts should be offered by the same presiding minister. If the bread and cup were accompanied to the table by a crucifier or torches, these may on festival occasions stand round the table during the Great Thanksgiving. The congregation stands throughout.

Opening Dialogue

During the Dialogue, the presiding minister may stretch out his arms to the rest of the congregation. In any case, the dialogue is an empowering exchange of the gospel; and this must show in everyone's posture.

MINISTER:	The Lord be with you.
PEOPLE:	*And also with you.*
MINISTER:	Lift up your hearts.
PEOPLE:	*We lift them up to the Lord.*
MINISTER:	Let us give thanks to the Lord our God.
PEOPLE:	*It is right to offer thanks and praise.*

First Act of Praise

During this "Preface," the presiding minister stands in a posture of prayer suitable to the congregation's customs—but this must not *be with bowed head or closed eyes. The following text is for Christmas.*

It is indeed right and salutary,
That we should at all times and in all places

Offer thanks and praise, O Lord, Holy Father, Almighty and ever-
  living God;
For the sudden beauty of the embodied Word has clarified our minds,
That as we see God born as Mary's child,
We may see humankind reborn in God.
Therefore with Mary, Joseph and the shepherd saints,
And with all the messenger choir of shining spirits,
We praise and glorify your name, forever saying:

Sanctus

This composite hymn must be sung, and by the entire congregation.
This is an irruption of joyful noise, a relaxation. Congregations do not
need to know what Sabaoth or Hosanna mean; such joyful and slightly
mysterious noises also belong to the word's more-than-propositional
reality.

Holy, holy, holy Lord,
God of Sabaoth,
Heaven and earth are full of your glory.
Hosanna in the highest!
Blessed is he who comes in the name of the Lord.
Hosanna in the highest!

Second Act of Praise

The presiding minister resumes his posture of prayer. The desideratum
of this prayer is comprehensive doxological narration: creation, fulfill-
ment, and the saving history that joins these.

MINISTER: You are indeed holy, O God:
             You are the Holy Father, the hope at the beginning of all
                things;
             You are the Holy Son, our brother and our Lord;
             You are the Holy Spirit, the power of our Lord's resur-
                rection.
             You are holy in all the works of your creation, and in the
                life that moves them.
             You are holy in the promise to remember all creatures in
                your love.
             You are holy in your works for Israel:

In her rescue from Egypt.
In her memory of Abraham and Isaac and Jacob,
In the victories of David and the defeats of the Exile,
And in her prophets' words, which will yet not be in vain.

PEOPLE: *Amen.   Praise be to God.*

Narrative of Institution

At the appropriate places, the presiding minister takes the bread, and then the cup and shows them to the congregation.   The gestures are demonstrative: this *loaf and* this *cup are those which now are the objects of the biblical mandates and promises.*

MINISTER: At the last you are holy in our Lord Jesus,
Who fulfilled and will fulfill all your mercies,
Who in the night in which he was betrayed,
Took bread,
And gave thanks,
Broke it,
And gave it to his disciples, saying:
Take and eat;
This is my body,
Given for you.
Do this, for my remembrance.
Who again, after supper,
Took the cup,
Gave thanks,
And gave it for all to drink saying:
This cup is the new covenant sealed by my blood,
Shed for you and all people,
For the forgiveness of sin.
Do this, for my remembrance.
For as often as you eat this bread and drink from this cup,
You confess the Lord's death
And proclaim that he is risen and lives.
Until he comes.

PEOPLE: *Christ has died.*
Christ is risen.
Christ will come again.

Anamnesis

The presiding minister resumes the posture of prayer. The "Maranatha" is restored here, as it surely should be.

MINISTER: Therefore, O God, with this bread and cup we recall before you the whole sacrifice of our Lord's life:

His preaching of your imminent Kingdom,

His life-giving signs of the Kingdom,

His eating with publicans and sinners,

And his inevitable death.

And believing the message of his resurrection,

We await his coming in power

To share with us the feast of hope fulfilled.

PEOPLE: *Amen. Maranatha. Come, Lord Jesus.*

Epiclesis

This prayer is continuous with the previous, and should involve no special "consecrating" gesture. The last line is from the Didache.

MINISTER: Send now, we pray, your Spirit,

The Spirit of our Lord and of his resurrection.

Let him be the Spirit of our feast,

That we and all who share it

May not perish at the last,

But may stand before you,

As now, so in the fulfillment,

To serve the eternal mystery of your love.

Let grace come and let this world pass away!

PEOPLE: *Amen. Come, Holy Spirit.*

Last Doxology

In this last burst of praise, the presiding minister raises the bread and cup to God, uniting word and gesture in God's praise. At the beginning, in the Preface, and at the end, the congregations' praises are joined to the praises of all the church and all creation.

MINISTER: Join our thanksgiving with the praises of your servants of all earth and heaven;

And unite our service with the eternal worship of our great High Priest,

PEOPLE: *By whom and with whom,*
               In the unity of the Holy Spirit,
               All honor and glory be yours, almighty Father,
               Now and forever.   Amen.

IV

The congregation prays the Our Father, the presiding minister adopting the same posture as they.   Then the presiding minister takes the loaf and breaks it; if it is to be distributed from more than one plate, he breaks it into the needed number of pieces.   This Fraction may be accompanied by prayer or a declaration to the congregation, or it may, with great impact, be done silently.

Thereupon the members of the congregation greet each other in the Lord's peace: V. "The peace of the Lord be with you." R. "And also with you."   The location of the greeting at this point is particular Western tradition, which we may as well continue.   The greeting is embodied, an embrace, for which various congregations will undoubtedly substitute a handshake or whatever gesture of intimacy they can tolerate.   On very formal occasions the greeting may start among the ministers around the altar, be carried by them down the aisles, and then be passed down the rows of seats. Otherwise, all simply turn to those around them.

V

We come to the eating and drinking.   How best to arrange for this? The very best would be for all simply to gather around the table; but usually there will be too many for this.   The great objective is to preserve the experience of eating and drinking *together,* while not prolonging the act into a meaningless waiting. The most varied expedients have been devised.

Processions to fixed "stations" of distributing ministers do not preserve the commonality of the meal; moreover, actual timing shows that the use of stations slows the distributing rather than accelerating it as intended.   Eating and drinking by discrete "tables" divides the congregation and is very slow.   Eating and drinking in the seats, passing the bread and cup from hand to hand, is better, but it misses an opportunity for congregational movement and leaves the table as a priestly preserve of the ministers.

Perhaps the best is for the people to form a circle—or a formation as close to a circle as is architecturally possible—around the table, for each communicant to leave when he has taken the cup, and for those waiting to fill spaces as they open. As the congregation begins to come to the table, the presiding minister eats and drinks and gives to those serving the table with him. As the presiding minister then moves around the circle with the loaf, and an assistant—the "deacon"—follows with the cup, a rotation is established in which each communicant joins and experiences a continuing fellowship involving the entire congregation.

The congregation is further unified in the meal if hymns are sung throughout by all: by those in the circle, by those waiting for place, and by those in their seats. These should not mostly be "communion" hymns, but hymns of the season, hymns of Easter, hymns to the Spirit, and generally hymns of praise. In no case should the organist play background music, for this again individualizes the experience. If there cannot be hymn singing and perhaps lusty organ or instrumental preludes to the hymns, let there be real silence.

The bread and wine should be *good*—amazing that one needs to say it! Whether the loaf is leavened or unleavened, let the presiding minister break for each a substantial portion that must actually be chewed, tasted, and swallowed. Let the wine be honest red table wine, and let the deacon give each one opportunity actually to *drink*. If the congregation is too poor, or too repressed by local prejudice, to use real wine, it should follow the lead of similar groups in the apostolic church and drink water. In no case may *artificial* wine, "grape juice," be used. Recipients may respond to the words of the ministers with "Amen" and mark themselves with the cross before leaving the table.

When all have eaten and drunk, and while a last hymn of praise is being sung, the ministers settle the table. If bread and wine are to be taken to the sick, the vessels for this purpose are filled and taken to the sacristy. The loving-cup and loaf are finished. The vessels are rinsed—if that is customary—and wiped, and if they were vested before the Supper, are revested; all this should be done briskly and matter-of-factly.

The service now quickly comes to an end. There is a closing prayer and a parting blessing, according to denominational custom. If there was a procession, there is another. And that is all.

PART FIVE

THE INSTITUTION OF BAPTISM

12

Mandate

I

A missionary community will necessarily have a rite of initiation, and that rite, whatever it is, will be at the center of its life and consciousness. Baptism is the Christian initiation. And baptism was the experientially and theologically dominating sacrament of the New Testament church, and of the church in all those centuries in which the reception of large numbers of converts continued to be the regular experience of congregations. As to why the particular rite of initiation is a *bath,* I am concerned with this question of origin only insofar as its discussion will help to explicate baptism's mandate.

There can be no doubt but that John the Baptist's "baptism of repentance" was somehow Christian baptism's immediate precedent. The role of John in the gospel tradition, the New Testament's unquestioned use for his action of terminology that is otherwise specific for Christian baptism,[1] and the peculiar business in Acts about those baptized "only" with John's baptism, are otherwise inexplicable. For an historian, this only throws the question one step back: what were *John's* precedents? But my purpose does not require this further question—though my guess is that John had and needed no more specific precedents than the obvious and almost universally exploited ritual possibilities of washing. The specific features of such models as Jewish proselyte washing or the washings of the Qumran sect seem to have had little importance for John's practice.[2]

John's baptizing was of and unto *repentance.*[3] John renewed the prophetic proclamation of God's triumph, and in so urgent a fashion as to leave room for only one more witness thereof, the one who would bring the very fire of judgment. In a time so qualified, the only possibility is repentance, i.e., self-abandonment to God's judgment and just so to God's will.[4]

The word that in *this* situation calls to repentance calls to the only possibility; therefore it is itself a saving word, and its speaker is a mediator of salvation. This call to repentance must therefore be sacramental. Upon those whom his audible word seized and upon whose bodily presence he could then act, John performed a visible word of repentance: with whatever suggestions from antecedent practice, he *washed* them of the past.

Nothing more than this washing by the preacher seems to have been essential to the act—at least, so far as we know. That the washing was immersion is, contrary to established opinion, unlikely or at least unproven; to John's washing, the *washer* was intrinsic, as is not the case with immersion.[5] The act was once-for-all-time; in the situation of eschatological urgency that created it, repetition was unthinkable. And like its audible cognate, this visible word was both summons and mediation, law and gospel.

Beyond any reasonable doubt, Jesus was baptized by John.[6] We do not and cannot know anything about the antecedent circumstances of Jesus' baptism,[7] but must suppose that somehow it too was a baptism of repentance. It seems also that Jesus later affirmed John's baptism in its own function.[8] I will argue that these simple circumstances played the chief part in the origin of Christian baptism.

But the event itself probably turned out to be more than an enactment of repentance, and became some sort of beginning for Jesus' special mission.[9] However much the theological freight of the existing accounts may represent later Christology, there must have been some reason why it was loaded on *this* event, which was an embarrassment as repentance and only an embarrassment if it was only repentance. If Jesus' baptism was his initiation, the question is whether this too played a part in the origin of Christian baptism.

As they stand, all four accounts are of God's public proclamation of the Messiah, shaped by Christian interpretation of Psalm 2:7 and/or Isaiah 42:1.[10] But it is hard not to suppose that we may retroject the development clearly visible from Mark to Matthew to Luke, to posit an earlier version which recounted a visionary experience of Jesus. Such an account must surely have been of Jesus' call to an office; and it is again hard not to think of the prophets' calls, especially in view of the importance of the *Spirit* both in the accounts of Jesus' baptism and for the revival of prophecy in the earliest church.[11]

The simplest explanation of the origin of Christian baptism would be that Jesus and his disciples, in continuing John's proclamation of the imminent kingdom, continued John's sacramental practice; and that after the resurrection the disciples, in resuming their discipleship, resumed also their baptizing. This may be the view of a tradition behind John's Gospel.[12] But there is no synoptic tradition of baptizing by Jesus, or by his disciples before the resurrection; and in such a matter the argument from silence is surely good.[13] It thus seems that the primal Christian community did not baptize as the result of a continuous development of its own practice, but by post-resurrection recourse to John's practice. Why would they have done that, especially since John's baptism was not an initiation?

To a point, the matter does not seem so difficult as is sometimes thought. Conversion to the resurrection's community, was eschatological repentance exactly in John's sense, even though it was not only that; and surely submission to John's baptism was the way in which many, if not all, initial members of the church had themselves repented. Moreover, the act had Jesus' own endorsement. That Peter and the rest baptized the penitents created by their preaching seems to me to need no further explanation. And given that repentance and entrance into the community coincided, it is also clear how the rite of repentance immediately filled the inevitable need for a rite of initiation, especially since the rite of repentance was once-for-all-time in any case.

But why then had not Jesus or his disciples baptized during his mission? I suggest that it was because Jesus' proclamation was not in fact a call to repentance in the sense for which John had established baptism as a visible word—"The bridegroom's people cannot fast while the bridegroom is with them."[14] But for the resurrection-created community, faith in the Lord's presence, however enthusiatic, dialectically included a fundamental experience of his absence. He is, after all, present as the *risen* Lord. Apprehension of this breaks out in the tradition in a variety of ways: in the explicit story of the Ascension, in such phenomena as the account of Jesus' "Touch me not" to Mary Magdalene,[15] in the eschatological longings of the Supper, and most fundamentally in the missionary impetus itself. After the resurrection, the church found itself in a situation which dialectically *included* the situation of John's proclamation, the situation of *preparation* for the kingdom. To this situation, a baptism of repentance was again appropriate.

Apprehension of these dialectics was by no means limited to Luke's special theology. But Luke did indeed set himself to think through this aspect of the church's situation thematically. The rubric under which this reflection is often put—"delay of the parousia"—is a misnomer; *any* time for the existence of the church is already a "delay," so that the renewed futurity of the Lord's presence belongs intrinsically to the situation of the church. Thus Luke's version of the risen Lord's final commission commands preaching, "in his name,"(!) "of repentance unto forgiveness of sin."[16] And in the Pentecost story, those who hear the apostles' preaching are accordingly "cut to the heart"; when they ask what they are to do, Peter sounds exactly like John the Baptist: "Repent; and be baptized . . ."[17] *It was the factual identity of repentance-preaching and mission in the post-Easter situation that established Christian baptism.*

II

This explanation seems to me sufficient. But Christian baptism of course meant more than repentance; and other motifs may have been additional factors in the rite's institution. Adherence to the church also meant faith in Jesus as Lord and anticipatory experience of life in the kingdom. Peter continues, in the Pentecost sermon: ". . . be baptized *in Jesus' name* . . . and you shall receive the *gift of the Holy Spirit.*"[18]

Submission to Jesus' lordship was enacted in a fundamental addition to John's baptism: Christian baptism was "into"/"in"/"upon" "Jesus' name."[19] The three prepositions are apparently used promiscuously. The New Testament use does not seem particularly obscure. "In Jesus' name" is used for any personal invocation—as "for the sake of Jesus" or "by the authority of Jesus"—of the sort where actually speaking the name would normally belong to carrying out the connection; nor does control by the latter factor seem lost from any New Testament case.[20]

The bath was performed with invocation of Jesus, by name. Whether this was a proclamation by the baptizer, or a confession or epiclesis by the neophyte, we do not know.[21] The meaning of the invocation of Jesus' name has been much disputed, precisely because familiarity with the act and its meaning is presupposed in all New Testament texts, so that these are never explicated. Eduard Lohse states the scholarly near-consensus: "In that the name of Jesus Christ is named over the neophyte, he is committed to Jesus as Lord, belongs to him, and owes him obedience."[22] But perhaps it would be better to say more generally that whatever new reality the neophyte enters by this rite of passage, is named as *Jesus'* reality.

From the earliest time for which fuller liturgical information is available,[23] the gift of the Spirit was enacted by the laying on of hands. Christian preachers called to repentance in view of the impending eschaton, as had John. But for *their* penitents, the eschaton no longer impended only as the coming day; it impended also in the eschatological existence of the congregation, to which converts could look forward. Thus the call was not only, "Be baptized and you shall enter the kingdom when it comes," but also, in "Spirit"-language, "Be baptized and you shall receive the gift of the Holy Spirit."[24]

Baptismal entrance into the life of the Spirit need not, however, always have been conceived as a gift of the Spirit directly to the entering individual. In some parts of the earliest church, it seems rather to have been conceived as consisting simply in entry into a community that included prophets and other charismatics. Then the connection between the Spirit and baptism will be in the Spirit's leading of the baptizer,[25] not in a special gift to the neophyte; and there will then be no function for a rite to invoke the Spirit upon the neophyte. The connection between baptism and the Spirit goes back to the very beginning;[26] and imposition of hands, as a communication of the Spirit, does also.[27] But it does not follow that the two rites were always and everywhere joined.[28]

Circumstances related also to these additional two motifs may have promoted the adopting of baptism. There have been many hypotheses along these lines.[29] As a sample, I give that of Heinrich Kraft, which combines both motifs neatly but not artificially:

"They were moved to introduce baptism by an experience in which they saw the fulfillment of Joel's prophecy: the outpouring of the Holy Spirit. By this outpouring, the primal church became the promised nation of prophets. Prophets become prophets by being *called*. As after Pentecost new members sought to join the community of prophets, one remembered that the Lord Jesus had been baptized by John, and called the new disciples in the same way and by the same sign . . ."[30]

The hypothesis is attractive.   If what I suggested earlier about the accounts of Jesus' baptism were right, and if Bultmann were right that they functioned as cult-legends of Christian baptism,[31] it would be insofar confirmed.   And in Acts 10:37–38, Jesus' baptism is described: "God anointed him with the Holy Spirit and with power . . ."

Other such hypotheses have a similar attractiveness.   Nevertheless, it is hard not to feel something arbitrary about them all.   Those motifs of baptism's practice that go beyond the practice of John do not seem to provide the stuff of historical knowledge.   There are clear phenomena in the texts that urge us to attempt such hypotheses; undoubtedly a multiplicity of factors led to the practice of baptism, as is always true of historical beginnings.   But actual attempts to fix additional factors turn out to be so reconstructive that we can never say more than that it *may* have been so.   As the tradition stands we seem blocked from taking hold of any but the one strand of the tangle.   I find this of the first importance for our next considerations.

III

Baptism is mandated in a way set by the circumstances of its adoption. Insofar as the command to proclaim the gospel is a command to proclaim repentance, the concrete reality of the mission-command is "Baptize."   Baptism, unlike the Supper, has and needs no explicit rubrics or separate "Do this" to establish it; for from the beginning no distinction is conceived between the church's missionary task and its baptizing.   Throughout Acts, it is assumed in the very vocabulary that to be converted from the past to the church, and to be baptized, are the same event.[32]   Paul assumes that all Christians are baptized;[33] and he includes himself, despite all his claims for immediacy to the Lord.[34] *That* baptism is the concretion of the repentance which the Christian mission opens, is of course historically contingent; had Israel lived and the church begun in the desert the rite would doubtless have been different.   But, in this sense, the entire origin of the gospel is contingent.   We are commanded to baptize simply insofar as we take the command to preach repentance in Jesus' name as addressed also to us.

The argument is closed in that the primal church understood its missionary action, including the practiced identity of conversion and baptism, to be commanded by the risen Lord.[35] In the longer conclusion of Mark (16:15f.), the risen Lord's missionary command is to "proclaim the gospel." The desired outcome of this preaching is that hearers shall "believe and be baptized," to which not to "believe" is by itself the opposite. The Matthaean mission-command (28:18–20) is even more densely theologically packed. Here the Lord's word is a proclamation of the universal authority which the resurrection has brought him. Then follow three verbs which describe the inner-historical reality of this authority and so also the content of the believers' mission: "make disciples . . . baptizing . . . teaching . . ." In view of the relation between "discipleship" and "teaching" we must understand "make disciples" of a whole action of which "baptizing" and "teaching" name parts. Since "teaching" was directed to those *in* the church, "baptizing" thus stands here for the whole disciple-making process up to the actual activities of membership.[36]

The apostolic community may, of course, have been mistaken in the understanding just described—but this is only to say that the church's apostolicity may in general be its apostolic deludedness. We must also remind ourselves that the truth or falsity of the apostolic church's understanding is not decided by whether or not there indeed occurred appearances of the risen Lord with a baptism-command as their experiential content. Yet the usual skepticism on this point is psychologically naive. Of course the baptism-commissions reflect the later practice of the church; but that may well be because such commissions in fact originated the practice. The factors which decided the practice of baptism (as discussed in II) may as well have become definite in the appearance-visions as in any other experiential context. Moreover, an excellent case can be made for the origin of Matthew 28:18–20 in the resurrection-appearances themselves.[37]

Thus the baptism-mandate which Scripture puts on us is extraordinarily stark. There are no full rubrics transmitted as deliberate instruction to the future church, as there are for the Supper; there is no "Do this, and this, and this." We merely read of "baptism" as of a well-known act, the undergoing of which is by the Lord's will indistinguishable from repentance and entrance into the church, and the performing of which is by the Lord's will inseparable from prosecuting the mission.

And we are invited to take up the mission. Only one rubric is added: this baptism is to be "in Jesus' name." But *how* Jesus is to be named is also unspecified.

If other reasons participated in leading the church to baptize, besides the provision to penitents of John's sacrament of repentance, these do not have place in the connections by which *we* may apprehend, in the documents of primal practice, a command to baptize. We hear no command: "Ordain prophets, by water-anointing," or "Initiate into Jesus' death, by representation." There is only: "Do for penitents what John did, in Jesus' name." We are to *wash*—any way that is real washing!—the penitents our mission calls, making it—somehow!—verbally clear that the community and obedience they enter is Jesus' and not another's.

NOTES

1. *baptisma, baptizein*—active and passive. See Joseph Ysebaert, *Greek Baptismal Terminology: Its Origins and Early Development* (Nijmegen: Dekker & Van de Vegt, 1962), pp. 12–63.

2. E.g., Werner Kümmel, *The Theology of the New Testament*, trans. John E. Steely (New York: Abingdon Press, 1973), pp. 28–30.

3. Hans Conzelmann seems to take a different position; see his *An Outline of the Theology of the New Testament*, trans. John Bowden (New York: Harper & Row, 1969), pp. 47–48.

4. Philip Vielhauer, "Johannes," in *Die Religion in Geschichte und Gegenwart*[3], Vol. III, col. 805.

5. "Zur Tauchtaufe bedarf es keines Tauerfers," p. 92 in Heinrich Kraft, "Die Anfänge des geistlichen Amts," *Theologische Literaturzeitung*, 100, pp. 82–98. It seems to me that this simple argument must prevail, since the purely linguistic evidence is—to say the least—indecisive and other evidence is lacking. The common opinion seems to rest on the long exploded historicist supposition that a word, here *baptizein*, must when possible be taken to mean what it used to mean. Thus Ysebaert, op. cit., p. 39, says, "In the New Testament period (these terms) have not yet become so technical among the Jews that the idea of an immersion is lost." But one searches his pages vainly for evidence that this was in fact the case. In itself, the evidence he so exhaustively and clearly presents would seem to show the contrary; and that is the conclusion drawn from similar evidence by Erich Dinkler, *Die Religion in Geschichte und Gegenwart*[3], Vol. VI, cols. 627–8, 634–5.

6. Kümmel, op. cit., p. 31.

7. All attempts to reconcile Jesus' repentance with his consciousness of

mission are vain, since we have no historical report of Jesus' work or intention prior to his baptism. On the one side, we do not know what we are trying to reconcile. The most respectable recent attempts on this line are those of Oscar Cullmann, *Baptism in the New Testament,* Studies in Biblical Theology 1, trans. J. K. S. Reid (London: SCM Press, 1950), pp. 15ff., and G. R. Beasley-Murray, *Baptism in the New Testament* (Grand Rapids: Eerdmanns, 1962), pp. 45–67, who knocks down Cullmann's construction easily, and then builds an even less plausible one.

8. Mark 11:30 par.

9. Kümmel, op. cit., p. 74.

10. On this much disputed matter see Beasley-Murray's sensible discussion, op. cit., pp. 59–61.

11. E.g., Conzelmann, op. cit., p. 39; Kümmel, op. cit., pp. 123f.

12. John 3:22; 4:2. But see also Rudolf Bultmann, *The Gospel of John,* trans. G. R. Beasley-Murray et al. (Philadelphia: Westminster Press, 1971), ad loc.

13. Beasley-Murray, op. cit., pp. 67–72, takes an opposite position and lists numerous authorities on both sides.

14. Mark 2:19 par.

15. John 20:17.

16. Luke 24:47.

17. Acts 2:38.

18. Acts 2:38. See Johannes Schneider, *Die Taufe im Neuen Testament* (Stuttgart: Kohlhammer Verlag, 1952), pp. 68f.

19. *eis* in Mt. 28:19; Acts 8:16, 19:5; 1 Cor. 1:13–15. *en* in Acts 10:48; 1 Cor. 6:11. *epi* in Acts 2:38.

20. Since this is a negative, passage-listing would reproduce the concordance, to which I therefore directly appeal. I see no reason in the actual uses before us to think of the rabbinic *LSM*; Eduard Lohse, "Taufe und Rechtfertigung bei Paul," *Kerygma und Dogma,* 11, pp. 308–21, n. 17.

21. Doubtless there was confession expected of new believers, as demonstrated by Günther Bornkamm in "Das Bekenntnis im Hebräerbrief" in *Studien zur Antike und Urchristentum* (Munich: Chr. Kaiser Verlag, 1959), pp. 188–203. But that this was the "naming" or indeed any sort of act within baptism, is not thereby established. For beautiful clarity on this whole matter, see Hans von Campenhausen, "Das Bekenntnis im Urchristentum" *Zeitschrift für die neutestamentliche Wissenschaft,* 63, pp. 210–53.

22. Lohse, op. cit., p. 313. So also Conzelmann, op. cit., p. 48; Gerhard Delling, *Der Gottesdienst im Neuen Testament* (Göttingen: Vandenhoeck & Ruprecht, 1952), p. 121; Kümmel, op. cit., p. 132.

23. Conveniently at hand in Burkhard Neuenhauser, "Taufe und Firmung" in Schmaus, Gieselmann, and Rahner, eds., *Handbuch der Dogmengeschichte,* Vol. IV, No. 2 (Freiburg: Herder, 1956), pp. 24ff.

24. Lohse, op. cit., pp. 311–13.

25. Acts 8:26–50.

26. Those who doubt this, as Conzelmann, op. cit., pp. 38–40, are surely refuted by such arguments as those of Kümmel, op. cit., pp. 131–32.

27. E.g., Delling, op. cit., pp. 134ff.

28. In connection with this whole paragraph, see Georg Kretschmar, *Die Geschichte des Taufgottesdienstes in der alten Kirche* in K. F. Mueller and Walter Blankenburg, eds., *Leiturgia, Handbuch des evangelischen Gottesdienstes*, Vol. IV (Kassel: Johannes Stauda Verlag, 1954), pp. 19–27.

29. Above all by Oscar Cullmann, op. cit.

30. Kraft, op. cit., p. 92.

31. Rudolf Bultmann, *The History of the Synoptic Tradition*, rev. ed. trans. John Marsh (New York: Harper & Row, 1963), p. 251f. But see Schneider, op. cit., p. 80.

32. Acts 8:12, 8:35, 9:18, 16:15, 18:8, etc. For a sensible discussion of the apparent narrative exceptions, see Beasley-Murray, op. cit., pp. 104–20.

33. 1 Cor. 1:11–17, 10:1–12.

34. Romans 6; 1 Cor. 12:13.

35. Lohse, op. cit., pp. 311ff.

36. Schneider, op. cit., p. 30.

37. Splendidly done by Beasley-Murray, op. cit., pp. 77–90.

13

Promise

I

The mandated action of baptism is itself starkly simple and carries little theological freight. Just this is the possibility of rich and varied theological interpretation, i.e., of rich and varied accession of the gospel-promise to the element. The biblical mandate of the Supper is detailed, its interpretation relatively uniform. With baptism it is the opposite. As we shape our practice and understanding of the connection between the gospel's promises and our repentance-washing, just this circumstance is our canonical guide.

There is no one New Testament interpretation of baptism. But there is one New Testament *way* of interpreting baptism; and it discloses aspects of the apostolic understanding of the gospel. Its structural characteristics should therefore appear also in our gospel-interpreting of baptism.

Let me state my results at the beginning. I find that biblical interpretations of baptism have the following structural characteristics: (1) interpretation of baptism is a function of the interpreter's understanding of the church; (2) when baptism is interpreted to those yet to be baptized, the interpreting is itself pure promise-making; (3) when baptism is interpreted to those who have been baptized, it is exactly this existence of a past-tense biographical fact that is made use of, to interpret believing existence as a whole; (4) the purpose of both interpretings is to prevent the subjectivizing of belief; (5) baptism is thus described as an alteration of the neophyte's reality; and (6) this change is effected by the Lord's presence.

II

The New Testament sometimes describes an offer of baptism to those not yet in the church. Our understanding of such future-tense interpretations is limited by the general difficulty of reconstructing early mission preaching. We are mostly limited to what appears in Acts.[1] Here the church appears as the community of the prophetic Spirit and its gifts.[2] To those brought to repentance by the mission, the church's preachers accordingly offer baptism with the promise, "You shall receive the gift of the Holy Spirit." Indeed, much of Acts is the story of this promise's fulfilling.

That which the community is and has is brought to word for the one not yet in it; just so, the act of entrance becomes for those who look forward to it the actual receiving of the gift. The church's present life is constituted by expectation of the fulfillment, its being-in-communication is the making and hearing of promise. The Spirit is the present fact that there is such fulfillment.[3] To penitents the church said, "Be baptized; and you will live by the power of the eschaton." The promise that thus accedes to the washing is straightforward and unconditional: penitents are allowed to look forward to eschatological existence as something that will certainly be theirs. And it is exactly the identification of this new life's initiation with an objective event that enables this unconditionality.

The New Testament has other things to say about the church besides that it has the Spirit; some of these will occupy us in the following. There is no reason that the eschatological promise to those not yet baptized could not be made in the language of any of them. Perhaps it was.

III

The more extensive interpretations are in the past tense, addressed to those who have been baptized. I will, like everyone else, begin with Romans 6:1–11. Paul faces the question, "Why not continue to indulge ourselves, if we will be forgiven anyway?" An obvious answer would be, "Because God will punish at least all who ask such questions"; and this indeed has its place in his response. But the doctrine of justification that provides opportunity for such a question also prohibits that this should be the whole response. Paul's answer in Romans 6 is, "Because

you are not the kind of beings who can meaningfully ask such questions."
They *used* to be; and this is the ground of their—now meaningless—
babbling. But something has happened to them to detach such questions from their reality: that something is baptism. The *past tense* of
all the passage's references to baptism is essential to their argumentative
force: to remove sin and good works from the sphere of subjective
choice.[4]

As the Romans ought well to know, they have been baptized "into
Christ Jesus," and that is "into his death" (v.3). The consequence is
that they now are related to Christ in a way that Paul states by using
of them a series of verbs that in their simple forms narrate Christ's own
work but to which "co-"(*syn*) is here prefixed: "we were co-buried,"
(v.4); "we have co-inhered," (v.5); "we were "co-crucified," (v.6);
"we will co-live," (v.8). Of these, all those in the past tense have to
do with that death into which the Romans were baptized. The Romans
now share Christ's death, and therefore share his *separation* (vv. 7, 10,
11) *from the old self*. There no longer subsists in their case that relationship of indulgence and need between person and world, to which
"why not continue. . . ?" could meaningfully refer.

The argument is fairly simple. On the one hand, "into Christ Jesus"
is probably short for "into the name of Christ Jesus";[5] thus connection
is made to the experienced event of baptism. On the other hand, this
formulation opens the whole resonance-system of *inclusion*-images which
constitute so much of Paul's thought. The baptized are "in" Christ and
so have died "with" him. Given this thinking, the argument is valid; if
baptism initiates into determination of life by the reality of Christ, it
initiates into determination by that event by which Christ has defined
himself—which, according to Paul, is the cross. But how does this
thinking work?

If we try to understand the passage only christologically, we are driven
to speak of "mysticism," etc., which may classify the discourse but does
not clarify it. We cannot follow the argument until we see that it
depends on the description of the church as "the body of Christ," that
the ecclesiological meaning of "in Christ" is not penumbral in the
passage but enables the argument. We are baptized into the church,
which is a "body," a given transpersonal object-reality in the world,
whose communal structures then quite unmystically include us and
determine our possibilities. But this community is *Christ's*; his self-

determination determines its structure and dynamics. It is through such relations of meaning that the discourse of Romans 6 works;[6] and when we see that, we see that Paul's claims for baptism are a function of his claims for the church.

One further matter should be noted. In verse 5 we find: "we have become united (literally "co-grown," or "coinherent") with the *homoiōma* (image) of his death." This *"homoiōma"* may be: (1) something other than Christ or his death, but *like* it or (2) Christ's death itself as a sharply profiled event.[7] In the first case, the like reality may be (a) our life, related by likeness to Christ's death or (b) a third entity, a likeness, by which we are related to Christ's death, which must then be baptism itself as a cultic representation of Christ's death. All these options have their promoters; but 1 (*a*) is grammatically difficult in the passage and is supported by few modern exegetes. Should 1(*b*) be right, we may reckon that the tradition of baptismal theology that appears in Romans 6 had generated liturgy: immersion. But somewhat to my disappointment, the grammatical difficulty also of 1(*b*), and the way *homoiōma* is used in this same letter at 8:3, have convinced me that interpretation 2 is correct.[8] We should paraphrase: "We have become united with Christ, insofar as he has died." Thus the baptismal interpretation of Romans 6 does *not* go by way of immersion as a cultic representation of death, and indeed does not even allow us to conclude that immersion was practiced in Rome.

IV

Other Pauline passages show the same sort of interpretation. Galatians 3:25–27 also makes baptism the pivot of faith by way of inclusion in Christ. In 1 Corinthians 12:12–13, the problem is very directly a problem about the church: its Corinthian disunity to which Paul opposes the church's essential unity as "one body," one given object in the world.[9] Then he fastens the Corinthians into this given unity by the equally given fact of their past baptism—*which is now interpreted as itself an abrogation of differences* in that it is "in one Spirit" and *so* "into one body" (v. 13).

According to 1 Corinthians 6:9–11, the Corinthians once were adulterers, etc.; *now* they can be such only by self-contradiction, for "you were washed . . , you were sanctified . . , you were justified . . ." (v. 11). All three verbs are doubtless pre-Pauline jargon for baptism, but the use Paul here makes of them depends on the sense they can have for *his* theology.[10] What that is, 1 Corinthians 1:26–31 has made clear: the church is the creation of the justification of the ungodly, the community of the "nothings" (v. 28) who nevertheless are something—only not in themselves, the community of those whose "justification and sanctification and washing" (v. 30) are outside themselves. Our passage says that baptism is entry into *this* community; thus Paul loads onto baptism his entire justification theology in its ecclesiological form. The three passively-possessed values of 1:30 here accrue to the Corinthians by an event denoted by the corresponding three passive verbs.[11]

Paul makes this move not for the sake of baptism but for the sake of justification. Paul could have argued, as our preachers regularly do: "You who are justified by grace must not continue to sin because that would be ungrateful." But such a word as the proposed object of the Corinthians' reliance would not defeat the dialectics of subjectivity: in two sentences the Corinthians could be either at the question of Romans 6, or in despair. By evoking justification as what simply did happen to the Corinthians at baptism, Paul makes of it an inexpungeable fact, and so brings it to word in a way that is above subjectivity's evasions.

1 Corinthians 6 also tells us why Paul can talk of baptism as he does. The new fact worked at baptism is worked "in the Lord's name . . . and in the Spirit . . ." (v. 11). These phrases refer to the standard marks of Christian baptism, but so as to make them the *agent* of the passive verbs; it is the naming of Christ and gift of the Spirit that sanctify. Linked in this fashion as joint agent, the naming of the Lord and coming of the Spirit amount to the risen Lord's personal presence; *he* has transformed the Corinthians' reality.[12]

V

John 3:1–8 divides humankind into two ontological sorts: those who are "Spirit" and those who are "flesh" (v. 6).[13] The distinction is ecclesiological, a reflective development of the Old Testament language by which all creation is flesh, the opposite of which is spirit, and of the Christian claim that the church is the community of the Spirit. But a change of great scope has occurred: John's shift to "the judgment is now" (3:18) shifts the dualism of the old age and the age to come sufficiently to establish a metaphysical dualism between two present realities; this in turn redefines the line between church and non-church as a line between two kinds of being. And belonging to one of the two ontological sorts is the same as having a certain *origin*: "from" flesh or Spirit (v. 6).[14]

There has been, for those in the church, a beginning by which they are now of the spirit-reality. This birth was, moreover, "again"[15] (v. 3); it was not from nothing but was rather a transfer from the other ontological sort. For our purposes, what happens in this text is that "of water and" in verse 5 identifies this Spirit-beginning with baptism. Quite apart from Bultmann's general theories about John's Gospel, one can sympathize with his feeling that "of water and" is tacked on to the scene.[16] But if the phrase was indeed added by a later hand, the purpose of the addition is the exegetical point, and whether the hand was a "churchly redactor" or someone earlier makes no difference for my purpose.

By specifying that the new origin from Spirit is also from water, someone achieved two things. John insists, first, that the possibility of new birth is the possibility of miracle, a possibility that is not ours.[17] But if that is *all* that can be said, it may as well not be. No doubt the Spirit blows unpredictably (v. 8), but if we also cannot say where he *has* been, Spirit-talk is empty and Spirit-being is pure arbitrary self-assertion. The identification of birth from the Spirit with birth from baptism's water makes the Spirit's coming a humanly specifiable event. If the phrase is indeed added by the qualm of an editor, his qualm was right.

Second, our passage is directly before renewed reference to John the Baptist.[18] His testimony had been that he baptized "in water" but that Jesus would baptize "in the Spirit" (1:33). According to 3:5, the origin-event in the church is *both* of these baptisms;[19] it is both departure from the old, and beginning of the new. Thus again, the reference to baptism serves to anchor the discourse about Spirit-beginnings to the present reality which, however much it may be passing away, has not quite gone yet, and *from* which the reality "from the Spirit" must therefore begin.

VI

A quick look at a few other passages will show the generality of the kind of interpretation I have found; I need select only those whose reference to baptism is unquestionable. Throughout the New Testament baptism is freely interpreted to suit whatever conception or need of the church the writer entertains. I will not expound these passages, but only point out how each is a case of this ecclesial malleability of baptismal interpretation.

In Hebrews 10:22 the church appears as the *priestly* community, living by its access to God's presence. Promptly, baptism is now described as the super-lustration that gives the purity demanded by such a super-cult.[20] And again, the point is what believers may now do, without further qualifying, since they *have* been thus purified. In 1 John 2:18–27 the congregation is addressed as the *prophetic* community, able to speak God's truth on its own authority and thus able to recognize and refute false teaching. That the congregation is made of prophets is assured by the fact of baptism, which to that end now appears as "anointing by the Holy One" (vv. 20, 27).

In Titus 3:5, an interpretation of baptism related to John's "rebirth" is used for Pauline purposes: to block the way back to sin by inserting baptism into the past.[21] 1 Peter, addressed to an—at least potentially—persecuted church, has "salvation" as its great word and the power of the risen Lord as its great message (1:3–21). Accordingly, we now hear without qualification that "now baptism *saves*" (v. 21) and that this occurs "by the resurrection of Jesus Christ, who is at the Father's right hand" (vv. 21f.). That the agent of baptism is the Lord reigning from the Father's power is not a motif we have previously found, but when ecclesiology suggests it, there it is. In Ephesians 5:25–27, the church appears as the bride of Christ who gives himself to sanctify her. The beginning of this sanctification is the water-lustration of baptism (v. 26).[22]

NOTES

1. Acts 2:38, 9:17, 19:1–7, etc.
2. Acts 2:16–21.
3. Romans 8:23; 2 Cor. 1:22, 5:5; Eph. 1:13f.
4. Otto Michel, *Der Brief an die Römer* (Göttingen: Vandenhoeck & Ruprecht, 1955), p. 129. On this text in general see Günter Bornkamm, "Baptism and New Life in Paul (Romans 6)" in *Early Christian Experience*, trans. Paul L. Hammer (New York: Harper & Row, 1969), pp. 73f.; G. R. Beasley-Murray, *Baptism in the New Testament* (Grand Rapids: Eerdmanns, 1962), pp. 127–45.

5. Johannes Schneider, *Die Taufe im Neuen Testament* (Stuttgart: Kohlhammer Verlag, 1952), p. 77; Beasley-Murray, op. cit., pp. 128–30.

6. Eduard Lohse, "Taufe und Rechtfertigung bei Paulus," *Kerygma und Dogma*, 11, pp. 308–21, 318. On the whole relation of baptism to church-as-body, Werner Kümmel, *The Theology of the New Testament*, trans. John E. Steely (New York: Abingdon Press, 1973), pp. 207–12.

7. On the possible senses of *homoiōma*, see Bornkamm, op. cit., pp. 77–79; Beasley-Murray, op. cit., pp. 134f.

8. The position taken here is taken by Bornkamm, op. cit., pp. 77–79; Michel, op. cit., pp. 130ff.; Hans Conzelmann, *An Outline of the Theology of the New Testament*, trans. John Bowden (New York: Harper & Row, 1969), pp. 272ff.; Beasley-Murray, op. cit., pp. 134f. Kümmel, op. cit., pp. 210, 217–20 adopts a different interpretation.

9. Hans Conzelmann, *1 Corinthians*, trans. James W. Leitch, Hermeneia (Philadelphia: Fortress Press, 1975), pp. 211f.

10. Conzelmann, *1 Corinthians*, p. 107; Lohse, op. cit., pp. 308–21, 322.

11. *apelousasthe* is a passive; Conzelmann, Ibid., p. 107, n. 44.

12. 2 Cor. 3:17–18, the whole argument!

13. Despite all problems, there is still no commentary on these texts to rival Rudolf Bultmann, *The Gospel of John*, trans. G. R. Beasley-Murray et al (Philadelphia: Westminster Press, 1971), pp. 131ff.

14. Bultmann, op. cit., 138 n. 1, asserts that the concept of origin has been detemporalized; however, apart from his systematics, there seems to be no reason to suppose this.

15. That *anōthen* here is "again" and not "from above," is both demanded by its use and here established by Bultmann's argument, op. cit., p. 135 n. 1.

16. Ibid., p. 138, n. 3.

17. Ibid., pp. 138–40.

18. John 3:22–30.

19. Schneider, op. cit., p. 59.

20. Ibid., p. 65.

21. Ibid., p. 63.

22. This passage has the fascinating phrase, *tō loutrō tou hudatos en rhēmati*, but I can neither find nor invent a satisfying explanation of it.

PART SIX

INTERPRETATION OF BAPTISM

14

The Logic of Baptism

I

Baptism's mandate and promise are differently related than are the Supper's. By the Supper's mandate the community is commanded to act as a whole, and the promise is to the community as a whole. Those who act according to the mandate and those who are acted upon by the promise, those who give on God's behalf and those who receive from God, are the same persons. Our practice and understanding of the Supper is therefore always liable to confusion between God's act and ours: whether by those who attribute to our act what belongs to God or by those who seek to honor God's act by grudging ours. Much of church history is shaped by the seesaw between these twin blunders, and many of my more arduous discussions have been necessary in order to warn against them.

Baptism's mandate, by contrast, commands the community to act upon persons not yet in it. Those who act have nothing to get from it; and those who receive have nothing to do. The mandate is to one group, the promise to another. Only if the biblical facts were so far forgotten as regularly to perform baptism upon persons who are in practice already members of the church could works-righteousness of either sort threaten. Thus there was—at first thought, surprisingly—no controversy over baptism between Rome and the paedobaptist Reformers.

II

Baptism is the Christian intiation. Over against much past and current malpractice, such as separation of baptism and first communion, this mere platitude is all the doctrine needed. But that Christianity

146

has an initiation, and that it is this one, are only necessary preliminary observations. Just so, Augustine observed that all religions have sacraments and that Christianity does too.

The force and justification of *Christian* sacraments, said Augustine, is their relation to the word of God. The truly theological question about baptism is what this particular embodied initiation does for the gospel. What our biblical studies teach, I suggest, is that baptism, first, lets the gospel be *unconditional* and, second, prevents the separation of faith from *community*.

In the mission proclamation, the fact of coming baptism lets the missionary point to the advent of new life as to a coming specifiable event. In the life of believers, the biographical fact of baptism makes possible a kind of discourse that sustains faith's extra-subjective authenticity. Whatever the church is or has, baptism makes a free and unconditional gift. If the church is described as the bride of Christ, baptism makes it possible to say to those yet outside: "You will be virginal in that bath," and to those inside: "You have been wedded to the Lord, and can not love another." If the church is described as a class-free political zone, baptism makes it possible to say to those yet outside: "The curse of your poverty (or) riches will be broken," and to those inside: "It is too late for submission (or) exploitation: you no longer have anything to gain from it." And such statements are to figure as factual propositions about the world.

That it is a bath which apostolic command and promise establish as the, future or past, biographical anchor of the gospel is, of course, contingent. But it would have had to be some ceremony of renunciation and new beginning, and a ritual bath is manifestly well-adapted to this. Given the canonical institution, the ceremony and the event are no longer separable. The past and future factuality of new life and community is a ritual bath of cleansing and refreshment, which authoritative command and promise bind us to do and trust.

As the church has always said, baptism is to be *used*. *Its sacramental function is to enable the gospel's claims to be more than moral exhortations or subjective appeals.* We have lately made little such use of baptism. Thus, e.g., the social-action preaching of the sixties was ineffective partly because it seldom transcended moralism and subjectivity. Preachers said to white congregations: "You ought to love your black neighbors, because God loves you." They should have said:

"It is too late for racial fears and hates—at least in your cases. In the kingdom to which your baptism destines you, these outsiders will be your priests and moral examples; and you might as well start getting used to it."

III

Whatever the church is or has baptism grants. The repentant can be told: "You will be saints," and the baptized told: "You are saints," and these sentences are to be taken as *true*. To a point there is nothing remarkable about this. If we are any group, we may induct persons into that group; and whatever it means to belong to that' group, we thereby make true for them. If we are the order of Elks, we make Elks by initiation, with all rights appertaining to Elkhood. If we are indeed the bride of Christ, we can wed persons to him.

But *ought* we? That is the interesting point. If when we induct persons into *this* group that we are, we make *such* visible promises, by what right do we do any inducting? Must not the church rather end with the first generation called by the Lord, or await its new members as miraculous gifts? The question of an agency beyond ours emerges, in connection with baptism, not because what baptism does is a supernatural act beyond our power, but because it is an eschatological act beyond our right.

Whatever it means to belong to any community that we are, we can and do make true for those we bring in. What it means to belong to the church is to live in expectation, for the church is the community of a coming Lord. This is the key to baptism's character as an embodiment of the gospel: the induction we can and do perform, as an ordinary human act, is into a community whose whole continuing existence is a great induction into the final community. My initiation into the church, just by being initiation, is the enacting of that into which I am initiated, which is itself the great initiation. If initiation into the church is legitimate at all, it is, just by being initiation, eschatological anticipation of entry into the kingdom, in the precise sense of "anticipation" defined earlier for the Supper.

But again, if when we induct into the church we anticipate entry into the kingdom, how may we presume to induct anyone? It is at this point that the basic sacramental argument applies to baptism. This initiation is indeed an embodied promise we cannot rightly make. If it is nevertheless rightly made, then the Lord is present to make it. The only *justification* of baptism would be the present agency of God in Christ. We are in fact commanded to baptize, and therefore do so, trusting in the giver of the command to justify our act. When we baptize, we initiate into that initiation which Christ conducts as the whole life of his church. Our act is the anticipation, the embodied and therefore present communication of his.

It is now also explicable that the New Testament connects baptism so regularly with the Spirit—as it does not specifically connect the Supper. In the Supper, there is a classic balance of representation and anticipation. With baptism, all is anticipation. From the fourth century, baptism has regularly been interpreted also as representation of Jesus' death and resurrection, and this interpretation shaped baptismal orders. There is nothing wrong with this, nor would there be anything wrong with now proposing orders with representational elements, for sensible reasons. But the mandated action itself involves no necessary representings. On the other hand, it is one great anticipation. Just so, the New Testament thinks the presence of the Lord to baptize mostly as the coming of the Spirit.

IV

With respect to the second function mentioned above, baptism is at once the rite of personal repentance and of initiation into the community, and this simultaneity is of its essence. Baptism means transformation of individual life, but *what* it means is whatever the church means. If the church means expectation of the eschaton, baptism will mean a radical break with the past. If the church is, at a time and place, the dominant social groups at prayer, baptism will be a religious addition to name-giving (and all the instructions of the clergy will not alter this one whit). In faith, the individual exists by grant of the community, and the community by contribution of the individual. Baptism is the event of this coincidence.

If baptism is rightly used, it is Christianity's main protection against the two chief communal temptations of all religion. Religion is regularly destructive of community by offering individuals escape from its problems. It is not the futurity of "pie-in-the-sky-by-and-by" that has made this sort of eschatology an economic and political evil, but the possible privacy of the future meal. There is nothing about the "heaven" of most evangelical piety that would necessarily keep God and me—or even just me!—from being its sole inhabitants. Into the "kingdom" proclaimed by any recognizable version of the gospel, on the other hand, we enter together or not at all. When baptism is the individual's ground of eschatological hope, the very event which assures him salvation has also made him one of a fellowship. The one whose hope is founded in baptism cannot have salvation by himself.

Vice versa, religion is regularly destructive of personhood by giving inviolable sanction to inherited communal structures. In a perfectly traditional society there would be no *persons*, for there would be no decisions to be made other than by social organs. To the extent that societies approximate this state, religion is their great support. Baptism grants believers the community by which their life is defined, but is itself an act of—necessarily—individual repentance. Precisely to the extent that any communal entity tries to become total, whether pre-morally as in "natural" societies or by modern totalitarian choice, the Christians within it are a monkey-wrench. For they belong to a community which defines all community for them, and into which one cannot be born, which one can enter only by an act of self-definition. This is so also when the would-be total society is the church itself.

Also in this connection the justification of our baptizing becomes questionable. From what vantage point do baptizers thus transcend the conflict between the individual and the communal so as to claim to resolve it for those we baptize? It is precisely the continuing historic impossibility of so organizing society as to fulfill individuals, and of so seeking personal fulfillment as simultaneously to build up society, that is "original sin." Baptism, the church claims, cures original sin. What justification is there for this claim?

The justification, again, is the present agency of Christ. As we have seen, in his risen life individuality and commonality are no longer opposed. Christ is present as that *church*-body into which the neophyte is inducted, and just so is personally present to perform the induction.

V

The reinterpretation of baptism by reinterpretation of the church has continued to the present, and rightly so. What baptism means, is whatever the church means, and the church's self-conception must vary historically, precisely to be true to its object. For the church's self-conception must articulate expectation of the *living* Lord, over against the believers' situation in each new time and place.

The shaping of baptism by the history of the church would only stop if washing in Jesus' name were to be practiced wholly as an individual gateway into private salvation. Such a ceremony would have nothing more to do with the gospel, which promises no such salvation and provides no such gateways. Indeed, this washing would be a different rite altogether from that instituted as baptism, merely exploiting some of the same general symbolic materials. Pending such disaster, when we ask how we have understood and practiced baptism, and how we are to understand and practice it now, we are inquiring into the structure and self-conception of the church in history and in the future.

If baptism is richly interpreted at a time and place and is a decisive event in the lives of those who undergo it, this both reveals and promotes a rich and sharply contoured believing community. If baptism as interpreted at a time and place is puny or speaks inappropriately to the gospel, it is most likely the actuality and self-conception of the church that are antecedently puny or remote from the gospel. And when we perceive such sickness, reshaping of baptism must be and often has been a chief means to reform the church.

The history of reinterpretation is best seen in the rite itself. Just because the mandated action is in itself so simple and undifferentiated, it is extremely malleable by the way those who do it conceive it. Presumably, if the rite were better described in the New Testament, we would see liturgical variation to match the varying interpretation we do see.[1] In any case, the process is clearly visible since *ca.* A.D. 200; something of this story is our next concern.

NOTES

1. For a convincing attempt to reconstruct something of apostolic baptism's liturgical variety, see Georg Kretschmar, *Die Geschichte des Taufgottesdienstes in der alten Kirche* in K. F. Mueller and Walter Blankenburg, eds., *Leiturgia, Handbuch des evangelischen Gottesdienstes*, Vol. IV, (Kassel: Johannes Stauda Verlag, 1954), pp. 20–36.

15

The History of Baptism

I

By A.D. 200, baptism had become a performance of some length and complexity, a drama in more than one act.[1] Two different orders are detectible, each embodying a different churchly self-conception, distinguished by a different liturgical relating of the bath and the rite of the Spirit. In large areas of the East, centered at Syria, baptism was conceived as one great anointing with the prophetic Spirit into a church characterized above all by asceticism and prophecy. The gift of the Spirit began with an anointing with oil and was perfected in the special Christian anointing with water.[2] In the West, baptism was conceived as intrinsically a sequence of *different* acts: the bath and its attendant confession of faith were above all the ending of old allegiance and the beginning of new, upon which followed the gift of the Spirit by prayer and the imposition of hands, as strength for the new obedience.[3]

The future belonged to a synthesis of these rites and perhaps also of these conceptions of the church. Ancient baptism's liturgical and experiential flowering centered on the turn of the fourth and fifth centuries, in the flush of the church's triumph over the ancient world and before the problems of that triumph became overwhelming. But remarkably enough, the earliest baptismal rite that we know in detail, that described by Hippolytus around A.D. 200,[4] was probably already the product of such a fusion of East and West, and better than any other single rite displays the common pattern to which the great ceremonies of the fourth and fifth centuries tended. Therefore, and for honor's sake, I will make it the outline of my discussion.

Ancient baptism was a drama in three acts: the ending of old life, the transformation, the beginning of new life. Intrinsic theological determinants of baptism had unfolded liturgically, each acquiring its own visible word and fitting into dramatic sequence.[5] Yet this unfolding might not, of course, have happened at all, or might have happened differently; by it the ancient church created the initiation appropriate to its self-conception and situation in the world.

II

The enactment of old life's ending took considerable time, most of it occupied by the *catechumenate,* which was not an independent educational enterprise—though it may partly have developed from such— but part of baptism. In Hippolytus' school at Rome, the catechumenate normally took three years.

Catechumens were not hangers-on, but believers committed to baptism. But as unbaptized, they were not admitted to the Supper or its attendant modes and signs of fellowship. They joined the congregation precisely insofar as *instruction* was part of its life; for the rest, they had their own communal institutions.

The content of instruction was in part, of course, the teachings of the faith. But it was not for the sake of this that the catechumenate was needed as a distinct step in Christian life. The ancient catechumenate was above all a period of ethical and religious testing. Those who applied for admission were presumed to have been brought to this step by missionary preaching and therefore already to have some understanding of the gospel; further growth in understanding would be the work of a lifetime in the church. What could not be presumed was, first, a candidate's readiness for the shock of the ethical transformation to which the congregation's discipline would hold him, and second, his emotional and practical freedom from the pagan gods. The catechumenate was above all a discipline of prayer, supervised good works, public moral examination—and the visible word of exorcism.

In general religious history, exorcism is a normal and unsurprising visible word. Mankind has anciently understood—better than moderns—that the divine is at once utterly desirable and utterly fearsome. Therefore worship has always been at once to draw near the divine and to keep it at its distance. Insofar as ancient religions were polytheistic, love and fear tended to sort themselves out among the divinities; exorcism was merely the worship appropriate to fearsome divinities.

The God of Israel could not be kept at a distance, and Israel could worship no plurality of gods. Therefore exorcism was forbidden in ancient Israel. But once Israel had interpreted the plurality of numinous powers as "angels," they practiced invocation of good angels and exorcism of rebellious angels.

The church inherited exorcism from Judaism. If all created reality is personally structured, exorcism makes sense. Insofar as God is person, we are persons, the collectivities of history and personality are brought into God's relation to us, and God's relation to us is determined by rebellion, there "are" demons. In that God yet addresses us in mercy *and* wrath, despite our rebellion, he brings the collective determinants of our historical existence to speech as participants of rebellion and messengers of wrath. And then, if he chooses, he may give us a word of the gospel in reply.

The ancient church saw the rebellious powers embodied and visible throughout ancient civilization: the *pagan gods* exercized in bitter fact the old age's emotional, social, and political hold on aspiring Christians. Therefore they exorcized their candidates for new life to break the hold of old life.

Modern orders regularly omit exorcism. In the eighteenth century, this is understandable. But that it should still be so, in the late twentieth century, is astonishing; as usual, the church is the last to catch on. The experience of evils that are less than all individual wills, yet manifest all the characters of individual will, i.e., the experience of "the demonic," is *the* experience of our age. If such forces can indeed not be addressed, nor execrated by the gospel, we are all lost in any case.

The content of Christian exorcism, in whatever context, is well summarized by the formula that still appeared in Luther's order for baptism: "I adjure you, unclean spirit, in the name of Father, Son and Holy Spirit, to come out and depart from this servant of Jesus Christ." The execration was always embodied, most often by imposition of hands, anointing with oil, blowing, and the sign of the cross, in one combination or another. The sign of the cross is a visible word of such primitive power and general application for Christians as to need no explication. Blowing is an obvious apotropaic gesture. Anointing and laying on of hands are fundamental actions of the baptismal tradition and will be discussed in a moment.

In Hippolytus' order, baptism was normally performed at the cock-crow of Easter. Final exorcisms and spiritual exercizes occupied the vigil of the night. These arrangements vary in other and later orders, but Easter remained the great time of baptism, and always there was intensified discipline in the last day or days. Then the candidates were taken to the place of baptism, separate from the congregation's assembly since baths are not taken in public. In Hippolytus' order, the liturgical mark of the beginning of baptism itself falls here: with the blessing of the font and its water by the bishop, that is, by the pastor of the congregation.

The blessing of the font was a necessary part of baptism in the ancient church. Hippolytus gives no text for the prayer, nor is there any one pattern in the later liturgies. But three motifs are reasonably constant: reference to baptism's institution, by the Lord's command and by his own baptism at Jordan, prayer for the coming of the Spirit to take the water into his service, and prayer that the bath may be a means of purification and healing.

This baptismal Epiclesis was not originally a consecration of the substance in the font, a manufacture of holy water; Hippolytus directs that the font shall if possible be a running fountain. But of course, once the conception had emerged for the bread and wine, the baptismal Epiclesis was inevitably also so interpreted; thereby the problems of ritual transformation were introduced also into baptism. Apart from this problematical function, the Epiclesis served at least two necessary functions.

First, it brought the particular washing now to be performed under the divine institution. Augustine interpreted the Epiclesis as the enacted bringing of the word to the element. This is a precise parallel to the function of the Narrative of the Supper's institution. Second, it established the unity of baptism: of the bath and the bestowal of the Spirit. The same Spirit who will be given by prayer and the imposition of hands is the Spirit who before then uses the water of the bath. A main purpose of the baptismal Epiclesis was to prevent any separation of "water baptism" and "baptism of the Spirit." One may in general say the same about the baptismal Epiclesis as about the Supper's Narrative of institution: if its functions are not fulfilled in this way, they must be fulfilled in some other way.

The bishop returned to the congregation, leaving the candidates with the presbyters and deacons. Then the candidates were stripped. Total nudity in baptism was the universal rule of the ancient church;

this was to be no partial cleansing, and neophytes were to leave behind all shows of the old life and begin again as naked as at the first birth or in the garden of the first creation.

Then the presbyters and deacons blessed the oils for anointing. Again Hippolytus gives no text; later prayers are closely parallel to the prayer over the water, except of course that there is some problem about an "institution." In many orders, the oils were not blessed now, but at the Supper. There will be no less than three anointings in Hippolytus' order, two of the whole body and one of the forehead. No ancient order was without at least one; in the Syrian orders the anointing was the main action.

In the Mediterranean world, rubbing oil was a necessity of life, for much the same reasons that still make it necessary on beaches. Athletes were anointed, the sick were anointed, bride and bridegroom were anointed, those going to a party were anointed. In the ancient world, anointing meant blessing, the gift of vital force—for the straightforward reason that it did in fact experientially renew life.

The church knew that the true power of all life, and definitively of the church's eschatological life, is the Spirit. To embody prayer for and proclamation of the Spirit's gift of vitality, the church followed the lead of Judaism and the Old Testament and used the universal medium of invigoration in such contexts as suggested it. We do not know how the practice originated. In the New Testament, only anointing of the sick is attested.[6] But by A.D. 200, baptismal anointing is assumed practice in both East and West and seems never to have occasioned controversy.

With the blessing of oils, the ministers' preparations were finished, and the candidates' great transfer of life began. A presbyter seized each in turn and bade him renounce the prince of the old age and all religious and social ties to him. In later liturgies the candidate faced West, away from where Christ would return. Three times he spoke: "I renounce you, Satan, and all your ceremonies[7] and all your works." The last exorcism followed immediately, an anointing of the whole body, with the words: "Let every demon depart from you."

Here all the orders make haste, since the candidate hangs between two lives; immediately upon renunciation of Satan, the candidate confesses faith in his new Lord. In the West and in Hippolytus, this was done as one act with the naming of Christ in the bath itself. A deacon took each candidate into the water, and asked: "Do you believe in God the Father Almighty?" The candidate replied: "I believe." Thereupon the deacon immersed the candidate. This was done three times, with what were essentially the three articles of our Apostles' Creed.

In the East, the renunciation of Satan was followed by a direct act of worship known as the Syntaxis, or by a creedal recitation, or by both. For the Syntaxis of a fifth-century Egyptian rite, the candidate turned from West to East, and said "I believe, and I bow down to you and all your ceremonies, O Father, Son and Holy Spirit."[8] Then the naming of Christ at the bath was accomplished by a declaration of the minister as he immersed the candidate: "N. is baptized in the name of . . .," again with three immersions and three declarations. In the tenth century this pattern, with the declaration in the second person, was adopted also in the West.

On emerging from the water, the candidate was again anointed over his whole body. In the West this may originally have been baptism's only anointing. In Hippolytus, yet another anointing by the bishop is to come. Whether one or two, the post-baptismal anointings were to embody baptism's gift of new life. The bath itself ended with the reclothing of the neophytes in white albs. Then they were led to where the bishop and the congregation waited.

The third act of ancient baptism had two scenes. The first was the rite of the Spirit: the bishop laid hands on the candidates, prayed, and— in Hippolytus and mostly thereafter—anointed their foreheads with blessed oil. In Hippolytus, the bishop's prayer is: "Lord God, who have made them worthy to obtain the remission of sin by the bath of new birth, make them worthy to be filled with the Holy Spirit and send them your grace, that they may serve you according to your will. For yours is the glory, Father and Son with the Holy Spirit, in your holy church now and forever. Amen." The second scene was first communion, where the neophytes received extra chalices of water and of milk and honey, the food of children and symbols of the promise they entered upon, of the land flowing with milk and honey.

The bishop's prayer, touch, and anointing were a main and vital part of the rite. Indeed, in a sense this "confirmation" was the climax. For the Holy Spirit here invoked *is* the new life that baptism grants, and the bond of the community into which baptism inducts. In the ancient orders, moreover, the Spirit, once invoked, drew the neophytes immediately into the actuality of that life and community, the Supper.

Touching with the hands is an undifferentiated but deep and universal visible word. We know it as the hand on the shoulder, the embrazzo, the handshake, or as an unformalized possibility differently realized on each occasion. These touchings say fellowship. They also say power, the power that is created and lives in fellowship: the power of leadership, of obedience, of discourse. Touching is a universal gesture to grant such power, to take into fellowship in some specific way that empowers.

Mankind has mostly conceived this power in the way for which anthropologists use the Polynesian word *mana*: as a sort of supernatural electricity that runs along the joints of community and just so can be channeled by a touch.[9] Christianity has known that the Holy Spirit is the true power of community, that our community, at least, lives only by and in eschatological hope. To embody prayer for and sharing of the Spirit, the church therefore naturally and from the very first used the universal human gesture of communal empowerment, therein also following Judaism.

In the New Testament, laying on of hands appears in four contexts, all of which reappear in the practice of the later church:[10] for general blessing, for healing, at ordination, and in connection with baptism. Whether or not Luke's picture of laying on of hands at baptism accurately depicts the primal church's universal practice, Luke thought it did. By fundamental conviction, the Spirit is given at baptism; Luke regarded imposition of hands as the ordained embodiment thereof, and the subsequent church mostly adopted his view. It would be saying too much to maintain that the act belongs to the integrity of canonically mandated baptism, but anyone proposing not to do it should have very weighty reasons. I know of none, of whatever weight.

By a series of historical accidents, the Greek-speaking church lost the imposition of hands from its rite of the Spirit, so that its "confirmation" has only anointing [1] Since the non-Greek-speaking churches of the Orient were decimated by the Arabs, imposition/non-imposition became yet another West/East distinction   Under the assumption that confirmation is "*a* sacrament," the "validity" of which must be located in some one essential element, and not wishing to say that the valid sacrament is missing in the Eastern church, Roman Catholic theology has tended theoretically to designate the anointing as the essential gesture of "confirmation," while commanding imposition of hands in practice. From a properly historical and Augustinian viewpoint, we need not follow these tortuosities. We need only recognize that baptism unfolded somewhat differently in different places. Our problem is how to shape it now. If there is to be a distinguishable rite of the Spirit, imposition of hands is surely what has to be done.

III

In unfolding inner determinants of baptism in the particular way just described, the ancient catholic church followed the lead of its situation and self-conception. The apostolic church had been a hasty gathering together of those who would, to carry the news of the immediately impending kingdom, and to prepare communally for it. In these circumstances, baptism was itself hasty; and there was little attention to what was being left behind.

By the end of the second century, things are very different. The catechumenate, a clear and regulated period of testing, fits a church that has decided it has some time, and has realized that the community its neophytes enter has itself a continuing life of its own quality, for which people must be trained.[12] The church was now also very conscious of the continuing society around it, as an alternative to its own life. It knew itself as the "City of God" amid the "City of Man," as a society set in another society created by quite other religion. Yet it was not a "sect" in the modern sense: it did not live in continual protest, and had—despite outbreaks of persecution—a *modus vivendi* with the established powers that allowed it to develop its own forms of life with some fullness and stability. The classical balance and order of ancient initiation is perfectly correlated to a church so situated in the world.

The history of baptism since *ca.* A.D. 500 can be told as the history of ancient baptism's disintegration.[13] At the same time, the ways in which this disintegration occurred were not merely accidental, and provided the medieval and Tridentine churches, mainline Protestantism, and even the sect-type bodies with exactly their appropriate initiations. From here on it is only the Western church with which I am concerned.

The universalized practice of infant baptism was the main disintegrat-

ing force. Manifestly, the initiation just described was designed primarily for adults—in straightforward response to the New Testament
mandate, which concerned, after all, a rite of repentance. Yet the
church had also baptized infants as far back as our sources allow sure
conclusions.[14] Until the fifth century, that "also" was the key factor.

The practice of also baptizing infants was and is a response to a real
and unavoidable problem. The church lives in expectation of the immanent triumph of Christ. At the beginning, this immanence was—
rightly or wrongly[15]—conceived chronologically: Christ was to triumph
in a few days or weeks or years. Thus none of the church's original
practices were designed for a second generation, its initiation included.

When the world nevertheless endured so long that the birth of children to those already baptized had to be regarded as the regular event,
what was the church to do? Was it to say that these persons, who
would be raised in homes ruled by the comprehensive discipline of the
church and might never know unbelief or the old heathen life, were to
be excluded from the Supper? We must understand precisely what the
question is: is baptism the sort of rite that *can* be performed on infants? For if it can, there is every other reason to allow it in such cases.

Whatever other difficulties the "delay" of Christ's return may have
caused the apostolic and subapostolic church, the need to baptize infants seems to have caused no controversy at all: Hippolytus assumed
it, and of the ancient writers only Tertullian made any protest.[16] The
history by which we arrive at the standard practices of A.D. 200 was
undoubtedly complex, but we know next to nothing of it. However the
decision was made, it was the right one.

The point of baptism is its *use* for the proclamation. The use of
baptism for missionary preaching is in any case lost for those born into
believing homes; *insofar*, baptism simply does not apply to them, whenever administered. Throughout church history, there have been attempts to force it to apply, by insisting on conversion for all, even if a
heathen life from which to be converted must be taken on assurance
or even invented. Such piety has regularly proved spiritually destructive. Moreover, unless the unbaptized children of believers are altogether treated as heathen, the works-righteous situation earlier mentioned results.

On the other hand, the use of baptism in preaching for believers is
in any case after the fact. There is no way this can be lost by early

baptism. As the discourse of the church becomes meaningful to the growing baptized child, the biographical fact is there to be used. Thus by baptizing infants of believers nothing of original baptism is lost that can be saved for them, and what can be saved is.

What such arguments show is that infants *can* be baptized, not that they always should be. In the first place the question of baptism does not arise—or anyway must not!—except for infants whose familial circumstances are such as to compel the judgment that they will surely be raised "in the fear and admonition of the Lord." And even with these, the most that can be argued is that the church community should not, from its side, exclude them as a group. Thus in the ancient church infant baptism remained an option, and those coming to baptism were a mixture of adults and infants.

So long as the mixture could be maintained, so could an initiation shaped primarily for adults. And so long as it could be, it was, since adult baptism is manifestly what the New Testament had in mind. But with the nominal Christianization of the whole Mediterannean population and civilization, the church's self-conception had eventually to change, and with it, baptism. With a dubiously committed population inside, and no more local mission field outside, the church ceased to think of itself as a fellowship to bring the gospel to those outside and began to think of itself as an institution to bring the gospel to those inside. In these circumstances, the infant baptism that had been permitted, became the standard practice. And the rite itself had to become a rite for this practice.

The catechumenate was simply destroyed, having no application to exclusively infant groups of neophytes. By the end of the sixth century, all that remained was left-over ritual. The consequence was profound: there is no longer any testing of readiness for baptism. But precisely this fit the self-conception of the medieval church: those born in Christendom were, with whatever theoretical reservations, treated as just thereby ready for baptism.

With respect to the left-over ceremonies of the catechumenate, the question necessarily arose of their meaning and necessity in the case of infants. Under the impact of this question, *all* of ancient baptism before the bath shrank. And with the scholasticism of the high Middle Ages, the question of need became the fatal question of "validity": what is the least we can do and still baptize? Following the right biblical texts to answer this very wrong question, scholasticism answered: get some water on the candidate, with a trinitarian verbal formula. Then everything before the bath became in principle superfluous. The shrinking continued right through the Reformation and into the eighteenth century; ironically, this peculiarly Roman and scholastic process reaches its fulfillment in very self-consciously Protestant orders.

The reduction of baptismal actions concentrated the whole task of visible speaking upon the bath itself. This might have produced an order of primitive biblical potency. But the disastrous question of validity eventually reduced even the bath: from the fourteenth century, actual washing slowly gave way to sprinkling—so long as some water touched the infant that was enough. Thereby the intrinsically meaningful gesture of washing, whose meaning the institution of baptism had once put to the service of the gospel, was itself removed, *and baptism was silenced as a visible word.*

Just in its silence, of course, this new baptism suited the medieval church and still suits the Western mainline denominations. For if baptism says anything at all, it says ending of the old and radically new beginning, right to the physical inconvenience of the bathing; and just this is what Western Christendom has not wanted said. Of course, so long as a ceremony of initiation occurs it says something. What meaningless baptism means, is that Christianity demands no renunciation and that grace carries no risks. One hears that in some places they "baptize" by shaking droplets from a rose.

IV

The bishop's part of baptism fared quite differently, going off on its own to become a would-be independent sacrament.[17] The great size of dioceses in northern Europe prevented bishops from regularly presiding at baptisms; but the bishops retained their part of initiation, the confirmation. Thus the regular custom came to be that initiation was begun by a local priest, and concluded when the bishop came around or the parents could go to the cathedral city. Then the high rate of infant mortality, and a legalistic doctrine of the necessity of baptism, led to the conviction that baptism should be as soon after birth as possible, and no longer be kept for the great Paschal festivals. Thus the postponement came to be temporally palpable.

The separation once made, mere apathy increased the interval: "If baptism without confirmation really does all that is necessary for salvation," parents and priests asked, "why should we chase after a bishop?" Through the Middle Ages, the church answered with decrees: "You must have your child confirmed by _____ years after baptism;" and each new maximum promptly became a minimum in practice. The process continued until the age reached the "age of discretion," whereupon a theological justification could be made up: "confirmation" became a Christian puberty rite, thus again providing for the needs of a church and civilization that were practically one.

As Western civilization and Christianity have in modern times again tended to separate, confirmation has become a rite in search of a function. It has been interpreted as a delayed rite of conversion, by pietists who insist conversion must come sometime; as a graduation ceremony, by pedagogues looking for a way to keep children in church school; or openly as a puberty rite, by secularists hoping to maintain some public ties to "religion." All of these justifications are irrelevant to a rite for bestowal of the Spirit.

There can be no justification of separated "confirmation." It establishes two stages of church membership, and so hedges the bet on infant baptism. If there is to be any rite that bestows the Spirit, not for special churchly roles but simply for Christian life as such, it must be part of baptism, for that is what baptism is supposed to do. If infants can be baptized, they must be "confirmed" then and there or never. If infants cannot or should not receive the Spirit, they should not be baptized. If we have a rite for the Spirit and separate it from baptism, we merely thereby make either baptism or this later rite meaningless, probably both.

Finally, the direct movement from baptism to first communion was broken by sheer historical inadvertence.[18] By all theological right, infant baptism must be accompanied by infant communion and was until the thirteenth century, when infant communion was incidentally terminated by the withdrawal of the cup from lay communicants. Infants had been given the cup, which they could always share one way or another, but not the bread, which the youngest could not swallow. When the cup was taken from the congregation, infants were left with nothing.

Afterward, the deed was justified by *ad hoc* and entirely false exegesis of Paul's demand to "discern the body," which was turned into a demand for some, variously specified, level of understanding of Christ's presence. This medieval rationalization is standard to the present day. Those who defend it have not usually been willing to test adult communicants in the same way—in which they are doubtless well advised.

In fact, the separation of baptism and first communion lacks all justification, and can only be regarded as a catastrophic deprivation, both of the baptized children and of the communing congregation. Whatever arguments could disqualify persons of such-and-such age or attainments from the Supper would disqualify them also from baptism. Moreover, there can be no such arguments; for while there are indeed considerations that tell directly against infant baptism, in the nature of the case there can be nothing against infant communion. The one thing we do well at any age is to participate in fellowship by accepting nourishment.

General infant baptism ended the catechumenate, silenced the bath, and created separate confirmation. Just so it provided the appropriate pattern of initiation for a church nearly identical with a civilization. My description of the process and its results has been unfavoring, since it is their negative aspects with which we have now to deal. But that is not to say that anything else could have been done at the time. Baptism's order and interpretation are rightly determined by the structure and self-interpretation of the church; therefore they must share the dialectics of the church's history, in which creation and perversion are at all times paired.

As the synthesis of the gospel with Western culture ends, worry about inherited forms of initiation increases. Whatever new relation emerges between the church and our society will create and be created by new patterns of baptism. Even the alternatives between "church" and "sect," and correspondingly between infant baptism and "believers' " baptism, are only exhaustive alternatives within the dying synthesis. I have some prophecies and proposals; they make the next chapter.

NOTES

1. For the historical sequences narrated in this chapter, see above all Georg Kretschmar, *Die Geschichte des Taufgottesdienstes in der alten Kirche* in K. F. Mueller and Walter Blankenburg, eds., *Leiturgia, Handbuch des*

evangelischen Gottesdienstes, Vol. IV, (Kassel: Johannes Stauda Verlag, 1954). My historical summaries are largely of his material; the interpretations vary almost entirely. Many of the texts are conveniently collected in English translation by E. C. Whitaker, ed., *Documents of the Baptismal Liturgy,* 2nd ed. (Naperville, Ill.: Alec R. Allenson, 1970).

2. E.g., the "Acts of Judas Thomas," English text in Whitaker, op. cit., pp. 10ff.

3. Clearly described by Kretschmar, op. cit., pp. 86–114.

4. In the edition of B. Botte, *Sources Chretien,* 11 (Paris: Editions du Cerf, 1946), pp. 68–95.

5. The dramatic reality of baptism at its full flowering in the ancient church far exceeded in richness and penetration what can be described here. For an evocation of how the ancient church experienced each step in the following, see Hugh M. Riley, *Christian Initiation* (Washington: Catholic University Press, 1974).

6. Jas. 5:14; Matt. 6:13.

7. "Pomps" were evidently religious processions.

8. "The Canons of Hippolytus," in Whitaker, op. cit., p. 80.

9. S. Morenz, "Handauflegung" in *Die Religion in Geschichte und Gegenwart*[3], Vol. III, cols. 52f.

10. H.-D. Wendland, "Handauflegung" in Ibid., col. 53f.

11. For a definitive discussion, see Louis Ligier, *La Confirmation: Sens et Conjuncture Oecumenique, Hier et Aujourd'hui* (Paris: Beauchesne, 1973).

12. Kretschmar, op. cit., pp. 63–69.

13. A clear and compendious such telling is provided by Frank Senn, "The Shape and Content of Christian Initiation," *Dialog,* 14, 2, pp. 97–107.

14. Kretschmar, op. cit., pp. 81–86.

15. If rightly, the mere passage of time has refuted the gospel.

16. Kretschmar, op. cit., pp. 81f.

17. The story is told, with a surfeit of documentation, by J. D. C. Fisher, *Christian Initiation: Baptism in the Medieval West* (Naperville, Ill.: Alec R. Allenson, 1965), pp. 1–77, 109–140.

18. Ibid., pp. 101–08, again with decisive documentation.

16

Some Liturgical Proposals

I

In our time, the entire matter of baptismal action before the bath itself will and must be reopened. When life in the church and life outside the church obey the same moral explications of life's value—however badly on one side or nominally on the other—Christian initiation will inevitably tend practically to begin with the bath; prior testing and discipline, and rites of departure from the old life, will not seem essential. Infant baptism will be the normal way into the church. But in our time—for good and ill—the Western world no longer even nominally affirms Christian or Jewish understandings of life's purpose. Unless the church is wholly unable to affect the needed separations from this culture and so loses its own self, it will again experience that those entering the church have to be prepared and tested for the shock of moral innovation.

It is not that the West now less obeys the good as the church understands it; it is rather that the West now less agrees with the church about what the good is. The gospel's vision of human good claims to be generally applicable, but it does not follow that the generality will always agree to its application. For example, the oldest surviving moral catechism of the sort taught to catechumans begins: "You shall not kill. You shall not commit adultery. You shall not commit paederasty. You shall not fornicate. You shall not steal. You shall not dabble in the occult. You shall not experiment with drugs. You shall not abort unborn infants, nor kill the newly born."[1] This was not intended as a list of moral platitudes; it was an expansion of three of the Ten Commandments, precisely to disavow some of late antiquity's accepted normalities. The list increasingly recovers its original force:

in late modernity, several of its items have their "liberation" movements, and one or two are already regarded as virtues.

Our civilization may achieve nihilism. Or it may acquire a new
morality, based on a nonbiblical religion. It may die. Or we may
realize a new civic religion, perhaps from cooperation between the needs
of democratic polity and the eschatological vision of Judaism and
Christianity. But such possibilities are not my present matter. In any
event, the church must now look to its peculiarities, and so to the
preparatory steps of baptism. The measures I will propose are designed
not for an unforseeable future settlement, but for the period of separating; congregations could adopt them now.

Adults preparing for baptism should submit to a period of instruction
and intensified spiritual exercise. If Lent were used for this purpose,
it would again have one. Most groups now require theological instruction for those joining the church; what must be added is instruction in
the moral dissensus between late modernity and the gospel: between
consumer humanity and loving humanity, between self-realization and
joint realization, between trust in weapons and trust in God. Such instruction is meaningless outside the practice of prayer and reflection:
the catechumens must meet daily for worship, discussion, and medita-
tion. In our society such requirements will be a sufficient test of commitment. Those who are irregular, or show no growth of insight, must
not be baptized.

When the church baptizes infants, it takes the promises of the parents
to raise the children in the faith as a substitute for instruction and testing. The problem is, of course, that most parents who now bring infants for baptism are wholly and manifestly incompetent to make such
promises. Those who do not live intensively in the faith cannot raise
anyone in it. Indeed, those who have themselves evaded the risks of
believing existence do not have the simple human right to commit
another person to them. A bit of pre-baptismal "counseling" is little
help; nor can it be effective so long as it is assumed that the child will
be baptized in any case. It is neither uncharitable nor legalistic for
the church to recognize incompetence and lack of right; nor need the
judgment pretend to infallibility. Thus there are many promises the
author of this book is incompetent to make: e.g., to build a house.
Should I nevertheless attempt to contract to build a house, no one who
loved me would sign the contract.

I suggest one possible solution. All will surely agree that Christian parenthood is a demanding and very special enterprise, for which training is essential. Those who first bring a child for baptism must be prepared for the difficult enterprise to which they thereby commit themselves. If there is any function for "parish education," surely this is one. Those embarking on Christian parenthood should submit to the same deliberately rigorous and lengthy course as adult catechumens, with additional practical help for home prayer and instruction of children. Thus all would be given opportunity to demonstrate or acquire competence to make the promises about their children.

If all parents submitted to this path, baptism would merely thereby be restored. But it should be understood that there is another equally appropriate and salvific way into the church, for the children of any who did not submit to this path or lapsed from it: that the children make their own commitments and undergo their own testing when they are adults. Probably we should anticipate that many nominal members would not attempt to qualify for the baptism of their infants; but it might also be that many nominal members would submit to the path, and become authentic members in the process.

The catechumenate of adult converts and new parents should have a concluding rite. If the catechumenate has occupied Lent, this could be any service of Holy Week except Good Friday or Easter itself. Appropriate Scripture should be read, including Mark 10:13–16 if parents are included. Adult converts are questioned as to their willingness to undertake the various obligations of church membership, including legal and financial obligations. New parents make their promises: to attend services regularly, bringing their children and explaining as the children grow, to teach and explain the Ten Commandments, the Our Father and the Apostles' Creed, to pray at meals and at other occasions, and to set examples of Christian commitment in their political and social involvements. The rite could conclude with a prayer for perseverance and a benediction.

II

Except in special circumstances, baptisms should be celebrated at a very few occasions during the year. The services on those occasions can be arranged to accomodate baptism's necessities; if the occasion is the Easter Vigil, this takes care of itself. In any case baptism terminates in the Supper, and therefore must fit into a congregational service, even when the bath itself occurs in a separate place.

Present circumstances demand that the baptismal rite itself again include opening acts of separation from old bonds. For this purpose there is every reason to draw on the ancient tradition. If practical, the service should begin elsewhere than at the font, to create internal dramatic structure. If there is a separate baptistry, the opening may be in the presence of the congregation, with a procession to the baptistry thereafter. The opening action comprises prayer, exorcism, and reading of Scripture. The opening prayer may be something like the following, the text is a slight reworking of prayers general in the Western tradition.

MINISTER: The Lord be with you.

PEOPLE: *And also with you.*

MINISTER: Let us pray.

Almighty God, Father of Jesus Christ, we pray for your servant(s) who seek(s) baptism and its gift of the Spirit. You have said: "Ask and you will receive; seek and you will find; knock and the door will be opened." We ask your blessing for this (these) your servant(s), and knock for his (her/their) admission, that he (she/they) may obtain the promises enacted in this washing, both now and forever. We pray in our Lord's name.

PEOPLE: *Amen.*

The exorcism follows. Where so much has been forgotten, proposals must be very tentative.

MINISTER: Dearly beloved, our life is full of peril: of seduction to moral despair, of political and social oppression, of encompassing violence. We also are told and experience that these powers of Satan especially hate those whom God brings to baptism. Join me, therefore, in prayer for ourselves and for this (these) servant(s) of God.

As the minister performs the exorcism(s) he marks the mouth and breast of the neophyte(s) with the sign of the cross.

MINISTER: In the name of Jesus Christ, I command all destructive and unclean spirits to depart from this servant of God and to keep from him/her all his/her life, making **way** for the Spirit of Holiness.[2] **Let all say "Amen."**

PEOPLE: *Amen.*

Now assistants may bring processional torches and stand with them as the Scriptures are read. The readings may be chosen by those to be baptized or by their parents. Then the torch bearers lead the procession to the baptistry or font.

III

Most urgent, of course, is that we in fact start *baptizing* again. Mere moistening is tolerable only on superstitious and unbiblical assumptions: that some sort of "mana" is transferred by blessed water. Otherwise, baptism's ability to speak, to be a visible word, depends altogether on the function of washing in everyday human life; baptism that is not in fact a washing is just not a possible Christian sacrament. Even after scholasticism had provided a sophisticated version of the superstitious rationale for sprinkling, the practice was so generally perceived as contrary to baptism's essential character that it was resisted for centuries. Thus Martin Luther rejected it precisely because baptism must *mean* what it *is*.[3] And the infusion then in question was still, after all, a fairly generous pouring.

With infants there is little problem. Let them be held undressed— or, for that matter, in diapers and water-proof pants!—in the font, and either dipped or laved, not necessarily over the head. Then they should be towelled—and if desired, they can be anointed with baby oil!

With adults, future practice will probably be most various. What is possible and meaningful depends on the development of culture and on the relationship between culture and the church—and both are going in all directions. There may be corners of the church where the ancient nude bath can be restored tomorrow—for all I know, it may already have been. In others the baptizing minister offends if he spoils a hair-do. Fortunately, there is a principle that can be followed in all situations: whatever change in the direction of actual bathing is possible in a given group will result in a practice which that group will indeed experience as washing, at least for a while.

In many congregations, for example, the following practice could be adopted and would be obedience to baptism's mandate. A woman comes in sleeveless clothes; a man removes his jacket and shirt. The neophyte bends over the font, resting his arms in it. The baptizer then pours water over the neophyte's arms, and with his own hands laves the forehead and face. Then the neophyte laves his own hands, arms, and face. Afterward, the neophyte towels himself.

I propose no use of anointing oil—at least, not with adults. Anointing's capacity for meaning depended, like that of washing, on a function in the whole of life. But anointing's function has mostly ceased; and nothing can be done about that.

IV

The first action at the font, or in the baptistry, is the Epiclesis. The text here suggested is adapted from Martin Luther's famous "flood prayer," taken by Cranmer into the *Book of Common Prayer* and one of the great items of the ecumenical heritage.[4] The baptizer stands by the font in a posture of public prayer. No other gestures are appropriate.

MINISTER: The Lord be with you.

PEOPLE: *And also with you.*

MINISTER: Let us pray to the God who by a flood of water once condemned an unbelieving world,

And in the flood mercifully rescued faithful Noah and his family;

Who drowned hard-hearted Pharaoh in the sea,

Through which he safely led his people Israel;

Thus by many signs prefiguring this bath of holy baptism;

And who by the baptism of our Lord Jesus consecrated and set apart the Jordan and all waters,

To be a saving flood and a cleansing washing.

Merciful God, send now your Spirit;

Let him be the Spirit of this washing,

That NN. may receive the gift of faith,

That the world of Adam's sin may be drowned in him/her/them by this saving flood,

And that secure in the ark of the church, he/she/they may serve you with joy and hope,

And at the last be made worthy of his eternal life.

In whose name we pray.

PEOPLE: *Amen.*

Then the baptizer takes each neophyte by the hand and bids him or her
renounce the religion and polity of the old age, and worship and confess
the true God.   If the neophyte is an infant, a parent speaks.

MINISTER: N., will you be baptized? (or) N., will you have N. be
                    baptized?
NEOPHYTE: *I will.*
MINISTER: Renounce the evil of this age (on N.'s behalf).
NEOPHYTE: *I, N., (on behalf of N.) renounce Satan, and all his cere-*
                    monies and all his oppressions.
MINISTER: Worship the true God (*on N.'s behalf*).
NEOPHYTE: *I believe in God . . .*

If the neophyte is an infant, an assistant holds him in the font.   If an
adult, he enters or bends over the font.   The baptizer washes the neophyte three times, proclaiming Jesus' name as Lord, with the following
formula or some other.

MINISTER: I baptize you in the Lord Jesus' name,
                    And in the name of God his Father,
                    And in the name of their saving Spirit.
PEOPLE: *Amen.*

When the neophyte is dried, he is clothed in a white alb, if the congregation otherwise uses these vestments.   If the baptismal congregation has been in a separate baptistry, it now returns in procession to
the chancel or choir.   The rite of the Spirit follows.

V

Each neophyte kneels or is held before the bishop or other pastor, depending on the rules of the denomination.   The pastor lays his hands
on the neophyte's head, and invokes the Spirit and his gifts.   The
prayer given here follows general Western tradition.   At the indicated
place, the minister signs the neophyte's forehead with the cross.

MINISTER: Almighty and everliving God, who have chosen to give
                    new life to this your servant and to forgive all his/her
                    sin,
                    Send your Holy Spirit upon him/her:
                    The Spirit of wisdom and understanding,
                    Of counsel and strength,

The Spirit of knowledge and true godliness,
And of your holy fear.
Mark him/her (†), O Lord, to be yours forever,
In the power of your cross and resurrection.
Let all say Amen.

PEOPLE: *Amen.*

The neophytes are led to places in the congregation. The Supper then continues, with participation by all. Infant neophytes are communed, if awake, with wine sucked from a parent's finger, and a crumb of bread.

It will have been noted that this proposed rite involves relatively little talking, except such as belongs to the actual baptismal actions where the rhetoric is allowed quite free rein. More than any other sacrament, baptism has recently been buried beneath quantities of extremely disembodied explanation and exhortation, and tenuously relevant prayer. This is partly in sheer compensation for vanished actions, lest the whole performance shrink to an experiential point. It is partly a futile last-minute attempt to make up for missed preparation and testing of the neophytes or parents. And above all, it is an entirely futile attempt verbally to impose meaning on a visible word too attenuated to speak for itself. At least for the foreseeable future, the motto of baptismal orders must be: less talking, more doing.

NOTES

1. *Didache,* II, 2 (my translation).
2. This is a composite of the traditional western exorcistic formulas.
3. See Bruno Jordahn, *Der Taufgottesdienst in Mittelalter bis zur Gegenwart* in K. F. Mueller and Walter Blankenburg, eds., *Leiturgia, Handbuch des evangelischen Gottesdienstes,* Vol. V (Kassel: Johannes Stauda Verlag, 1969), pp. 350ff. and especially 303–395.
4. The idea of using this prayer as an Epiclesis comes from the Inter-Lutheran Commission on Worship (North America). It is most appropriate, since Luther's prayer drew on the motifs of the ancient Epiclesis. I have tried to solve the problem of the second-person ascriptions of traditional prayer by incorporating them into the *Oremus,* a device of possibly wider application.

PART SEVEN

THE CORRELATES OF BAPTISM

17

Penance

I

The practice and theology of *penance* are part of the practice and theology of baptism. Baptism mandates (1) the necessity of community discipline, (2) the necessity of mutual forgiveness, (3) the connection between the community's discipline and forgiveness and those of the Lord Jesus, and (4) the need of believers to seek forgiveness from the church also when not publicly convicted. The various practices which have succeeded one another in the history of the church, for which we use the general label "penance," are all attempts to satisfy these four interrelated mandates; and the grave theological problems which have hexed these practices—problems which indeed make much of Western theological history—arise from the interplay among the same four.

First, baptism mandates community discipline. The baptized community originates in an event which means separation from the old age and its life; the church's very definition could be that it is the company of those who have already repented in face of the last judgment. For this community, such acts as adultery or apostasy or destructive gossip therefore cannot be "human frailty" or "the way things go"; they are sheer anomaly, occurring impossibility, "offenses."[1] Nor can such anomalies be ignored or defined away. Attempts along that line were made very early: devotees of the free Spirit in Corinth and elsewhere said that since they had already been detached from the old life, whatever they did had to be good since they were the ones doing it.[2] All such attempts fail, for baptism establishes the holiness of the community inseparably from its mission to those outside it, and so submits the community's holiness to judgment by publicly definable and applicable standards. When baptized persons so live, as by such standards to disprove baptism's claim about their detachment from the way of the old world, the community must somehow separate itself from them.[3] If it does not, it loses its mission.[4]

But, second, baptism also mandates unlimited mutual forgiveness. For baptism *is* forgiveness and initiates into a community whose bond is the Spirit of love, whose Lord rules his disciples by unlimited acceptance. Even if the community must exclude, it can never say good riddance.[5] The baptized person has an eternal claim on the community, to which it must always respond. The history of penance is mostly the history of the various arrangements which the church has made for this claim and response.

The arrangements have varied because the problems involved in making them are not permanently soluble.[6] Exactly *how* disgraceful must someone's behavior be before it constitutes contradiction of baptism? Do we readmit someone just excluded simply because he turns around and asks? If not, exactly what more should we require? Are there no sins so grave as to exclude permanently? How many times can we repeat readmission before it becomes ridiculous? Clearly, the best that can be done with any of these questions is to find the least objectionable answer for a time and place. So far as the New Testament lets us see, the apostolic church both excluded for cause and readmitted the repentant with no controversy whatever about the need or justification of either act.[7] But the problems just listed arose already: "Lord, how often shall my brother sin against me and I forgive him? Seven times?"[8] Already 1 John 5 distinguishes classes of sins and their consequences for church fellowship.

Third, baptism does not allow us to treat exclusion and readmission as our option only, or as judgments that we make only in our own name. For both are intrusions upon the Lord's baptismal judgment. Exclusion can only be a suspension of or qualification of baptism; and readmission can only be a repetition or restoration of baptism. No more than baptism can either be rightly done as if we were the sole doers. The apostolic church affirmed this straightforwardly.[9]

Finally, the individual believer does not wait for the discipline of the community. The new life into which baptism inducts is, for the community as such, identical with its mission to the world. Just so, the individual believer cannot separate his value for himself from his value for that world to which the church is sent. And whereas the community is concerned with his behavior only insofar as it is an obtrusive factor in the community's relation to the world, for the believer himself the relation of all his life to his fellowmen is visible. From this dialectic arises the particular character of the Christian consciousness of "sin" and "forgiveness," and the need for *communal* mediation of the latter.

The great theological problem of penance should already be plain. Our judgment to exclude from or readmit into our community cannot be neatly separated from the Lord's decisions to admit into or exclude from his fellowship. How exactly are we to understand this? On the one hand the practice of exclusion and readmission is imposed by the structure of the community, and is no different from the sort of thing every living human community must do. Yet on the other hand, the individual's relation to God is implicated.

Precisely what sort of sacramental mandate and promise does penance have? The necessity of some arrangements for and practice of communal excommunication and penance is given with the essential character of baptism; and this relationship was recognized and affirmed by the apostolic church. Such arrangements as the church at a time and place has for this purpose, will be an institutionalized form not merely of the word of the Christians, but of the word of God. This too is given with the essential character of baptism, and was so understood by the apostolic church. We are to say, "Return to the fellowship," or "Be secure in the fellowship," and to speak for God when we do so.

No particular embodiment of this gospel-form is instituted in Scripture—or, for that matter, universally later. Necessarily, the plea of the penitent and the word of reconciliation will always be embodied somehow, and at any time in such a way that the visible action will be experienced as essential. For as a communal act over against an individual, penance will necessarily be ceremonial. And the word to be spoken is to be, almost in the extreme sense of a direct oracle, a word of God. But penance does not have a contingent beginning of its own, in which some one rite would have been instituted, thereafter to be taken or left. Penance arises as the necessary consequence of such a contingently instituted rite, baptism, and therefore has always had the character of a rite created from time to time as needed in a given situation.

Whether the complex of necessities and theological connections just described, and the biblical affirmations of them, make a "sacrament," depends on definition and is of no substantive importance. What is important is to recognize the particular complex that in fact subsists and to think how we may obey its command and understand its promises.

II

Penance is a correlate of baptism. As we cannot understand baptism without knowing something of its history, so with penance. And unsurprisingly, the epochs of baptism's history are also those of penance.[10]

The church's practice of penance becomes historically visible around A.D. 200, because only in the immediately preceding decades had it become an object of the kind of explicit worry that creates historical visibility. The worry was created by reforming protest against that very settling in of the church for a longer haul which also created elaborated orders of baptism.

If the church is to be here for a while, it cannot demand quite the spiritual breathlessness that might be appropriate to a year or two before the end comes. Prophecy and glossolalia will not seem the most necessary leadership gifts; Paul's advice not to marry so as to travel light will not seem so urgent; church discipline will take more account of the difficulties of life in the meantime. As these changes of atmosphere occurred, precisely the most fervent protested, and in their protest made more of prophecy, asceticism, and rigid discipline than the church had before. In the years before A.D. 200, the most radical protest was a movement—Montanism—first led by prophets from that very part of the church where baptism was not an ordered initiation but a sudden prophetic anointing. Montanists and other rigorists pressed for enforcement of a sort of eschatological purity by free use of expulsion and drastically restricted readmission, both under the control of charismatics. Those feeling their way toward creation of the ancient catholic church expelled less quickly, readmitted more freely, and regarded both as the prerogative of the congregational clergy. Out of the conflict, a reasonably consistent practice emerged, at least in the West.

The bishop was the judge of what sins were occasions of excommunication. Probably, at this period, those expelled for apostasy, murder, adultery, or fornication were never readmitted.[11] Others were admitted to do penance at the judgment of the bishop. They were required—or rather permitted—to provide evidence of their renewed charity and to confess their sins to the congregation, dressed in the garments of mourning. The congregation joined in prayer for God's mercy. The actual readmission was accomplished by the imposition of hands, with prayer to God for forgiveness. The process could not be repeated.

The severe persecutions around the middle of the third century created masses of apostates, many of whom wished to return when the pressure eased. In the ensuing controversy, ancient penance took its classical form. Apostasy also could now be forgiven, and with it the other "deadly" sins; indeed those now became the chief occasion of regulated penance. Expelled or self-confessed grave sinners applied for "admission to penitence." The explicit confession took place then. Penance of from a few days to a lifetime was imposed, following widely-accepted rules, but also according to the bishop's judgment of the case. Penance consisted in attendance at services without full participation, fasting and other ascetic disciplines, including sexual abstinence, and regular prayer for forgiveness with imposition of hands. Except for excommunication, the penitent was to live after the pattern of an ascetic. Readmission occurred as before.

This entire institution perfectly matched baptism as practiced, and in that correlation made eminent sense. The period of penance was a correlate of the catechumenate: its increased severity and its signs of mourning marked the new beginning in experienced failure. Visibly, the community said to the applicant: "Last time we took your commitment partly on your word and it proved faulty; now we need additional evidence." Reconciliation was effected by a correlate of baptism, also in its ceremonial form. Penitence could not be repeated; for repetition of *this* process would make fools of the community and its Lord.

The identity and difference between the church's judgments and the Lord's were very delicately reckoned with. The one readmitted to the church was readmitted by a sacramental act performed upon him, the content of which was the forgiveness of God. Yet the audible word of readmission was not a declaration to the penitent, but a prayer for this forgiveness. So also those permanently excluded were not thereby excluded from God's mercy or the love of the congregation. The congregation prayed for them to death and beyond, and had also for them the missionary word of the gospel. But they could not again belong to the missionary congregation itself.

III

Ancient penance was overwhelmed by the same flood of nominal converts that overwhelmed ancient baptism. Faced with whole congregations of "deadly" sinners, the bishops moved in two directions. On the one hand, they attempted to combat the demoralization of the communities by increasingly severe penitential regulations: penances of from ten years to life were assigned for long lists of crimes. But on the other hand, excommunication practically dropped out of use; by A.D. 600 it was only a churchly weapon for great public cases, and remained so through the Middle Ages. Once discipline at admission is impossible, it is merely tyrannical to try to restore it by severity later; when the congregation is the mission field, nothing is accomplished for the mission by expelling people. Thus penance became mostly a voluntary undertaking by persons who had *not* been excommunicated, but knew— of their own accord or on advice of their pastors—that they *should have been,* and that their relation to God was implicated in this misrelation to the church.

Finally, the increasing severity of the renunciations demanded by penance, and its unrepeatability, drove voluntary penitents to undertake the actual labor only at the end of life. The penance established by the rules of the ancient church became heroic preparation for death by the very pious or very wicked. Therewith it became a sacrament detached from the church's public discipline and directed to the individual believer's need, but one unavailable when most needed. And the normal life of the congregation was left with no penitential system at all.

The vacuum could not remain. For the moral standard of the faith continued to be taught and preached as those of the community gathered at the Supper. Therewith the burdened conscience of the one who is at the Supper but knows he is not rightfully there—and that it is God's Supper—was left without aid. In the early Middle Ages, a whole variety of practices were sucked into the vacuum. One triumphed: "private" penance.

The isolated church of Ireland had met the crisis of ancient penance in a way very different from the ecumenical norm. The Irish church was centered in great monasteries, and its practices were influenced by the intense pastoral care possible in monasteries. Regular confession of sins—of whatever gravity—was urged on all believers, this to be made privately to a pastor.   Periods of penance were imposed that did not involve unworkable excommunications, and which might or might not involve any public manifestation.   The whole affair could be repeated as often as necessary.   In the eighth and ninth centuries, Irish missionaries were the spiritual leaders of the European churches, and they brought their penitential practice with them.   It was the very thing wanted.

Penance on the Irish pattern was soon generally regarded as the necessary preparation for the Supper, so as not to come in a state worthy of excommunication and so unworthy of the Supper.   All sins were confessed, and each had its penalty.   Since the period of penance involved no actual excommunication, it was soon perceived that there was no need to wait until its conclusion to perform the renewal of fellowship and assurance of divine forgiveness.   By the eleventh century, the order was established: admission to penance by confession and imposition of works of penance/ reconciliation on the same day/ works of penance.

The reconciliation had meant the forgiveness of the community and just therewith the forgiveness of God, with the relation of the two carefully but not narrowly specified by the rite.   In the reconciliation's new location, it no longer had a practical function for church fellowship; its original primary meaning therefore fell into abeyance.   The reconciliation thus became purely a rite of God's forgiveness and since its visible form as a sacramental act performed upon the penitent remained, it became something the church had not before practiced, a direct sacramental mediation of the mercy of God simply as such, an "absolution."

This new sacrament of the forgiveness of sin was the experientially dominating sacrament of medieval Christendom.   And in it the theological problems of penance's whole history became inescapable.   This was a rite whose direct content was man's confession and God's mercy— to the occurrence of which the satisfaction of churchly conditions was made integral.   It is one thing to require proofs of sincerity from lapsed believers seeking to return to the congregation—under circumstances, this may be the only reasonable procedure.   It is quite another regularly to subject practicing believers to a rite by which the forgiveness of God is to be granted, admission to which is conditional upon undertaking of stipulated good works.

Medieval theologians saw the problem and expended enormous ingenuity on distinctions designed to mitigate it. But the problem was not to be overcome without attacking the rite itself. Instead, penance overcame the theologians, and became the fixed occasion of medieval theology's pervasive works-righteousness—which was sometimes marvelously subtle and sometimes marvelously gross, but was always dominant in actual instruction to believers. It was above all the medieval theology of penance that compelled the Reformation.

IV

In the "95 Theses," Martin Luther wrote, "When our Lord said, 'repent,' he meant the whole life of the Christian to be repentance." Therewith Luther finally said what the whole history of penance demanded to be said. The problem of penance is: if baptism is a break with the old age, how are we to understand what happens in the meantime before the new age comes? Luther's answer is the only one possible, even if it took the church nearly fifteen centuries to come to it: life between the ages has the before-and-after of baptism, the departure from old life and the advent of new, as its *structure*. The return to baptism is not a particular act we do sometimes, when we are aware of "sins" or are in trouble with the church community; it is what happens for believers in every action of life.

That which penance does for the believer in good standing is thus identified as entirely independent of churchly *discipline,* though not of churchly *mediation.* Penance had attempted to satisfy two needs at once: the need of believers to live always by the forgiveness of God and their fellow believers, and the need of the believing community to maintain its missionary authenticity. So long as the whole church was a practicing missionary society, the ambiguity was not fatal, though it had been a problem since the third century. But in the Middle Ages the church ceased to be a missionary society.

To overcome the confusions, Reformation church orders continued private confession, *without* imposition of works of churchly satisfaction. Thereby they created a pure sacramental enactment of the individual's sin and God's unconditional forgiveness: simply a preaching of the gospel, but directly to the person's individual need as he himself defines it in the confession. It would indeed be reasonable that the penitent "prove" something about his sincerity also in this case; but the gospel is not here reasonable. This sacrament of forgiveness is, like all previous form of penance, a community act, but the community does not appear as a wronged party, only as the mediator of forgiveness.

Our sin is always, of course, against community, but the wronged community is not the church, but humanity, for whom only God is advocate. The church is an offended party only when my sin destroys its unity or cripples its mission—which has nothing to do with abstract grades of "seriousness." Then the church must indeed decide what to do with me, and it may very well decide it must expel me. If I seek readmission, it may have to demand evidence. And in both judgments, God's baptismal judgment is implicated, but only insofar as he seeks me for his missionary, not insofar as he seeks me as his child—that the two can be thus distinguished is precisely the anomaly of sin after baptism. The church is the kingdom's missionary presence in the world, but the last judgment is nevertheless free over against the church's judgment.

The church needs *two* sacraments of penance. It needs the kind of individual unconditional application of the gospel in the lives of faithful Christians, which the Reformation's confession and absolution provided. And it needs a rite of excommunication and reconciliation. As to the form of the latter, the only thing the matter with the rite of the ancient church was the lack of an accompanying rite of the first type.

V

The immediately preceding discussion must, of course, seem curiously empty, neither such sacrament being now much practiced. Another long stretch of history has intervened since the Reformation. During that time, the Roman Catholic church defended itself against Protestantism by becoming a walled-in enclave of the medieval order, with medieval penance as the chief bulwark. Those walls are now falling; no one knows what will come of it. In Protestantism, various individualistic influences gradually destroyed the Reformation's sacrament of confession and unconditional absolution; also this story would be instructive, but I must stop some place. And the Protestant bodies' frequent attempts to create an evangelical discipline of excommunication and reconciliation have always been defeated by the same relation to society whose early stages undid ancient penance. The present outcome is that there is little actual practice to which the affirmations of the preceding paragraphs could apply.

It is impossible that, if the world and the church continue, this situation should also. In that the church now lacks effective missionary discipline, we are in clear contradiction to the mandate of baptism. But reforms would be artificial until baptism is itself reformed. As Western civilization and Christianity find their way to a new relation—one may hope of mutual aid and respect—we may labor for new disciplines of admission and of missionary authenticity that will respond to the church's hard-won insight into its own calling.

In that Protestant bodies lack a rite of individual absolution, the burden has fallen on "pastoral counseling." In itself, the pastoral counseling movement offers great promise; in the one-to-one speaking of the gospel, the more knowledge of human behavior, the better. So far, however, most pastoral counseling has been guided much more by the therapeutic goals of the helping professions and so by social definitions of "illness" or "need," than by believers' need of the gospel or by a biblical understanding of sin. So long as this continues, much excellent counseling will continue to be done, but it will also continue to be very little "pastoral." Indeed, insofar as such counseling replaces absolution in believers' experience, it is destructive of faith. What we must hope for is creation of a genuine rite of confession and absolution, informed by and making place for the exercize of the high psychological expertise now available to the church.

In the meantime, stop-gap measures are needed. Those currently most often practiced are less helpful than they could be. In most Protestant orders, the chief device is a general confession of sinfulness and correspondingly general assurance of forgiveness, located somewhere in the Synaxis before the Supper. This is made to carry the burden of the missing private penance, and is generally understood by worshipers as "preparation" for the Supper. The arrangement usually fails.

In these rites, the confession of sin must be so generally stated as to fit anybody at all; and so it can fit nobody very well. Repeated confession that one is by general principle a sinner can only have the effect of transforming the proposition into a platitude, and confession into a formality—unless, of course, this *theologoumenon* is uttered in a context where moral struggle is otherwise communally and pastorally maintained, as it was in the centuries from which we have inherited such fine general confessions as that of the *Book of Common Prayer*. Few congregations now provide such a context.

The ministerial response to a general confession of sin is an even greater problem. Is the minister to absolve the entire crowd? Most liturgical committees, envisaging themselves in the situation, have lost their nerve, and provided either a conditional absolution or a dogmatic discourse on the general availability of grace. The formulas of my own denomination provide a choice of these disasters: "Almighty God, our heavenly Father . . . forgiveth us all our sins . . ." or "The Almighty and merciful God grant unto you, being penitent . . ." In the one case, believers hear *about* forgiveness without ever receiving any; in the other case forgiveness is not only made conditional on an achievement by the penitent, but on an achievement, "being penitent" or "truly believing," which is never certainly present. Repeated experience of such addresses can only cultivate works-righteousness, and of a particularly desperate or trivial sort.

Pending the historic changes which might enable new institutions of authentic penance, the best stop-gap provisions would be of three sorts. First, there is undoubtedly need for acknowledgment that we come to the Supper not in our own worthiness, but by the mercy of God. This can perhaps best be done by a prayer at the Offertory, on the order of the Anglican "Prayer of Humble Access." Such a prayer was suggested in Chapter 8. There should *not* be an absolution or pseudo-absolution.

Second, there should be provisions for congregational confession and absolution that are at least a little closer to life than "general" confessions can be. Most practical, perhaps, would be special congregational services of confession and absolution, held from time to time but especially at the beginning of Advent and during Lent. Confessions of sin should be written for each such occasion, confessing the recent failures of the congregation as a community—indeed, the confession might very well be composed on the spot, drawing from an open discussion by those present. If such a confession is of the community's real transgressions, and not merely of a theoretical average of individual transgressions, a genuine and unconditional absolution can responsibly follow: "By the authority of God and of my holy office, I declare to you the forgiveness of your sin, in the name . . ." Those who think they must say less, should say nothing.

Third, where medieval private penance is still viable, it might— whether by rulings of denominational judicatories or by accomodation of confessors—be bent in the direction of an authentic rite of individual turning to the gospel and unconditional speaking of the gospel. The Reformation once attempted this, but was defeated by the growing atomization of modern life. Perhaps Roman Catholics or "catholic" Anglicans might now be more successful.

The sacraments of penance are in abeyance. They will not forever remain so. In the meantime, we must make do as best we can. And when history makes new penitential arrangements possible we must be ready not to retrace the dead-ended paths of the past.

NOTES

1. Rom. 6, etc.! 1 John 1:6–7; Matt. 18:6ff.
2. 1 Cor. 6:9–20; 1 John 1:8.
3. Matt. 18:15–18; 1 Cor. 6:9–11, 5:6, 9–11; Gal. 5:9; 2 John 11.
4. If the Bornkamm-von Campenhausen exegesis of 1 Cor. 5:1–5 is correct, the passage is a remarkable statement to this point. The notorious adulterer must be removed from the fellowship to save the *congregation's* "spirit." See Hans von Campenhausen, *Ecclesiastical Authority and Spiritual Power*, trans. J. A. Baker (Stanford: Stanford University Press, 1969), pp. 134–35.
5. Matt. 18:21–22; Luke 17:3–4; 2 Thess. 3:6–16; Gal. 6:1.
6. von Campenhausen, op. cit., p. 136: "These two seemingly opposite tendencies . . . are in fact complementary. Both in their stringency and in their tolerance they reflect the needs of one and the same community, which has to defend its purity and solidarity against attack from without, and to preserve peace and quietness within."
7. 1 Cor. 5:1–5; 2 Cor. 2:5–11; Gal. 5:19ff., 6:1ff.
8. Matt. 18:21f. See the whole section, 18:10–35.
9. Matt. 16:9, 18:18; John 20:23.
10. On this history, see the writings of Bernhard Poschmann, most compendiously the section on "Busse and Letzte Ölung" in Schmaus, Geiselmann, and Rahner, eds., *Handbuch der Dogmengeschichte*, Vol. IV, (Freiburg: Herder, 1956), pp. 10–123. See also the essay by Peter Meinhold in *Die Religion in Geschichte und Gegenwart*[3], Vol. I, cols. 1545–54.
11. But see Poschmann, op. cit., passim.

18

Ordination

I

As baptism is initiation into the believing community, ordination is initation into a community within the believing community. As it is the historical reality of the church which we must above all understand to understand baptism, it is the historical reality of "the ministry" which we must above all understand to understand ordination.

It cannot be said that any particular rite is instituted for ordination with final scriptural authority. But the ministry itself, as a group into which persons must indeed somehow be initiated, belongs to the church's essential nature and is explicitly so regarded in Scripture; and some appropriate rite or other will necessarily achieve the initiation. Through the church's history since the middle of the second century, one rite has in fact been used, from beginnings in the New Testament church: laying on of hands by predecessors in the ministry with invocation of the Spirit. Appropriately, the rite reproduces the "confirmation" part of baptism, with different petitions. And like baptism, the rite is simple and undifferentiated; its specific meaning depends on the nature of the ministry as a communal structure of the gospel-community, which is then what I have in the first place to discuss.

The church is not and cannot be an essentially undifferentiated collection of equivalent individuals, who then may or may not choose so to organize themselves as to create offices with various authorities. The church is from its origin and nature a community structured by the existence of internal communities related to each other by varying functions and authority. In particular, without the internal community of the ministry, possessed of its defining authority, there is no church. The church is of this nature, because *both* the church and the ministry were instituted by the *same* event, the call of the apostles.[1]

The apostles[2] were those whose proclamation of the gospel was the creation of the gospel—whoever and however many they were. If the gospel is "Jesus is risen," its first proclaimers must have been witnesses of the resurrection, persons who could testify at first hand to his aliveness—whether their testimony was then believed or rejected. And if the gospel is the word of God, its first proclaimers must have been called and sent by God to speak for him: they must have been *prophets*. That is precisely what the New Testament, especially the Letters of Paul, documents: a limited group of those to whom the risen Jesus had appeared, for whom Jesus' appearance had been a call to go and proclaim the "gospel" of his resurrection, and whose self-understanding was modelled on the prophets of Israel. In the fluid language of the earliest church, other authorized messengers of the gospel, otherwise called "evangelists," were sometimes also called "apostles": missionaries of missionizing congregations like that at Antioch and charismatics called by prophets.[3] But *"the* apostles" were the authorized witness-messengers of the resurrection itself.[4]

On the one hand, the apostles performed a complex of functions in the church which would have arisen simply from the needs of the community, following laws that apply to all communities, and which would have had to be arranged for somehow. That is, the apostles filled an *office*. The believing community lives by the word of Christ, by the gospel of his resurrection, and by the encouragement to new life which the entire discourse of the community variously unfolds. Such a community must have within it an authoritative interpretation of its word; in the later phrase, there must be a "teaching office." Since the church is to be eschatologically lively, its teaching office cannot be filled by a mere "deposit" of doctrine, but must be filled by living persons. In the original church, the apostles were those persons.

Any community, even a community of the eschatological gospel, will have difficult and sometimes disputed choices to make precisely about the nature and obligations of the community. Some recognized way of making such choices thus belongs to the necessary structure of every actual community. In an eschatologically lively community, this authority will be personal; and in the community of the gospel, it will be legitimately exercized by persons given to "the service of the word."[5] In the original church, such authority was exercized by persons in a variety of forms of service, but final such authority belonged wholly to the apostles.

But on the other hand, though the apostles filled a communally inevitable and needed office, the communities had not created the office nor installed the apostles in it. It was precisely a necessary character of an apostle, that his service and authority were not derived from human initiative nor granted him by human designation.[6] On the contrary the apostles were there before the church was; their service and authority were precisely to create the church. Or, if anyone prefers, at the very first the apostles *were* the whole church. "The gospel" was and is simply a label for that message which these men in contingent fact spoke, following a certain event in their lives; and the church is the community of those brought together by the speaking and hearing of this gospel.

Thus the notion of a state of nature when everyone had the same service and authority does not at all apply to the church, not even as myth or as a purely theoretical model. The church's internal differentiation of service and authority was never created by a general decision to organize and delegate. The ministerial differentiation of the church and the church's own existence are precisely coeval and mutually dependent. Insofar as some Protestants have supposed that the church is originally an undifferentiated mass, whose communal structure is created by social contract of the members, this is an error with no biblical justification whatever.

II

The apostolate was not only the church's initiating office; it was also the church's only fully appropriate office. When the church lasted more than one generation, it was permanently bereft of the one leadership that could wholly fit its essential structure; since then, arrangement for the ministry has been an historic task at once necessary and not enduringly solvable.

The church is the community of a word that is simultaneously the narrative of a past event and eschatological promise to its hearers at any time. The servants of this word have thus both to speak with the utter freedom of the last future, the freedom that is the Spirit, and faithfully to cultivate the tradition of what happened in the past with Jesus. A ministry fully appropriate to the church would be at once a "charismatic" ministry of self-authenticating proclaimers and an established institution of historical continuity; and it would be each by virtue of being the other.

The audible and visible speaking of the gospel is the coming of the *Spirit* in that the gospel's promise is of the last future which can fulfill all possible prior events, which is subject to no conditions. It is the *unconditionality* of the gospel that is the Spirit's coming. Just so, when the New Testament describes services and authorities in the church as "charisms," as gifts and organs of the *Spirit,* it is the unargued immediacy of their claim that is in view.[7] A "prophet" does not *argue* for what the risen Christ's will must be for a specific decision the church must make, e.g., about how many times to forgive backsliding members; he simply cries, "Thus says the Lord . . ." And when Paul can list business management and sick calling as charisms, the point is the same. The "charismatic" business manager has not argued his qualification and plans and been appointed on this justification; he has simply started to do the work.

The prophet's oracle, or any other offered service, may of course be wrong, and it is the responsibility of the whole Spirit-filled congregation to judge. But acceptance or rejection is of the claim to prophecy, not of the evidence or reason behind a particular oracle; either the prophet is a false prophet or his speech for the Lord is unarguable. The apostolic church accepted that some charisms involved preternatural phenomena: ecstasy, glossolalia, etc. But the presence of such phenomena was not regarded as essential to any charism but itself, and did not constitute *evidence* of the Spirit's coming; for the devil's coming could equally well produce them.[8] The prophet says his word; the congregation gives or withholds the "Amen"; and that is all there is to it. Just this immediacy is the mark of the eschatological freedom that is the Spirit.[9] And so analogously for each charism. The only standard of the spirits is the remembrance of the Crucified[10]—which brings us to the other side of the church's ministry.

The speaking of the gospel remains authentic—to be the coming of *God*'s Spirit and not another's—only by faithfully remaining the news that *Jesus of Nazareth* in particular is risen. Every community that is to perdure through some palpable extent of time must maintain its self-identity through that time by fidelity to whatever it was by which the community once identified itself. The "institutions" of communities are simply those arrangements—whatever they may be—which they make for this purpose. The believing community identifies itself by the *One in whom* it believes. He is identifiable for the community as an object of historical recollection. Therefore all the institutions of the believing community are for the cultivation and purification of the tradition about him; and, vice versa, the church must in fact have institutions, for that very purpose. Most especially, the church must have an instituted ministry to be the cadre of those charged to "minister to" the historical continuity of the gospel-tradition, to labor at the proclamation's fidelity to its recollectable content.

With the apostles, these two assignments perfectly coincided. On the one side, the immediacy of their proclamation could not be transcended. Whatever they preached was the gospel, just because they preached it. On the other side, the apostles were the church's sole guarantee and possibility of fidelity to the object of its faith. So long as the apostles lived, all question of the proclamation's fidelity could and had to be finally answered in only one way: "Ask an apostle." The apostles were the ultimate charismatics and the ultimate communal institution. And they were each precisely by virtue of the other. Their immediacy as organs of the Spirit could not be challenged just because of their immediacy to the beginning of the proclamation. Vice versa, their function as guarantors of the tradition's historical continuity was enabled by their being themselves the originators of the tradition, i.e., by the great act of the Spirit, the original pentecostal bursting-out of the cry that "He is risen."

Manifestly, the apostolic ministry could not be perpetuated beyond the death of the last apostles. When the church lasted to a second generation, the two necessary sides of its ministry could no longer coincide: charismatic freedom and institutional continuity became and remain rival determinants. Charismatic freedom could no longer be the freedom of persons whose fidelity to the gospel's origin could by very definition not fail; and historical continuity could no longer be the task of persons in whom this continuity was the very work of the Spirit. Provision of an appropriate ministry became and must remain a continuing struggle—until he comes. *Ordination is the sacrament of this struggle.*

III

In the apostolic church, a great and probably only partly recorded variety of ministries functioned under the ministry of the apostles. In the later church, these then became the material of the historical struggle for an appropriate post-apostolic ministry. Insofar as the New Testament tells us about them, we find three very different types of designation. Some ministers are designated by the charism that possesses them, some by their official position of authority in the congregations, and some by the function they perform.

It seems clear that the apostolic church knew two great groups of ministers designated by their charisms: after apostles, there were "second prophets, third teachers."[11] These seem to have been found in all branches of the church.[12] In Paul's congregations and perhaps in other congregations stemming from the mission of such centers as Antioch, they were the whole proper ministry. Indeed in Paul's congregations, the entire structure was charismatic,[13] and Paul's long lists of charisms provide at least one for each member; but only apostles, prophets, and teachers were specific groups of ministerial persons.[14]

The specific forms and contexts of *prophets*'[15] ministry are not easily made out. But enough for our purposes can probably be said. Prophets were those able by immediate authority to speak the word of the risen Lord. Their appearance in the congregations was regarded as a renewal and extension of Old Testament prophecy, in fulfillment of Old Testament hopes for the last days.[16] They were proclaimers of the coming kingdom of the risen Lord Christ and spokesmen of his will for the meantime. Thus they were chief preachers in the gatherings, who were not to be squelched. They seem also to have been leaders in prayer, especially in Thanksgiving at the Supper, for also prayer is the word of God.[17]

Teachers[18] were exegetes of the Old Testament, and perhaps cultivators of the tradition about Jesus. Since their exegesis of the Old Testament was eschatological, its results were themselves prophecy, and exegesis thus a charism. We know little of the circumstances of the work of these Christian rabbis; but it will not have differed greatly from those of their Jewish antecedents and colleagues.

We come next to a group who derived their position quite differently; where *Elders*[19] appeared, the structure of the congregations differed greatly from that of Paul's congregations. "Elders," or in Greek, "presbyters," are simply the acknowledged experienced persons of a community. Leadership of a community by a panel of such persons is a standard practice of the human race, and was early adopted also by some Christian congregations. A regular group of presbyters first appears in Luke, at Jerusalem, and a Jewish-Christian origin of the institution is indeed possible.[20] In congregations with a board of presbyters, some might belong by virtue of their charisms—e.g., prophets or teachers, others by virtue of appointment to perform certain standard functions—e.g., somewhat later, "bishops" or "deacons" as below, and others simply by virtue of year-proven experience or good judgment.

The position of elder is thus not defined by charism or function; it is defined precisely as a *position,* to be filled on bases otherwise defined. That is, it is a proper office, an institution, a continuing place of honor and authority subsisting independently of those who follow each other in it. Presbyterial organization may well seem less appropriate to the free gospel's communities than the purely Spirit-created Pauline structure. Yet it rapidly triumphed in the immediately subapostolic church, by the time of the Pastoral Epistles being regarded as standard also in Paul's old congregations. The reason is obvious. The charismatic structure provided for historical continuity only by the apostolate; when a congregation survived its apostles, it had to reorganize. Since the presbyterial office was defined exactly by experience, it was well-adapted to bolster that continuity with the beginning which the absence of the apostles most immediately threatened.[21]

Finally, there were *functions* that defined identifiable ministries. Two stand out: "oversight"—in Greek *episcope,* and "service"—in Greek *diaconia.*[22] In Paul's congregations we find specific persons whose charisms are to "take care of" and "work for" their fellows,[23] and these activities are on both his lists of principal charisms.[24] These persons then appear explicitly in Philippi as outstanding, designated persons, the congregation's "bishops" and "deacons."[25] There may also have been such functions elsewhere on a non-charismatic basis.[26] In any case, as the presbyterial order comes to be generally established, we find bishops and perhaps deacons as presbyters holding particular functions, those of oversight and service.[27]

The origin of the titles "bishop" and "deacon," and the original functions of their bearers are obscure; but it is hard not to think of a connection with "overseeing" and "serving" the primal communal meals[28] which, since they included the Supper, were at once the church's chief institution of economic sharing and, as it developed, its chief liturgy. It was probably over rules of purity at these meals that the Hellenistic-Jewish Christians first became a separate group from the Jerusalem congregation under James and strictly Jewish Christianity generally.[29] To affect independence, it will have been precisely new table overseers and servants who had to be appointed for the Hellenists; and these will then have been the initial ministers of the new congregations. The account in Acts 6 is most easily explained as the reflection of such a development.[30] And such an origin of the bishops and deacons would also explain their later dominance, which was in fact based on control of the congregations' economic community and liturgy.

Manifestly, these three types of ministry exemplify separated aspects of appropriate Christian ministry, held together by subordination to the apostles in whom all aspects were one. When there were no longer apostles, a struggle began to create again a system of ministry which could provide at once institutional continuity with the beginning and spirited freedom of eschatological proclamation, and would be functionally differentiated. Various solutions no doubt briefly appeared, most no longer describable.[31]

A relatively stable solution established itself through the second century. In each larger central congregation there came to be one "monarchical" bishop-presbyter,[32] whose position and work were those of what we would now call the pastor. Under him were a number of assistants for liturgical and economic matters, the deacons;[33] bishop and deacons made the functionally differentiated, "professional" clergy. Around the bishop were the other presbyters, a college of instituted preachers, sacramental leaders and spiritual authorities. By A.D. 200, most disciplinary and sacramental functions were regularly performed by these instituted congregational ministries, but the appearance of prophets was reckoned with and in fact continued[34]—indeed, it has never ceased.

It would be too much to call the three-fold, episcopally-centered, occasionally charismatically open ministerium of the ancient church "classical." Yet in fact later orderings of the ministry have resulted mostly from its fragmentation and from hypertrophy of one or another fragment; nor can, in my view, any be regarded as an improvement, even for the needs of its own day.

Despite catholic claims for the three-fold order, it manifestly is not mandated by Scripture, and even by the most tenuous continuities does not go back to the beginning of the church. So far as I can see, however, it satisfied the demands on Christian ministry considerably better than the system which has replaced it: the system of local congregations each with its presbyterial minister, and of various semi-detached chaplancies and bureaucratically organized services. This system holds also among Roman Catholics, Anglicans, and episcopalian Lutherans, who maintain the three-fold ministry in theory; for the bishop is distant and precisely not a regular pastor in the congregations' lives, and deacons are either a fiction or substitutes for "real,"- presbyterial ministers.

The instituted community of ministry can provide and manifest the unity of office, charism, and function only by an internal differentiation such that different sorts of ministers represent different poles while together making one ministry. In the three-fold ministry, the episcopacy was defined both by office and function, the diaconate by a functional relation to the episcopate, and the presbyterate by office without function. The bishop and deacons made the "professional leadership" of the congregations, but were surrounded by a college of those without such clearly delimited function but with equal spiritual authority.

Precisely this anti-monolithic structure of the instituted ministry left it open for interruption by self-authenticating messengers of the Spirit. Whenever any one kind of minister has become dominant, as when bishops came utterly to rule in the ancient church or as in modern pastor churches, the inevitable tendency has been for the ministry to close against charismatic intrusion. Yet interrupting too secure continuities of the instituted ministry is finally something only the Spirit himself can guarantee, and through history the Spirit has done his work; such events as the Reformation should be understood also in this connection. That the openness of the ministry must occur as occasional historical discontinuities rather than as assured integration of charisms, is but another feature of the post-apostolic burden.

Every ordering of the ministry is an attempted simultaneous satisfaction of the several polar demands upon Christian ministry. After praising the ancient order, I must say that it too was only a partial success, and that our present goal should not be to repristinate it, but to improve on it. Indeed, the problem of Christian ministry can never, after the apostles, be more than partially solved by the structure of the ministry itself. It is precisely the *deficit,* which the rite of ordination seeks to make up.

IV

A rite of ordination appears in the New Testament church only for the presbyterially structured sort of ministry. From 1 Timothy 4:14[35] we learn that a bishop-presbyter was chosen by the word of a prophet and given his position by the laying on of the presbyterate's hands.[36] That there was also prayer is likely, both intrinsically and from Acts.[37] The visible word itself, the touch of hand to head, is the typical act of communal empowerment: it is acceptance of a believer into the internal sub-community of the presbyterate and granting of this community's rights and duties. But that a particular person is chosen is an act of the Spirit; and, more important, *what* is granted is precisely a charism. The rite is an achieving of institutional continuity, but the identity of the institution lies in a particular activity of the utterly free Spirit.

What cannot after the apostles be fully united in the structure or practice of the ministry is united in this sub-apostolic rite of initiation *into* ministry. The rite which originated in the presbyterial congregations of the New Testament church, is precisely the visible word ministers need to have heard, as all believers need to have heard the word of baptism. It was thus adopted for the whole ministry as soon as there was such a thing; and its main features have maintained themselves through all the ministry's subsequent vicissitudes.

As soon as the three-fold ministry was established there was ordination for all of its parts. The earliest preserved texts and rubrics are again in Hippolytus.[38] The three services are essentially alike, with varying biblical typology; that for presbyters follows.

When a presbyter is ordained, let the bishop put a hand on his head and let the presbyters also touch him, and let the bishop pray . . . saying: God and Father of our Lord Jesus Christ, regard this your servant and grant him the Spirit of such grace and wise judgment as belongs to presbyters, that he may uphold and govern your people with a pure heart—even as you regarded your chosen people and commanded Moses to choose elders whom you filled with the same Spirit you had given to him.

Texts for the prayer have been written and forgotten in profusion;[39] and around the simple heart of ordination elaborate unfoldings and disastrous perversions have come and gone. An account could be written of ordination's response to and shaping of the ministry's self-conception, as of baptism and the church's self-conception. But the elaborations of ordination do not seem quite so much to have been unfoldings of the act's inner determinants, and the perversions accordingly not to have penetrated so deeply. I may therefore perhaps be justified if I plead lack of time and space and do not rehearse the history.

In the Western church, certain ritual elements have been more or less constant. Ordination is celebrated during the Synaxis of the Supper. There have been two main prayers for the gift of the Spirit to the ordinands: one of the people, in the form of a litany with concluding collect, and the other of the ordaining minister, always on the general lines of the prayer in Hippolytus. With large numbers of candidates, the minister's prayer came to be said once for all, and the imposition of hands therefore to be done in silence; then later again, the silence was filled with briefer declaratory formulas: "Receive the Holy Spirit, for the office . . ." These variations make no great theological difference; but in general it would be desirable to maintain the original practice of prayer *with* the imposition of hands. Later additions were the vesting of the newly ordained in the vestments of their offices, anointing, and the delivery to them of symbolic instruments of their function, e.g., chalices and patens to new presbyters. In all post-Reformation branches of the Western church, practice has chosen from these elements;[40] and there is now generally a tendency to reclaim all but anointing, in one arrangement or another. It should be clear, however, that the visible word for which a truly weighty institution can indeed be claimed, is the simple act of prayer with imposition of hands, done by some acknowledged organ of the ministerium itself.

V

Ordination is installation into an institutionalized office—by a rite which bestows a charism. It is incorporation into the presbyterate—by bestowal of the Spirit of prophecy and inspired exegesis. Just this implausible combination is its essence.

We must be careful not to mislocate the miracle. We have seen

that a charism of the Spirit is a particular freedom in and for the believing community, a particular justification of unconditional action for
God within and over against the church. The community of faith,
whose freedom is the Spirit, can bestow any charism it chooses—just
as it can initiate into the Spirit by baptism.

If, of course, a charism were either the manifestation of ecstasy
which may appear to others or the experience of inspiration which the
person may have, the community could not bestow it—though it might
induce it. But also in the New Testament it is well understood that
these phenomena can as well be produced by a demon as by the Spirit.[41]
The charism *itself* is the justification of otherwise unjustified service
and authority, the foundation of otherwise unfounded appearance on
God's behalf. The charism itself is the sheer fact that, as it by God's
choice happens, some person who claims to speak or act for God really
does. The charism itself we can bestow. The question is not whether
we *can* bestow the charisms of the Spirit, but whether, since they are
the charisms of the *Spirit,* we *may.* The matter is exactly the same as
with baptism: by what *right* do we ordain persons to speak for the
gospel over against their fellows, i.e., to speak immediately for God?

We dare to baptize because we are commanded by Scripture and
trust Scripture's Lord to make it right. There is no such direct command to ordain. What there is, is the sheer necessity to ordain, if the
church is to continue beyond the apostolic generation, and canoniza-
tion of documents that show the immediately post-apostolic church
acknowledging the necessity by measures that include the beginnings
of ordination. But since the formation of the canon was itself part of
this undertaking by the post-apostolic church, the situation is circular.
Finally, ordination is simply a venture on baptism.

The baptized are to carry on with the church's mission until the Lord
comes. The departure of the apostles before his return may mean that
he is not coming and our hope is vain, that baptism is empty. If not,
then it is in obedience to the mandate laid on us by baptism that we
carry on with a would-be apostolic ministry, that we induct persons
into a continuing inner ministerial community by a rite that claims tc
give a charism. And the promise to our action is baptism's promise
that the differentiated life of our community is the very life of Spirit.
If indeed the church ought not have ended with the apostolic generation, then ordination is rightly instituted. And if rightly instituted, then

it is indeed the coming of the Spirit. When the church's ministers induct a new minister, they do so with prayer that the Spirit will take her or him into a specific part of the Spirit's freedom in the church. If baptism is true, that prayer cannot fail. I must now say what this charism is.

Specifically ministerial freedom is freedom to speak and act upon God's word not only as a member and servant of the community, entrusted like all members with the community's mission, but also independently of the community, *over against* the community. The community's own proper life necessarily draws it away from the gospel. The community is called to do works, and the gospel is a message of hope beyond our works; the community is called to live now, and Jesus was a long time ago. By very fidelity to its mission, the community is exposed to temptation to bowdlerize the gospel on both of its essential sides: to proclaim in Jesus' name a hope less than eschatological, or to proclaim hope in some other name than Jesus. The ministerium is those God and the community set free to worry about this, to take the authenticity and vivacity of the gospel as their special responsibility against all comers. The ministry's charism is the gospel's freedom *from* the community *for* the community.

Ordination is God's permission to speak and act for that gospel which invented the church and is not invented by the church, to speak and act for the gospel over against the community as a whole, if need be, in defiance of the community as a whole. It will happen that the community agrees, e.g., that persons of varying color should hear the gospel in separate assemblies, or that "It doesn't matter in whom you believe, so long as you believe hard enough," or that salvation is a private matter. Then the ordained ministry are those recognized precisely by the community to say to the community: "That may well be what you and I and all of us want to say and call it Christian; but we are wrong." The ministerium is those liberated to speak and act over against community opinion about the gospel on behalf—tautologically and fantastically—of the gospel itself. From the minister's side, ordination is a sort of liberating oath: to preach and teach the gospel in accord with nothing but the gospel. The church rightly worries also about how much truth the world can stand, or about what will best motivate folk to the many works that need doing in the world, or about how not to offend the marginal with too much gospel; but ordination is permission to certain persons to worry in the opposite direction.

It is because the ministerial charism is this independence within the total community, that ministers are ordained by their predecessors, not by the community as a whole. The necessity and right of ordination is the baptism of the whole baptized community, and it is the whole community that, by whatever organ or representation, chooses those to be ordained. But it is the ministerium itself, by whatever organ or representation of its own, that ordains. If the visible word is imposition of hands, it is predecessor ministers whose hands alone are relevant.

Despite being thus told to behave like apostles, ministers are not apostles and do not even belong to a continuing institution with the apostles—the ministerium is precisely that institution made necessary by the apostles' *absence*. Therefore the call to apostolic freedom makes the ministry an insoluble task, defined by dialectics that can never come to rest: "Who am I to say what the gospel *really* is?" "To take such risks with the peace of this congregation?" "What does the Spirit say to me that he does not say to others?" Therefore every actual exercize of ministerial freedom proves its authenticity only by unanimity with the real apostles: the ordination promise to preach and teach in accord with the gospel is concretely and historically a promise to preach and teach in accord with apostolic Scripture—which of course only complicates the passions and uncertainities of the calling.[42] It is as a visible word of the gospel to those who must live with these questions that ordination is a sacrament.

Finally, I must briefly touch the matter of ministerial authority. In the life of the communities, their ministers must have whatever sorts of authority are necessary for the success of the particular ministerial responsibility. Ministerial responsibility for the independence, eschatological vivacity, and historical faithfulness of the gospel is not fulfilled by monopoly of any particular functions: the pastor of a congregation is not to be its only preacher or teacher or liturgical leader, and most assuredly he is not to replace the congregation in its mission to the world. The ordained ministry is rather to share the mission and life of the community, fulfilling its special responsibility by the *way* in which its participation is shaped. The functional actuality of the ministry may therefore be expected to change from time to time, and so also the particular sorts of authority which the ministry must have. Yet certain functions and authorities have inevitably been constant. One is important for a later matter in this chapter: since the Supper is the occasion when all aspects of the gospel and of Christian life concur, it will in all normal situations be essential for presidency of the Supper and authority over its celebrations to belong to the ordained ministry.

VI

For the rest of the community, ordination makes visible the gospel's claim to be prior to the community. To the one ordained, ordination's sacramental function is precisely congruent to that of baptism. Ordination makes a biographical fact, which anchors the ministerial charism just as baptism anchors faith as such. Those volunteering for the ministry are and ought to be caught in a subjectively intolerable dialectic: by what right do they propose to set themselves over against God's people? The coming fact of ordination makes it possible to say to them: God will free you from yourself and your need for justification. More important, the past fact of ordination makes it possible to say to ministers: whether you have so far done ill or well, whether or not you ever should have become a minister, it is too late for hesitation. God has cut you free from all the prudences and securities you should otherwise have clung to.[43]

This does not mean that ordained ministry does not require dedication and learning and skill, which no rite produces; or that there is excuse for ministry that lacks them. Indeed, the time-serving and the foolish will never even come to those questions in response to which ordination is the visible gospel. To an incompetent minister, the only appropriate word is that he must become competent or cease to inflict his incompetence on the community. And yet for him too, should he repent, and the fact of past incompetence then seem to invalidate past ministry and prohibit all future ministry, his ordination enables a word of permission to go on.

Ordination can thus no more be repeated than can baptism: each of us has one life, and a biographical fact is there for all eternity. My baptism exerts no ulterior force upon my life; despite it, I may sin grievously or leave the church. But if I return, it is precisely to my one baptism that I return. Just so, ordination bestows no special powers or virtue; once ordained, I may be unfaithful in my work, leave ministry for good reasons, or even be expelled for cause. But if I return, it is my one ordination that enables the word of gospel which welcomes and sustains me. As for reordination of ministers transfering from one denomination to another, it is either a declaration that the other group is not the church, or a blasphemy against the Spirit.

The unrepeatability of ordination led medieval theology to a doctrine that ordination impresses a sort of permanent mark on the soul of the minister. And within an understanding of human being that could conceive the continuity of a human life only as the persistence of some one interior substance, the irrevocability of biographical fact could indeed only be conceived as an alteration of that substance. This anthropology is inadequate; but reforming it cannot be my present task. What is important to our present concern is that this way of understanding ordination's permanence has repeatedly combined with the ministry's necessary authority over the Supper, and with the notion of consecration, in a disastrous way: as if ordination bestowed a *power* to make the real presence happen, a power that the unordained lack.

It must be said bluntly: there is nothing the ordained *can* do that the unordained *cannot,* though there are always things the ordained *may* do that the unordained *ought not.* If an unordained person presides at the Supper, those who participate are robbed of nothing; though his act will ordinarily be irresponsible and in a particular case may be wicked. It is not by adding new capacities that either baptism or ordination change persons—human nature is anyway not appropriately conceived as a collection of capacities. It is by making the Spirit's advent a biographical fact that baptism and ordination change persons.

If I have been ordained, I have been committed to the Spirit in a particular way. My opportunity and burden is to hold the community to the gospel, which means to the community's own and the world's last future; and the power of the future to grip the present is what the Spirit is. The Spirit "blows where he wills," he makes faith and creates the church "when and where God chooses." The outcome of my work is therefore unpredictable, more unpredictable even than ecstasy or prophetic vision. Ordination is visible permission to affirm this unpredictability, to find in it the very freedom to go on.

NOTES

1. Hans von Campenhausen, *Ecclesiastical Authority and Spiritual Power,* trans. J. A. Baker (Stanford: Stanford University Press, 1969), pp. 13f.

2. On the following, Friedrich Hahn, "Der Apostolat im Urchristentum," *Kerygma und Dogma,* 20, 1, pp. 54–77; H. Kraft, "Die Anfänge des geistlichen Amts," *Theologische Literaturzeitung,* 100, pp. 13–81; Hans von

Campenhausen, "Der urchristliche Apostelbegriff," *Studia Theologica*, 1, pp. 96ff.

3. In Gal. 1:1 there are apostles *ap' anthrōpōn* and apostles *di' anthrōpou*.

4. Most recently and clearly, Hahn, op. cit., pp. 61, 75–77.

5. Acts 6:2–4. Note the clearly terminological distinction between *diakonia tou logou* and *diakonein trapexais*.

6. Gal. 1:1 and Paul's whole argument in that letter.

7. On the whole subject of spiritual gifts, see Ernst Käsemann's article in *Die Religion in Geschichte und Gegenwart*[3], Vol. II, cols. 1272–79. On the nature of the charismatic ministries, see von Campenhausen, *Ecclesiastical Authority and Spiritual Power*, pp. 67–70; Kraft, op. cit., pp. 81–84.

8. von Campenhausen, *Ecclesiastical Authority and Spiritual Power*, pp. 189f.

9. Ibid., pp. 62ff., 182–86.

10. 1 Cor. 12:3.

11. 1 Cor. 12:28. Compare Acts 13:1; Eph. 4:11, 2:20; Rev. 18:20.

12. They are attested in all branches of the Synoptic tradition, by Luke in Acts, in the Johannine tradition, and by Paul for his congregations and Rome.

13. von Campenhausen, *Ecclesiastical Authority and Spiritual Power*, pp. 55–62.

14. Ibid., pp. 60–61.

15. On the New Testament prophets, see Ernst Käsemann, "Sentences of Holy Law in the New Testament," *New Testament Questions of Today*, trans. W. J. Montague (Philadelphia: Fortress Press, 1969), pp. 66–81; Philip Vielhauer, *Die Religion in Geschichte und Gegenwart*[3], Vol. V, cols. 633–34; Kraft, op. cit., pp. 91–93; von Campenhausen, *Ecclesiastical Authority and Spiritual Power*, pp. 60–63.

16. Acts 2:18–21.

17. 1 Cor. 14:13–25; *Didache*, V, 5.

18. On the Christian rabbis, see von Campenhausen, *Ecclesiastical Authority and Spiritual Power*, pp. 61, 192ff.; Kraft, op. cit., pp. 93–4.

19. 1 Peter 5:1–2; Acts 11:30, 14:23f., 15:2–6, 21:18; 1 Tim. 4:14, 5:1, 17–19. See von Campenhausen, *Ecclesiastical Authority and Spiritual Power*, pp. 76–123.

20. Acts 11:30, 15:2–6. von Campenhausen, Ibid., pp. 76–77.

21. von Campenhausen, Ibid., p. 78f., 149–53.

22. Ibid., pp. 63–65; Kraft, op. cit., pp. 95–98.

23. 1 Thess. 5:12.

24. 1 Cor. 12:28: *antilēmpseis, kybernēseis*; Rom. 12:6–8: *diakoniou ho proistamenos*.

25. Phil. 1:1. von Campenhausen, *Ecclesiastical Authority and Spiritual Power*, pp. 67f.

26. 1 Peter 4:11; Acts 6:6.

27. 1 Peter 5:12; Acts 20:18–28; Titus 1:5–7; 1 Tim. 3:1–13. In regard

to the latter vital passages, see Martin Dibelius / Hans Conzelmann, *The Pastoral Epistles*, Hermeneia, trans. Philip Buttolph and Adela Yarbro (Philadelphia: Fortress Press, 1972), pp. 54ff. (the best in this commentary is the legacy of Dibelius). In von Campenhausen, *Ecclesiastical Authority and Spiritual Power*, pp. 82–107.

28. In spite of von Campenhausen's objections to this traditional view (Ibid., pp. 63ff., esp. p. 68 n.81), which fail on the simple consideration that since the primary economic affair of the earliest congregations was precisely the meal which included the Eucharist, charge of economics was *never* a secondary unspiritual sort of function with them, and was indeed the best possible starting point for the development of the bishops' later spiritual authority.

29. Gal. 2:11ff.; Acts 6:1ff.

30. Kraft, op. cit., pp. 95ff.

31. E.g., in the Johannine writings, we find an "elder" with charismatically-based authority over a whole group of congregations; so von Campenhausen, *Ecclesiastical Authority and Spiritual Power*, pp. 122f. In the *Didache*, XI, 3–6, we find post-apostolic "apostles."

32. A. Adams in *Die Religion in Geschichte und Gegenwart*[3], Vol. I, cols. 1300–02.

33. W. Jannasch in Ibid., Vol. II, cols. 159ff.

34. von Campenhausen, *Ecclesiastical Authority and Spiritual Power*, pp. 178ff.

35. See also 1 Tim. 1:18; 2 Tim. 1:6. On all of these passages see Dibelius / Conzelmann, op. cit., ad loc.

36. The rite was probably taken over, more or less whole, from the contemporary Jewish ordination of rabbis; see Eduard Lohse in *Die Religion in Geschichte und Gegenwart*[3], Vol. IV, cols. 1671f.

37. Acts 6:6, 13:3.

38. The Western tradition is handily collected by H. B. Poster, *The Ordination Prayers of the Ancient Western Churches* (London: SPCK, 1967); Hippolytus is on pp. 1–11.

39. Ibid.

40. An excellent account of the development in one tradition is by Paul F. Bradshaw, *The Anglican Ordinal: Its History and Development from the Reformation to the Present Day* (Naperville, Ill.: Alec R. Allenson, 1971).

41. von Campenhausen, *Ecclesiastical Authority and Spiritual Power*, pp. 182ff.

42. It is probably time to acknowledge that my repeated references to scriptural authority raise serious problems. For their attempted solution, see Robert Jenson, "On the Problem(s) of Scriptural Authority," *Interpretation*, 31, pp. 237–50.

43. It is precisely in this capacity that ordination first appears, in the Pastoral Epistles: 1 Tim. 1:6ff., 1:18f., 4:14; 2 Tim. 2:2.

Afterword

Throughout this book, I have clung as tightly and exclusively as I could to the Augustinian starting maxim: sacraments are visible words, they are modes of the saying of the gospel. Readers may have been disturbed by this single-mindedness in a way I could not assuage in advance of the actual attempt. Precisely those best informed by the tradition may repeatedly have asked: is what a sacrament *says* to us all it *does* to us? Is the author not leaving something out, and that perhaps the most important thing: a presence or action of Christ independent of what may or may not be said by the sacramental performance?

The felt need to ask this question—and I too have wanted to ask it at every step—results from a certain character of sacramentology's Western tradition, a character which I judge to be incompatible with the gospel and which I have willed to overcome. Throughout the tradition, when the "Augustinian" line was followed, it was followed in the assumption that there was another line which might have been followed. It has been supposed that the question about what a sacrament says and the question about what a sacrament is and does are at least in principle two questions, e.g., that what the Supper is to say to us and the reality and effect of Christ's presence in it overlap but logically need not be congruent. Well-balanced theologians have therefore wanted to say something on both lines: e.g., both something about what the Supper should communicate and something about the "real presence" that, in a "valid" celebration, in any case occurs. And also those more single-minded thinkers who have followed a more exclusively Augustinian line have supposed there was another line they might have followed had there been scriptural warrant, other assertions they might have made had they not instead been led to deny them.

From time to time, however, Christian reflection has attained a more radical and evangelical interpretation of reality. It has been noticed that over against the events of the gospel, the question about *says* and the question about *is* and *does* are not at all two questions. This point is not quite adequately made by such dicta as that the sacramental gospel "does what it says" or "gives what it promises," as if saying and effecting were fundamentally two, but the gospel were an extraordinarily potent saying. The point is not adequately made even by noting that the gospel is the word of God and that what God commands must come to pass—true though this is. The way the gospel addresses reality makes an ontological revolution. When we speak the gospel, we are pressed to rearrange the fundamental structure of inherited language: to relate "is" and "ought" and "will be" by different rules, to use such words as "divine" and "human" in unheard of contexts, to locate reality by new clues. With respect to our present concern, if the gospel is a right address, then *to be* is *to be in converse*; for the gospel's God *is* his Word with himself. "Says" and "is" are, about this God's sacraments, two words for the same thing.

It is this sporadic insight of Christian theology which I have tried consistently to carry through. I have tried at every step to describe what happens in a sacrament, including the presence and power of God in it, precisely by analysis of the sacrament's particular structure and context as a communication event. This is not done to attenuate the reality of the sacramental event but to grasp it in the mode in fact appropriate to it. Thus the Supper is not *both* a visible word of the gospel and the place of Christ's real presence; it is either in that it is the other. And even this last formulation is wrong; for the language which requires us first to speak as if there were two phenomena, in order then to identify them, is still shaped by a false ontology. Overcoming that language has been an agenda of this book.

The Western sacramental tradition has tried to explain the sacraments in a language that separates "says" and "is," in a language which therefore is in fact inimical to there being any specifically Christian sacraments at all. In consequence, our theology has been on a tightrope from which it has almost programmatically fallen off, now to the one side, now to the other. Catholic theology has tended to suppose that in moving from preaching and teaching to sacramental occurrence we move from distributing information about God's reality and presence to the real giving and experience of them. Protestant theology has tended to suppose that in moving from preaching and teaching to sacramental occurrence we move from the real giving and sharing of God's reality and presence to the illustrating and celebrating of them. Both tendencies are disastrously false. As we move between proclamation and sacrament we simply move inside the borders of *one* event: God's real self-communication to us, which is always at once audible and visible in order to be the communication of the particular God who in fact is.

Indexes

General Index

This index is not a subject analysis of the work. It lists matters which, it seems likely, users may want to look up, and which cannot immediately be located by the table of contents. Where whole sections or even chapters are the relevant reading, they are the reference.

Biblical Index

Matthew
6:13—165
11:19 par.—63
16:9—187
18:6ff—187
18:10–35—187
18:15–18—187
18:21–22—187
26:26–29—67–74,
  79–84
26:28—63
28:19—134

Luke
12:18—63
17:3–4—187
22:15–18—64, 65,
  78
22:15–20—67–74,
  87
22:19–20—79–84
22:20—76
24:13–35—65
24:36–43—65
24:47—134

Acts
2:16–21—142
2:18–21—204
2:38—134, 142
2:46—65, 76
6:1f—205
6:2–4—204
6:6—104, 105
8:12—135
8:16—134
8:26–50—134
8:35—135
9:17—142
9:18—135
10:38ff—65
10:48—134
11:30—204
13:1—204
13:3—205

14:23f—204
15:2–6—204
16:15—135
18:18—135
19:1–7—142
19:5—134
20:18–28—204
21:18—204

Mark
2:15 par.—63
2:19 par.—134
10:13–16—168
10:35f par.—63
11:30 par.—134
14:12–17 par.—
  64, 75
14:25 par.—65, 78
16:14–18—65

John
3:18—140–141
3:22—134
3:22–30—143
4:2—134
6:51–59—84–85
20:17—134
20:23—187
21:1–14—65

Romans
6—135, 140, 187
6:1–11—137–139
8:3—139
8:23—142
8:25—70
12:6–8—204

1 Corinthians
1:11–17—135
1:13–15—134
2:26–31—140
5:1–5—187
5:6, 9–11—187

6:9–11—139–140,
  187
6:9–20—187
6:11—134
10—64, 66
10:1–12—135
10:14–22—85–86
10:16–17—76
11—64, 66
11:17–34—86–87
11:23–26—67–74,
  79–84
11:25—76
11:26—63, 71
12:3—204
12:12–13—139
12:13—135
12:28—204
14:13–25—204
16:22–23—66, 88
16:23—76

2 Corinthians
1:22—142
3:17–18—143
5:1–11—187
5:5—142

Ephesians
1:13f—142
2:20—204
4:11—204
5:25–27—142

1 Timothy
1:6f—205
1:18f—205
3:1–13—204
4:14—197, 204,
  205
5:1, 17–19—204

Hebrews
10:22—142

1 Peter
1:3–21—142
4:11—204
5:1–2—204
5:12—204

1 John
1:6–7—187
1:8—187
2:18–27—142
5—177

Galatians
1:1—204
2:11f—205
3:25–27—139
5:9—187
5:19ff—187
6:1ff—187

Philippians
1:1—204

1 Thessalonians
5:12—204

2 Thessalonians
3:6–16—187

2 Timothy
1:6—205
2:2—205

Titus
1:5–7—204
3:5—142

James
5:14—165

2 John
1:11—187

Revelation
18:20—204
22:20—76, 88

Index of Authors Cited

212

LaVergne, TN USA
13 July 2010
189324LV00003B/17/P